College Reading and Study Skills

College Reading and Study Skills

A Guide to Improving Academic Communication

FOURTH EDITION

Nancy V. Wood

Director, Integrated Program in Reading,
Writing, & Critical Thinking
University of Texas at Arlington

Holt, Rinehart and Winston, Inc.
Fort Worth   Chicago   San Francisco   Philadelphia
Montreal   Toronto   London   Sydney

Publisher:	**Ted Buchholz**
Acquisitions Editor:	**Michael Rosenberg**
Developmental Editor:	**Leslie Taggart**
Project Editor:	**Publications Development Company**
Production Manager:	**Tad Gaither**
Composition and Design:	**Publications Development Company**
Cover Design:	**Margaret E. Unruh**
Cover Illustrator:	**Audrey McCaffrey**

COPYRIGHT ACKNOWLEDGMENTS

George Athan Billias. Excerpts from *The American Revolution, Fourth Edition,* by George Athan Billias. Copyright © 1990 by Holt, Rinehart and Winston, Inc. Reprinted by permission of publisher.

Melvin D. Joesten, David O. Johnston, John T. Netterville, and James L. Wood. Excerpts from *Chemistry, Impact on Society* by Melvin D. Joesten, David O. Johnston, John T. Netterville, James L. Wood. Copyright © 1988 by Saunders College Publishing, a division of Holt, Rinehart and Winston, Inc. Reprinted by permission of publisher.

Spencer A. Rathus. Excerpts from *Essentials of Psychology, Second Edition,* by Spencer A. Rathus. Copyright © 1989 by Holt, Rinehart and Winston, Inc. Reprinted by permission of publisher.

Henry L. Tischler. Excerpts from *Introduction to Sociology, Third Edition,* by Henry L. Tischler. Copyright © 1990 by Holt, Rinehart and Winston, Inc. Reprinted by permission of publisher.

Library of Congress Cataloging in Publication Data

Wood, Nancy V.
    College reading and study skills : a guide to improving academic
communication / Nancy V. Wood. — 4th ed.
       p.   cm.
    Includes bibliographical references and index.
    1. Study, Method of. 2. Reading (Higher education) I. Title.
    LB2395.W63   1991
    378.1′70281—dc20   90–43810
                                          CIP

ISBN 0-03-054063-1

Requests for permission to make copies of any part of the
work should be mailed to: Permissions, Holt, Rinehart
and Winston, Inc., Orlando, Florida 32887.
Printed in the United States of America.
1 2 3 4 016 9 8 7 6 5 4 3 2 1

Holt, Rinehart and Winston
The Dryden Press
Saunders College Publishing

For Sam, David, and Joe

Preface to the Fourth Edition

Significant shifts in the past few years have influenced and changed traditional approaches to teaching reading and study skills. New theories about how people learn, how they read, and how they accept and integrate new skills and learning strategies into already existing frameworks have been generated partly by research but also by the practical experiences of many sensitive teachers who have experimented and reported on what has worked in their classrooms. Learning styles research, for example, demonstrates that students develop individualistic, but still effective, ways of studying, learning, and communicating in academic settings. Other research shows that if students become more aware of how they learn, and if they also evaluate and monitor what they do, they become more active learners who are in charge of their own learning processes both inside and outside of the reading and study skills classroom. To become active learners students must have room to experiment, negotiate, and personalize their reading and study skills if they are to use them consistently.

The major changes in this fourth edition have been made in response to these new perspectives on teaching reading and study skills. New materials and exercises are designed to promote active learning, individual learning styles, metacognitive, selfawareness, transferability, and personal ownership. The teacher's challenge is to teach every student to understand, to think, to experiment, and finally to use new methods and approaches that will result in independent learning. The following is a list of the most important changes and new materials in this edition.

NEW TO THIS EDITION:

- A chapter on setting goals
- A section and exercises on comprehension monitoring
- Materials on learning styles and teaching styles
- Materials on collaborative and cooperative learning
- Acknowledgement of the returning student with new examples
- Emphasis on reading as an interactive process
- Expanded materials on prereading including backgrounding, predicting, and asking questions
- Expanded materials on reading comprehension including textual clues to main ideas, recognizing organizational patterns, and reading difficult material
- Instruction on writing summaries and making organizational maps
- Materials and activities that stimulate critical, creative, and self-reflective thinking
- Materials on preparing for and taking standardized exams
- Information on using computers for composition
- Information on collecting material for research papers
- Material on preparing and delivering oral reports
- Many new examples: revised lecture notes, a written summary of a reading assignment, a sample time schedule for a working student with family responsibilities, a demonstration of how to use reading material to generate critical thinking, and a model outline of an oral report. Other examples of student work from earlier editions have been retained.
- Many new exercises: comprehension monitoring exercises, group exercises, summary writing exercises, and three extended reading exercises from current college textbooks
- New Evaluation Guides: students can now read, evaluate, and assign holistic scores to one another's lecture notes, textbook marking exercises, essay exam answers, written papers, and oral reports.

PURPOSE AND ORGANIZATION REMAIN UNCHANGED

The purpose of this edition, like the others, is to provide students with the skills necessary for success in college classes. Especially emphasized are the basic communication skills as they are used in the academic setting. There are chapters to help students learn to *read* textbooks and library materials, to *listen* to lectures, to *write* papers and examinations, and to *speak* in class discussions and give oral reports. When students can do a good job of communicating, they possess the skills most essential for academic success.

The sequence of topics follows the sequence of tasks that students are expected to perform when they enroll in college. In Part 1 students are encouraged to consider their reasons for coming to college, to set goals, and to decide how to organize and approach their studies. They are also taught ways to improve their concentration and motivation.

In Parts 2 and 3, they are taught how to learn during class time and how to read their textbooks. Part 4 teaches students to take examinations successfully, and Part 5 teaches students a process for doing written assignments. Part 6 summarizes the skills taught in the book and invites students to make a final evaluation of their own skills via a checklist of study techniques.

CLASSROOM TESTING

The first edition of this book, before it was published, was classroom tested with two groups of students. The first was a group of early-admission students, and the second was the group of provisionally admitted students referred to in To the Student. Both groups read the preliminary text and responded to a questionnaire. Specifically, they were asked to identify difficult vocabulary, confusing passages, and chapters that were too difficult or too long. These students' readings of the manuscript resulted in some significant changes. If enough students indicated they would not follow a particular suggestion, it was eliminated. Exercises were included only when there was nearly unanimous agreement that they were worth doing. Chapters identified as too difficult were simplified, and chapters identified as too long were shortened. The resulting chapters can be read by most students, with ease, in less than thirty minutes.

Since publication of the first edition, I have continued to test the theory and exercises in this book with at least a thousand additional students each year. A team of colleagues who taught the course in which this book was used have met with me weekly during the past twelve years to discuss and experiment with better ways of teaching these materials. Our students have also evaluated this book each semester. The new ideas and exercises that emerged from our weekly planning sessions and from student questionnaires were then tested in our classrooms. Those that worked best are included in this fourth edition.

INSTRUCTOR'S MANUAL

The following resources are available in the Instructor's Manual.

- The ten reading labs that appeared in the Appendix of the first three editions are now in the *Instructor's Manual*. Their purpose is to extend students' ranges of reading speed, to encourage students to develop the habit of selecting and reading books for pleasure, and to teach students how to skim when special situations call for this skill.
- Multiple choice tests include section tests, and a 100-item comprehensive test that can be used as a final exam. Essay tests.
- Answer keys to multiple choice tests and textbook exercises.
- Class designs and class syllabi for full semester as well as shorter courses.
- Additional ideas for class activities and exercises.
- Student information forms.
- Student evaluation forms for evaluation and conferencing on student work.
- Course and instructor evaluation forms.

To obtain a complimentary copy of the Instructor's Manual, write to the English Editor, Holt, Rinehart and Winston, Inc., 301 Commerce Street, Suite 3700, Fort Worth, Texas 76102.

Acknowledgments

In preparing the manuscript for this fourth edition, I have had valuable help from the tutors and the instructors who make up the staff of the Study Skills and Tutorial Services department at the University of Texas at El Paso. I would like to thank them and the students who participate in this program. Both groups have contributed much to this edition. In particular I would like to thank Gladys Shaw, Evelyn Posey, Maryann Burlingham, Melissa Wiseman, Rene Berta, Andrea Berta, and Mary Lou Gibson for their contributions and their care in testing the new ideas and exercises for this edition in their classes. James A. Wood has helped me generate and develop many ideas for all editions of this book. Helen Bell has contributed to the material on doing library research. Exam questions in Chapter 12 were drawn from actual examinations given by the faculty at the University of Texas at El Paso and at the University of Texas at Austin. Claire Weinstein of the University of Texas at Austin has had an influence on the basic perspective of this edition. I am indebted to her for the approach to setting goals in Chapter One and also to her research and writing on metacognition and learning theory. Karen Schwalm of Glendale Community College gave me the idea for the Evaluation Guides. Judith McDowell, Chair of the English Department at the University of Texas at Arlington has provided invaluable support and encouragement. Tammy Dyer and DeAnn Coffin have been exceptionally helpful with the preparation of the final manuscript. I also want to thank those who have read and commented on the manuscript during its various stages of revision: Greg Alexander, Portland Community College; James L. Brother, Hartford State Technical College; Gladdys W. Church, SUNY at Brockport; John H. Corcoran, Glassboro State College; Timothy E. Dykstra, Franklin University; LeAnne Higgs, Franklin University; Harold N. Hild, Northeastern Illinois University; Vance Rhoades, Brewton-Parker College; Norma V. Spalding, San Jose State University; Carlene Walker, University of

Texas at El Paso; Colleen Fairbanks, University of Michigan; John Howe, Community College of Philadelphia; Linda Knight, York Technical College; Becky Patterson, Anchorage Community College; W. Donald Smith, Lane Community College; Rory Stephens, Northeastern Illinois University; Bette B. Williams, Eastern Connecticut State University; Evelyn T. Silliman, Alice Lloyd College; Sally Powers, William Jewell College; Barbara Henry, West Virginia State College; Judith Olson-Fallon, North Harris County Community College; Thomas J. Buchholz, University of Wisconsin-Stevens Point; Donna McKusick, Essex Community College; Susan Lipscomb, Wharton County Junior College; Gladys Shaw, University of Texas-El Paso; Jackie Lumsden, Greenville Technical College; June Bracken, West Virginia Wesleyan College. When they see that I have followed much of their advice, they will realize how much I have valued their comments.

I extend my sincere thanks to the Holt staff: Michael Rosenberg, Leslie Taggart; and Nancy Land of Publications Development Company. These individuals have provided me with the editorial guidance, encouragement, and professional expertise that was indispensable for completing this project.

N.V.W.
Arlington, Texas

To the Student

When you pick up a study skills textbook, you have the right to ask two questions. The first is, "Are there really study skills I can learn that will make me more successful in college?" The second is, "Will this book help me learn these skills?"

In the first edition of this book, to answer these questions, I told about a group of freshman students who had not met ordinary admissions requirements at the University of Texas at El Paso. They were admitted with the provision that they make C's or better their first semester or they would have to drop out. Some of these students took the study skills course I was teaching and used this book. This group of students learned and practiced the material in this book for one semester. More than three-fourths of them made the grades required for regular academic status. Less than one-fourth of the other provisionally admitted students, who had no study skills training, were able to achieve the same status.

Since that time I have tested the material in this book with at least 12,000 additional students, 8,000 of whom were provisionally admitted. Nearly all of the provisional students who made the grades to continue at the university also completed the course in which this book was used as the textbook.

All of these students were successful because they learned and used certain skills that the other students did not have. These skills often make the difference between staying in school successfully or getting poor grades and becoming discouraged.

To do well in college you will need to learn to concentrate, listen, read and write well, join in class discussion, adapt to different types of classes and professors, and make efficient use of your time. This book will provide you with the information and practice exercises to help you learn these skills.

You will have to use what is in this book rather than just read it, if it is to work for you. The students who gave this text its trial run were willing to use it, apply it, and experiment with it in all of their classes. Some student went even further—they changed and adapted some of the skills to meet their own individual preferences or particular needs in other courses they were taking. The information in this book will help you, too, if you use it as these students did.

Contents

College Reading and Study Skills

PART ONE

Getting Started

1 | Knowing What to Expect and Setting Some Goals

When you have finished reading this chapter, you will know the following:

1. The major skills and qualities that you need for college success.
2. How developing these skills and qualities will improve your chances of finding employment after college.
3. How to set short- and long-term goals and create plans to meet them.

THE SKILLS AND QUALITIES YOU NEED TO DEVELOP FOR ACADEMIC SUCCESS

Not long ago the faculty members at a large university were asked, "Are there skills that you wish your students had but that you yourself have neither the time nor the desire to teach?" They were also asked, "Which skills do you consider essential to earn an A in your class?" Before you read further, make your own list of some of the skills and qualities you think college students should have in order to be successful learners.

1. _Reading Comphnession_
2. _Goal + time management_
3. _Writing skills_
4. _Critical thinking_
5. _Computer literacy_
6. _Library skills_
7. _Math skills_
8. _Oral skills_
9. _Note taking skills_
10. _Listening skills_
11. _Study skills_
12. _Memory + Concentration_

Now compare your list with the twelve qualities and skills listed by the faculty. Make a check by the ones that are similar to or the same as the items on your list. You can develop all of the qualities and skills in the following list while you are at college. Furthermore, when you have read and worked the exercises in this book you will have a good start toward developing every one of them. Continued practice and experience in other classes will enable you to develop expertise in all of these areas.

1. Develop your writing skills.   All of your professors, whether they teach math, English, history, or physical education, expect you to be able to write clearly and legibly. Everything you write should be well thought out, well organized, and written in complete sentences. Type papers if possible. Double-space and write in ink when you can't. Your handwriting need not be pretty, but it is essential that your professors be able to read it.

2. Improve your reading skills.   Your professors expect you to be able and willing to read difficult material. You will have to read for all of your classes. In some you will read greater volumes of material than in others. You probably should not take more than one or two heavy reading classes each semester. Then you will have time to read for every class as closely and thoroughly as possible. Reading skills considered especially important by university professors are as follows: reading the textbook regularly; reading and interpreting graphs; thinking about what you have read and evaluating it critically; reading and interpreting test questions.

3. Improve your speaking and listening skills.   Your professors will assume that you can listen, take notes, and remember the material from long, complicated lectures. Furthermore, they will expect you to be able to participate in discussion and give oral reports in the smaller classes you take. If you are not satisfied with your present skills, take a speech course while you are in college.

4. Develop some degree of computer literacy.   Even if you never work directly with computers, your life will still be affected by them both while you are in college and after you graduate. You should plan to learn some uses of computers, develop a minimal computer vocabulary, and learn the rudiments of operating a personal computer.

5. *Develop an adequate math background.*   Your professors will assume that you have an adequate math background for those courses that require it. A basic background in math, algebra, and trigonometry is important for most university science classes and for virtually all engineering and math classes. If you don't have a good math background, and intend to take classes that demand math, you will have to develop it. See if your university has facilities to help you remedy a weak math background. If it does not, you may have to take some math classes at a nearby high school or take individual instruction from a math tutor.

6. *Learn to do library research.*   Most professors take it for granted that you will be able to find the books, magazines, and other materials in the library that relate to their subjects. Learn to discover what information you need, where to find it, and how to use it.

7. *Plan to think while you are in college.*   Your professors all want you to think. Of the more than 100 professors polled, 86 percent said that an ability to reflect on and understand the concepts taught in their classes was essential to success. They expect you to apply what you are learning to everyday examples, to make what you are learning useful. They also expect you to elaborate on what you learn, to associate it with what you already know, and to ask critical questions. Most professors will be far more interested in your ability to think about their subject than in your ability to parrot back what they have said.

8. *Take time to memorize.*   The ability to memorize is important, however, and should not be slighted. If you are to think and reflect, you must have something to think about. So, first, you must memorize material as a prelude to, and sometimes as a companion to, reflective thought.

The ability to memorize is essential in languages, chemistry, biology, and math classes. In such classes you must memorize material daily in order to keep up. Even though most college history professors do not usually demand that you know the exact date for every historical event, they do expect you to know approximately when things happened. You will find it useful to plot and memorize a time line that encompasses major historical events. Such a time line will serve you over and over again in many other courses besides history, such as English literature and the history of art or science.

9. Develop self-discipline, a certain degree of self-confidence, and a willingness to take responsibility for learning.   In other words, your professors want to be able to count on you. They expect you to come to class. Furthermore, they expect you to get the assignments straight and to finish them on time without much supervision. They expect you to keep the quality of your assignments consistently high. If you miss a class, they expect you to take the initiative to find out what you missed and to do something about it. They expect you to be willing to work both in class and outside of class. In cumulative subjects, such as math, science, and foreign languages, in which the material of the class builds on all that has gone before, your professors expect you to learn material daily and to review and relearn it regularly so that new material will make sense to you. Finally, they expect you to be an active learner who concentrates, understands, and knows what to do when it is difficult to understand.

10. Learn patience and determination.   You should not, your professors say, expect instant answers to everything. Reading and listening in college are more time-consuming and much more difficult than in high school or most other settings. You may be able to comprehend ideas quickly, but to master and remember them takes time. You should resign yourself from the outset to putting in one, two, and sometimes three hours of study time outside of class for every hour you spend in class. This much is expected of you, and you will experience greater success if you accept and meet these demands.

11. Seek help when you need it.   Your professor is on your side and wants to work for you and with you. Don't be shy about seeking your professor's help. One third of the professors polled said they would like to have more contact with students. They cannot seek you out, however. You must go to them, and the best time is during their posted office hours.

12. Develop the ability to learn during class time.   It doesn't matter what you wear to class so long as you come with notebooks, pens, and the textbook if it is to be discussed. Then, work to overcome your shyness. Participate in class. Establish eye contact with the professor. Don't be afraid to ask questions, even if you are afraid they may be dumb ones. Three out of four of the professors polled indicated that students had to be able to learn during class time in order to get a good grade.

THE SKILLS AND QUALITIES ESSENTIAL FOR THE WORLD OF WORK

Now, look back over this list of twelve skills and qualities your university professors expect you to have. They are exactly those qualities your future employers will also be seeking. The College Board recently sponsored some dialogues with 200 business leaders and educators, and the general conclusion reached by these individuals was that both professors and employers expect you to have the same skills, qualities, and special competencies to succeed in college *and* in the workplace. Both expect you to be proficient in the basic communication skills and in mathematics and both expect you to be able to study and do research, think, and know something about computers. The reason for this conclusion is obvious. The most successful people in the workplace are those who have learned how to learn and who then continue learning throughout their lifetimes. Those are the individuals who get ahead.

You have three main tasks to accomplish in college: getting an education; getting an idea of what you want to do when you leave school; and developing the skills and abilities described in this chapter. If you accomplish these three tasks, you will be both educated and employable when you leave college. And those are accomplishments that almost every college student would admit are worth the time necessary to obtain them. You will accomplish these tasks more easily if you do some long-term planning and goal setting.

A SYSTEM FOR SETTING GOALS

Psychologists tell us that we lead much happier and more productive lives if we are working toward goals. We need long-term goals that help us visualize our future jobs, families, lifestyles, and accomplishments. We need short-term goals to help us with more immediate planning and also to help us determine how to meet our long-term goals. Short-term goals may include plans for a day, a week, or even a few months. Finally, we need some alternate goals because sometimes our primary goals do not work out. We often set goals that are either impossible to reach or in some way a mistake. Alternate goals then provide us with a fall-back plan.

Successful companies, businesses, educational institutions, and other organized groups create goal plans on a regular basis. These plans provide them with direction and measures of success. You can follow their example and create personal goal plans of your own.

FIVE FEATURES OF EFFECTIVE GOAL PLANS

1. Effective goal plans are specific.   Write out in detail what it is that you want to do. Examples of specific goal statements might be: I want to become a dental hygienist so that I can work part-time in a dentist's office while I am raising my family. Or, I want to get a general business degree so that I can learn what I need to know to set up my own small business in packing, crating, and shipping. Both of these examples describe long-term vocational and professional goals as well as the major discipline required to meet them. Notice that they are more effective long-term plans than general goal statements with no specific details such as, "I want to enter a health profession," or "I want to go into business." Shut your eyes and visualize yourself five years from now. Create as much detail as possible. "See" what you are doing and how you are living in order to create a *specific* goal statement.

2. Effective goal plans are measurable.   Examples of measurable goals might be: I will need to take an average of fifteen hours each semester and go to summer school one summer and take six hours to get my degree in four years. Or, I will need to take six hours a semester at night for the next six years in order to complete my degree. Or, I need to maintain a B average or better over the next three years in order to be competitive in the job market when I graduate. Notice how much easier it is to monitor your progress toward your goals when they are described in specific and measurable terms. Many students attend college for years without knowing exactly what classes or grades they need to graduate.

3. Effective goal plans are challenging.   Your motivation and energy levels will be at their highest if your goals represent what you *really want to do* and also if they are challenging and exciting to you. The way you feel about your goals is extremely important. If your goals seem dull or if they fill you with dread, you should change them.

Furthermore, your goals should put you under a reasonable amount of pressure. Too little pressure may cause you to lose interest and procrastinate. Too much pressure may depress or paralyze you. The right amount of pressure will energize you and keep you working on the goals that are important to you. For example, a short-term goal to write a successful major paper for a class would best be planned over a period of weeks to be effectively challenging. You would need to set interim deadlines for deciding the topic, completing your reading, doing your planning, draft, and finally rewriting and typing the paper. Part of the challenge would be to meet each of these deadlines and to see steady progress toward a good final paper. It would not be challenging to try to plan and write such a paper months before it was due because you happened to be worried about it, or, worse, to try to write it the day before it was due because you have procrastinated. The first situation would not pressure you enough. The latter would put you under so much pressure that it would be difficult to think or write.

4. Effective goal plans are realistic.   You should be reasonably certain that you can reach the goals that you set for yourself. Unreasonable goals can be discouraging and depressing, and you may abandon them finally altogether, leaving yourself with no goals and no challenges and excitement. For example, it may not be realistic to decide to be a pilot if you have poor vision or to decide to be a lawyer if you dislike research. It is important, instead, to determine your strengths and then to set goals that use them in realistic ways to make your goals attainable. You can often get ideas about realistic goals for yourself by taking a battery of tests and by seeking counseling in the career information center at your college.

5. Effective goal plans have a stated completion date. Ditch diggers can always look over their shoulders at the end of the day to see how much they have dug. For most of the goals you will be pursuing both while you are in college and after you graduate, there will be no such obvious measures of success. Thus, you need completion dates for both your short- and long-term goals so that you will know when you have "dug the ditch" or completed a goal plan. For example, you may decide to finish a reading assignment that is due Monday by Friday afternoon so that you can leave town for the weekend. Or, you may plan your classes so that you will graduate on a certain date. Should something happen that interferes with your progress as time goes on, you can then immediately set a new, more realistic completion date.

GENERATE A DEGREE PLAN

A degree plan is a list of the classes that you need to graduate in a particular major. It is usually written out by your advisor on a special form provided by your college. You can select a tentative major, even if you are not certain that you will stick with it, and either consult your college catalogue to learn the requirements for graduation in that field or make an appointment with an advisor to help you set up a degree plan for graduation. Either of these will give you an accurate idea of what you need to graduate. Many students change their majors two or even three times while they are in college. When you decide to make a change, create a new degree plan as soon as possible.

At the Very Least . . .

This chapter has described some of the skills and qualities that students need for success in college and has also set forth a description of successful goal planning. If you can't follow all of the suggestions in this chapter immediately or even soon, *at the very least* do this much:

1. Select one of the twelve qualities of a successful student and make a plan for improving in that area.
2. Select a tentative major and make a degree plan.
3. Set three short-term goals that meet the five tests for effective goal planning.

SUMMARY

When asked to identify the special skills and qualities important for academic success, most faculty agree that students should be able to read, write, think, speak, and listen well. They also emphasize the importance of an adequate math background, a certain amount of computer literacy, and the ability to do research in the library. They believe students should be able to memorize, should be responsible for their own learning, should not expect instant answers or instant success, should seek help when they need it, and should come to class prepared to work. These same skills and qualities are essential to success later on the job or in a profession. Setting goals can help students become successful during college and later. Goals can be long-term or short-term. Alternate goals are important when original goals do not work out. Effective goal plans are specific, measurable, challenging, realistic, and they have a completion date. An example of educational goal setting is the degree plan which all students should create with the help of an advisor and the college catalogue, even if it is changed at a later date.

EXERCISES

A. Class Exercises

The class exercises in this book are designed to be done in class either by individuals, in small groups that later report back to the class, or as a whole class effort. Small group work is usually done with 3 or 4 students. The group as a whole makes decisions and shapes the report. One model for such group work is as follows. One member of the group serves as the recorder and writes down the ideas and decisions of the group. Members of the group either agree with one another or agree to disagree. The recorder then reports the results of the group work to the rest of the class. More information about other ways to participate in group work appears in Chapter 7.

1. *Small Groups.*   Compare the items you predicted would be on the professors' list with the actual items on the list (page 3). Add additional items that you think should be on the list. Make sure that they can all be learned or developed. Evaluate the professors' items and remove any that you think should not be there. Report back to the class on your group's description of an effective college student. Create a class list that reflects the thinking of all of the groups in the class.

2. *Small Groups.*   Go back through the list of items that describe a successful college student, and select one item that every one in your group agrees is important. Create a goal plan to describe how to work to improve in this area. Describe the goal in specific terms, add some measurable objectives, evaluate it to decide if it is sufficiently challenging, decide if it is realistic, and set a completion date. Report your plan back to the class.

B. Application Exercises

The application exercises in this book are designed to help you take the material you are learning out of this classroom to use in your other classes and in your personal life.

1. Select an item from the list of qualities of a successful student that is the most important one to you. It may be the one you worked on in class or a different one. Write a goal plan to improve in this area that includes the five qualities of an effective plan, including setting a realistic completion date. Begin to work on this plan and submit two progress reports to your instructor, one at mid-semester and one at the end of the semester, to report on how you have worked to achieve this goal. Your degree plan may simply be a list of the courses that you need to graduate. Or, if you work with an advisor, these courses will be listed on the form that your college provides for that purpose.

2. Select a tentative major even if you are quite certain you may change it later. With the help of the college catalogue, your instructor, or an advisor create a degree plan that details what you will need to graduate in that major.

3. Set a long-term goal for five-years from now. Write a goal plan that includes the five steps for planning. Write, first, a detailed description of how you will be living and what you will be doing both during work and leisure hours. Then create some measurable interim goals, test your goal for sufficient challenge, and decide whether it is realistic for the five-year time

frame. Write a list of short-term goals for this semester that will help you begin work toward your goal. Put this list in the front of your notebook and check off the goals as you complete them.

C. *Topics for Your Learning Journal*

The journal topics in this book are designed to encourage self-evaluation and reflection about what you are learning. By thinking about why you are trying something new and also by evaluating how you feel about it, you are more likely to continue to use new ideas and systems. Buy a spiral notebook and write in responses to the following questions. Write fast and naturally, as though you were writing a letter to yourself. The beginning of a *sample* entry is provided after the first question to help you get started.

1. How do you feel about the list that was finally created in class of the qualities of a successful college student? Evaluate your present level of development in each area. What more do you need to do? Create a realistic plan for yourself to improve in key areas. Try to make your plan exciting and motivating by thinking of the areas in which you *want* to improve and by planning activities that you *want* to do.

   Sample journal entry:

   I feel sort of intimidated right now by that list. I know I am weak in most of those areas. Still, I can read and this course should help me learn to do it better. A visit to the library would help me get started there. I have no idea about computer skills. I wonder if I will have to take a class in computers, or if there would be some other way to learn. Speaking and listening are ok. Writing needs improvement, but I'm taking a writing course. All of this isn't going to happen at once. I have time for this...

2. What are your special interests and abilities? What college majors might be good possibilities for you? What are some possible career goals for you?

3. Look back through the chapter and write about both the most useful ideas in it and the most useful ideas it has caused you to think about.

2 | *Improving Your Concentration and Motivation*

When you have finished reading this chapter, you will know the following:

1. How to concentrate on reading this and other textbooks.
2. How to maintain a high level of motivation.
3. How to deal with problems that can interfere with concentration.
4. How active learning strategies can improve concentration.

CONCENTRATION AND STUDYING

Most students, if asked what their single biggest problem with studying is, will answer that it is concentration. It is often difficult, especially when learning new and unfamiliar material, to keep one's mind focused and at attention. This chapter will present some active learning strategies that you can start to use today to help you keep your mind on the new material you are encountering in your classes and your reading. It will also give you some insights into the types of distractions that can interfere with concentration and what you can do to minimize them.

IMPROVE YOUR CONCENTRATION AS YOU READ

Even though you have read only a few lines so far in this chapter, your mind may already be starting to wander. Here is a system for reading, then, that will help you immediately to concentrate. (Find more details on this system in Chapter 9.)

1. Underline the words and phrases in a paragraph that state the central thought.

2. Jot two or three words in the margin that state what most of the paragraph is about.
3. At the end of each section, in your own words, write a brief summary of the main points.

The following section of material has been marked for you. Study it as an example, and then continue to mark this book, and your other textbooks, in this way. You will find that you have to concentrate to jot down main ideas and summary points.

IMPROVE YOUR MOTIVATION TO HELP YOU CONCENTRATE

You need strong <u>motivation</u> to be a successful student. Think for a few moments about what motivates you. Are you motivated primarily by <u>outside factors</u> such as making more money, impressing your teachers, making good grades, doing what your parents want you to do, or trying to get a particular job or into a particular graduate school when you finish college? <u>Or,</u> are you motivated primarily by <u>internal factors</u> such as interest, enjoyment, and the satisfaction and challenge of the work itself? Recent research suggests that <u>internal factors</u> actually may provide <u>stronger motivation</u> than external factors, and that people do their best when they are interested, challenged, and engaged with their work.[1]

[margin note: internal or external motivation]

<u>Setting goals,</u> as you did in the last chapter, is one way to stay <u>motivated</u> because goals remind you of both the internal and external factors that are important to you. The following <u>five additional suggestions</u> will also help you stay motivated.

[margin note: 5 ways to stay motivated]

1. Have a boxed:reason for going to <u>college</u> and keep that reason in mind. Questionnaires administered to college freshmen over the past fifteen years show that students' reasons for being in college are serious and that they do not change very much. Figure 2.1 summarizes the responses that 572 freshman students gave in response to a questionnaire asking them to check off their reasons for being in college. As you read through the list, check your own reasons for coming.

[margin note: ① have reason for college]

Most students checked three or four different reasons. Look at what you checked. Do you agree with the majority?

[1] Alfie Kohn, "Art for Art's Sake," *Psychology Today*, September 1987, pp. 52–57.

I Am Going to College . . .	% of 572 Students Polled	Which Ones Would You Check?
a. because I don't want to get a job right now.	4%	_____
b. because I'm afraid I won't be able to get a job without a college education.	41%	_____
c. because I want to prepare myself for a specific job or profession.	97%	___✓___
d. because my parents want me to and I want to please them.	19%	_____
e. because I want to find a husband/wife.	2%	_____
f. because my best friends decided to go and I wanted to stay with them.	2%	_____
g. because I want to become an educated person.	86%	___✓___
h. because I had heard about college social life, and it sounded fun.	5%	_____
i. because I want to occupy a particular place in society (e.g., middle or upper class).	37%	___✓___
j. because I want to change careers.	2%	_____
k. because I was bored and needed new interests, friends, and ideas in my life.	5%	_____
l. because I need more education in order to advance in my present career.	22%	_____
m. because I want to use my V.A. benefits.	2%	_____
n. other	10%	_____

Figure 2.1 The age range of these students was 16–55. Sixty percent were members of ethnic minority groups, and 52 percent were female.

The <u>reasons</u> checked <u>most frequently</u> were "because I want to become an <u>educated person</u>" and "because I want to prepare myself for a <u>specific job</u> or profession." You need to <u>remember</u> your <u>own good reasons</u> for coming to college in order to stay motivated.

2. Create 「*interest*」 *in every class.* <u>Search</u> for material in every class or assignment that is <u>interesting</u> and <u>important</u> to you. Try to <u>relate</u> such material <u>to</u> the <u>goals</u> that brought you to college in the first place. Refresh these goals in your mind when your interest lags. Remember, also, that college can help you learn to enjoy your leisure time. Explore

② create interest

various fields and find out about subjects new to you. <u>Variety</u>
will help you stay <u>interested</u>.

3. Work to guarantee |*early success.*| Start immedi-
ately in each class to do your best work. This way you will
<u>give yourself the best opportunity for some immediate suc-</u>
<u>cess.</u> Early success earned by work well-done will motivate
you and make concentration on future projects easier.

*③ do first
assignment
well*

*success =
sucess*

4. Reward yourself for reaching your goals.   Plan
regular rewards for meeting your daily short-term goals so
that you will finish your work and also have something to
look forward to at the end of the day. Remind yourself also of
the internal satisfaction and rewards that come from accom-
plishing what is important to you.

*④ rewards
[shoot pool,
call a
friend]*

**5. Think of the consequences of not meeting your
goals.**   On days when concentration is particularly difficult,
<u>visualize the life you are likely to lead if you do not meet your</u>
<u>educational goals.</u> Most students quickly rekindle an interest
in school assignments when they contemplate a lifetime of
working at the jobs they hold in the summer or after school.

*⑤ think:
what if
I don't?*

*Stay motivated by both internal and external forces. Remem.
5 ways: Remem. reason for coming, create interest, 1st
assign. done well. Rewards. Remem. consequences of not doing.*

CONTINUE TO READ AND MARK THIS BOOK IN THIS WAY.

This method not only helps you to concentrate on your reading,
it helps you to remember what you have read by employing some of
the psychological factors that influence learning. (1) It enables you
to perceive the author's *organization of* ideas (note the summary that
captures the organization) and this aids both comprehension and
memory. (2) It encourages you to *react* to the author's ideas (note the
reader's comment in square brackets in the margin). And (3) it forces
you to *repeat key ideas* in your mind as you write them in the margin
and rewrite them in your own summary.

LEARN HOW TO HANDLE INTERNAL DISTRACTIONS

You can further improve both your concentration and motivation by
coping with the thoughts and emotions that cause your mind to

wander while you are studying. Some of the most common distractions can be dealt with as follows.

1. Take care of the small jobs you suddenly remember. You have two choices of action when you suddenly think of something you need to do: either stop and do it immediately, or write it down, along with a time for doing it, so that it will not continue to distract you.

2. Avoid worrying about problems that have no immediate solutions. Vague, unstated problems cause worry that can interfere with both motivation and concentration. Isolate and understand a problem by writing or talking about it. Then, think of solutions, even though they may not be perfect ones. Discuss the solutions with a friend or counselor or write them down. Finally, work to solve your problem. When you have done everything you can, put the problem out of your mind and resume work on the goals that are most important to you.

3. Daydream productively. An extremely successful businessman once told an interviewer that he daydreamed all the time, always about future business ventures. His success came from translating his daydreams into reality. You can learn to daydream about completed assignments and then work to make your daydreams real. Avoid other nonproductive daydreaming while you are studying.

4. Take a break or switch subjects. If you get tired of studying one subject, switch to another, and if you get tired of studying, take a break. You do not have to switch or take a break, however, if your concentration and motivation remain at a high level. Some students can maintain a high level of interest while studying for several hours at a time. Others need to take a break every hour or two.

5. Work to improve your confidence. Build confidence by doing difficult things that are important to you. Getting started on a difficult job is often the hardest part. It gets easier as you get closer to the end. When the job is completed, you will have gained some confidence, and confidence from various successes will accumulate and will improve your ability to concentrate.

6. Learn to deal with nervousness or tension. Anyone who spends his or her life doing challenging and difficult things has not totally banished nervousness. Its cause is excess physical energy that is generated by your body to help you do something that is important to you. The best way to deal with nervousness is to try to figure out what is pressing you and then get to work on it. Your nervousness will gradually go away as you concentrate on completing your project. If you still feel nervous when you have finished, work off your excess energy through physical activity. When you have worn yourself out, take a long hot bath or shower, get to bed early. You'll feel better the next day.

7. Cope with depression. Its cause can be loneliness, homesickness, anger, or disappointment with yourself. Family, illness, and money problems can also cause depression. If you are subject to depression, you should know that you can make things worse by not eating regularly, by not sleeping enough, by getting a bad hangover, and by not getting regular exercise. Fight depression by regulating your living habits and by trying to figure out what is depressing you. Talk to a friend or a counselor in your college's counseling office. Such help is usually free. If you're having a bad day, try to find something to salvage it. Do a job that you have been putting off for a long time. Your depression will usually lift faster if you give yourself the satisfaction of completing something that has been bothering you.

8. Work yourself out of mental dead ends. When you are blocked by a difficult assignment and feel that you cannot concentrate, break it down into parts and calculate the order in which you will do them. Next, physically isolate yourself from all distractions. If you can't find seclusion in the library or your room, find an empty classroom or even an empty car. Then start on the first step. As soon as you can, set a deadline so that you can see the end of what has bothered you for so long. Give yourself a big reward when you finish. You will deserve it.

9. Use positive self-talk. Turn negative statements that filter through your mind into positive statements. Instead of thinking, "I'm tired, I'm bored, I can't do this," consciously think instead, "This is the best part of my day, I feel energetic, this is interesting, I can do this." Include positive self-images with your positive self-talk. Stop imagining yourself as poor in math or poor in English or unable to concentrate, and relabel yourself as a success. Visualize yourself receiving your diploma, successfully interviewing for a job, working at something you really like to do. Frequently remind yourself of the value of the work you do now and later both to yourself and to others.

LEARN TO AVOID EXTERNAL DISTRACTIONS

Make a list of the external distractions that interfere with your efforts to concentrate. For most students this includes televisions, radios, telephones, refrigerators, magazines, friends, and family members. Shut off, shut out, and shun all of these during those periods of time you have set aside for study.

One exception to this rule are those students who concentrate better with music playing. Music can shut out other more distracting noise if it is not too distracting itself. It can also signal you to start concentrating on your studying as soon as you turn it on. Music will not help everyone concentrate. Many people require complete silence.

LEARN TO AVOID THE COMMON WORK DODGES OF STUDENTS

Getting an education is hard and sometimes painful work. When this is the case, it is human nature to find ways to avoid it. And when you successfully avoid your work, you never give yourself a chance to develop your powers of concentration. The internal and external distractions just described can interfere with concentration, as can the following very common work dodges. Learn to recognize and avoid them.

1. Avoid idle conversation. It's fine to talk to your friends if you really have nothing that has to be done or if you are rewarding yourself for something you have just finished. Most students, however, must learn to say, "I have to study—I'll see you later," or they may talk their way right out of college.

2. Know when you are rationalizing. Common rationalizations or excuses you hear students use are, "The professor is no good"; "The textbook is boring"; "This place doesn't really care about students"; "That professor's test questions sure don't come out of the book or his lectures"; "I studied everything for ten hours and I still got an F"; "I don't have to read the textbook in this class because it isn't important"; "I don't have to go to class because I read the textbook"; "Everyone in the whole class flunked the test, so it must have been a bad test"; and "I've studied two hours. That's enough for one day."

It's all right to say these things if they make you feel better temporarily. After you finish rationalizing, however, you should take a good look at the *real* reasons why you said what you said and then do what you can to make the situation better. There will be a lot of suggestions in this book to help you solve your *real* problems in school.

3. Avoid drugs and alcohol when you are studying. Don't tell yourself that you can think and remember while you are drinking or high because you can't.

4. Stay healthy. Some students get mild illnesses frequently. If this is one of the ways you dodge work, start studying in bed. You'll get well faster.

Exercise, walk, run, or play sports several times a week. Students who never move become lethargic and have difficulty concentrating. Regular exercise, worked into your schedule at appropriate times, will make you more alert, more energetic, and will improve your ability to concentrate.

5. Stay awake when it is time to study. When you sleep a lot in the daytime and play most of the night, you are dodging your schoolwork. If you get so tired you can't think, set the alarm for short, fifteen-minute naps. They are more refreshing than a three-hour nap. Then get back to work.

6. Go to class and do all assignments. Of all the advice given so far to improve both your concentration and your motivation, this may be the most important. No one can stay motivated to concentrate on material that contains great gaps caused by missed classes and assignments.

LEARN TO MONITOR YOUR COMPREHENSION

Pay attention to what you understand and what is confusing you. If you do not understand something, ask for clarification, go back and re-read, stop and think about it or write about what you have learned. *Insist* on adequate understanding.

To help you understand and also remember what you read, look away from your book at times and explain to yourself, in your own words, what you have just read. When you leave a class, you can also mentally rehearse in your own words what you have just learned. Then go a step further and think about what you have learned. Try to relate it to what you already know by making connections and associations.

USE ACTIVE LEARNING STRATEGIES

The text marking method that was demonstrated in this chapter and that you should be using right now as you continue to read forces you to be active and to concentrate. Active strategies that will help you concentrate in class include listening, taking notes, asking questions, and participating in class discussions and group work. The other active learning strategies sketched out so far in this chapter for reading and taking notes, improving motivation, dealing with distractions, learning in class, monitoring your comprehension, and rehearsing and thinking about what you have learned, are a preview of what is to come. They are discussed briefly here so that you will have some immediate strategies to employ during the early days of the semester when your motivation is strong and you need the sense of early success. All of these strategies along with many others like them will be taught in the following chapters. As you read this book, remember that the study skills and strategies presented here are not just to be studied. They are to be *used* in all of your other classes.

Once they have one good semester behind them, most students go on to make a success of college. Select classes and a class load you think you can handle. If you've made a mistake by signing up for too much, cut back. Then use what you can from the following chapters to make each semester a successful one.

At the Very Least . . .

This chapter has dealt with some ideal ways of improving your concentration. If you can't follow all of the suggestions every day, *at the very least* do this much:

1. Start underlining and writing notes in all of your textbooks.
2. Start taking some notes in all of your classes.
3. Start monitoring your comprehension to be aware of what you understand and what you do not understand. Take steps to improve understanding.
4. Analyze the distractions in your life and start managing them.
5. Discover what motivates you.

SUMMARY

Improving your ability to concentrate and remain motivated can make you more successful in college. Marking your textbooks as you read is one way to guarantee good concentration. Having a reason for being in college, generating interest, working for early success, and rewarding yourself can help you stay motivated. You can also improve concentration by avoiding internal and external distractions and avoiding the work dodges common to students. Taking notes in class, monitoring your comprehension, and rehearsing and thinking about what you learn can also help you achieve a consistently high level of concentration. If you can successfully complete one semester, other successful semesters will usually follow.

SELF-TEST

Do you know what will be demanded of you as a college student? Not knowing what to do or how to do it can be a major distraction that can interfere with your concentration and your education. Test yourself on what you know and don't know right now. Answer each question by checking Yes or No.

Look at your No answers. If you have answered No to 75 or 80 percent of the questions—that is, all but three or four—you are a pretty typical beginning college student. Notice that to the right of each of your answers is the chapter number where you can start reading to change your No answers to Yes. When you can answer all of these questions Yes, this book will have done for you what it was intended to do.

	Yes	No	*Find Out How in Chapters*
1. Do you know what kind of notebooks best keep your class materials organized?	____	✗	3
2. Do you know how to figure out what each professor expects of you so you will get a good grade in each class you take?	____	____	4
3. Do you know how to take notes on a fifty-minute lecture and how to study them later?	____	____	5
4. Do you have a method for spotting and learning the specialized vocabulary and concepts in a college class?	____	____	6
5. Do you know how to make worthwhile contributions to class discussion?	____	✗	7

	Yes	No	*Find Out How in Chapters*
6. Do you know how to read and take notes on a textbook and three or four supplementary paperback books for one course without the constant supervision of the teacher?	_____	_____	8–10
7. Do you know a quick and efficient way of taking notes on your reading?	_____	_____	10
8. Do you know how to improve your memory of what is said in class and what you read?	_____	_____	11
9. Do you know how to think about and reflect on what you are learning?	_____	_____	11
10. Do you know how to study for and take exams?	_____	_____	12 & 13
11. Do you know how to analyze a failed exam in order to keep from failing the next one?	_____	_____	13
12. Do you know how to plan, research, write, and revise a term paper?	_____	_____	14
13. Are you able to find a book and a magazine article on a particular subject in a large university library?	_____	_____	15
14. Do you know how to find specific information for research purposes without reading the entire book?	_____	_____	15
15. Do you know how to give oral reports?	_____	_____	16

EXERCISES

A. Monitor Your Comprehension of This Chapter

Write quickly using phrases rather than complete sentences, all of the information in this chapter that you understand and remember. Look back and add what you left out. Is anything unclear? Jot it down to ask about in class. Has reading the chapter caused you to think of new insights or examples of your own? Jot them down.

B. Class Exercises

1. Small Groups.   Make a list of all of the internal and external distractions that interfere with your concentration. Look back at the lists on pages 16 to 19 to see if you have forgotten any that you would like to add to the list. Now decide what you can do to minimize the negative effect of these distractions. Report back to the class on what you decide.

2. *Small Groups.*   Make a list of all the ways you now work to improve your concentration. What else might you do? Go through the suggestions in this chapter and add the ones you think would work for you. Modify them when necessary to make them work better. Report back to the class on your list of ways to improve concentration.

3. *Whole Class.*   Brainstorm and list on the board everything that the class can think of that helps them stay motivated to do well in college.

4. *Whole Class.*   Make a list on one side of the board of some causes of worry, stress, and depression. On the other side of the board, make a second list of ways to cope with these negative feelings. The purpose of this exercise is to demonstrate that negative feelings need to be identified and dealt with so that they do not interfere with your success.

C. Application Exercises

1. Continue to mark this book as demonstrated in this chapter. Expect occasional book checks when your instructor will ask all of you in class to open this book to a particular page and hold them up to show that you are reading and marking them. Begin to take notes in your other textbooks also.

2. Monitor your comprehension on one reading assignment for another class. Circle all of the words and mark with a line in the margin all of the passages that you don't understand. Reread the assignment and see if you understand more. Describe in writing what you understand, what you don't understand, and what you can do to understand more.

D. Topics for Your Learning Journal

1. Write a plan to help you improve your concentration. Include in your plan all the things that help you concentrate.

2. Describe causes of worry, stress, or depression for you along with ways to cope with each of them. Write a brief plan for yourself that includes all of the ways you can best manage your stress and other negative feelings.

3. Try some positive self-talk. Make a list of all your unique abilities and characteristics.

> Sample: *I am very alert between 8 p.m. and midnight and can study then. People can count on me to do what I say I will do.*

4. What motivates you? Make a list and then identify which are internal and which are external motivators. Which are more powerful motivators for you, those that are external or those that are internal?

3 | *Organizing Your Study Materials, Study Place, and Time*

When you have finished this chapter, you will have decided the following:

1. What kind of notebooks to buy.
2. Where you will keep your study materials.
3. Where you will study.
4. How you will manage your time.

FREE YOUR CREATIVE ENERGIES

You will free your creative energies and improve your ability to concentrate if you make some initial decisions about routine at the beginning of the semester and then turn those decisions into daily habits. Think what a waste of time it would be to have to decide each day whether or not to brush your teeth. You will also waste time by deciding more than once about the matters discussed in this chapter. Turn as many of your daily activities as possible into routine habits so that you can use your creative energies to concentrate on new material and ideas you are learning in your classes.

ORGANIZE STUDY MATERIALS IN NOTEBOOKS

When final exam time comes, you must be able to put your hands on the material to study. All lecture notes, reading notes, class handouts, returned exams and papers, and mimeographed information need to be in some order so that you can find them easily. The important thing is that you have some kind of system.

Be ready to start taking lecture notes at your very first classes. Buy your notebooks and have them full of plenty of standard size paper (8½ by 11 inches). Don't buy smaller paper. It is easy for professors to lose, and it's hard for you to study small pieces of paper. Take two pens with you to your first classes.

There are at least three basic ways to organize your study materials in notebooks. One of them or a combination of them will work for you. Whatever system you choose, remember to keep all materials for each course separate from each other.

Spiral Notebooks

Advantages

All lecture notes for each course are bound together separately and permanently.

At the end of a semester class notes can be filed and easily found months or years later.

Disadvantages

No convenient place to put handouts and other loose papers such as missed notes (unless you buy notebooks with pockets already bound into them). Easy to take the wrong notebook to class by mistake. (Write subject of each notebook on front in big black letters.)

Loose-Leaf Notebooks with Dividers

Advantages

All materials for all courses can be kept together.

Loose materials can be punched and inserted next to the material they are meant to accompany.

Easy to xerox borrowed notes and insert them where they belong.

Disadvantages

If you fold and stuff loose materials into notebook because it's too much trouble to punch holes, you end up with a mess. Some papers tear loose and need to be repaired.

Folders with Double Pockets

Advantages

Lecture notes may be kept separately in right-hand pocket along with blank paper for future note taking.

Other materials, such as mimeographed pages, assignment sheets, and returned papers, may be kept in left-hand pocket.

Disadvantages

If you drop a folder, the papers fall out. Can be disastrous on a windy day. (Best to carry all folders in a zipper bag or briefcase at all times.) Folders are somewhat fragile. They may begin to fall apart before semester is over and have to be replaced.

Advantages (Continued)
You can loan notes without loan-
    ing entire notebook.
No need to punch holes.
Ready to file permanently at end
    of semester.
Folders are cheap.

DECIDE WHERE TO KEEP ASSIGNMENTS

Make assignment sheets for each class before the first day (see Figure 3.1). Put them where you can find them easily in your notebook. Record all assignments on this sheet in as much detail as possible. Cross them off as you complete them. Always write the due date for each assignment so that you'll get your work in on time.

You may prefer to buy an assignment book or a week-at-a-glance appointment book. Whichever system you use, make certain to always write down every assignment along with the date it is due.

ESTABLISH A HEADQUARTERS AND A PLACE TO STUDY

You will need a "headquarters" where you can keep not only lecture notes and other materials you accumulate in class, but also textbooks, library books, supplementary paperback books, xeroxed copies of

Assignment *History*	Date Due
Read pp. 21–75 of text	Mon., Sept. 21
Quiz on first 75 pp. of text	Fri., Sept. 25
Read 1st half of Uncle Tom's Cabin	Thur., Oct. 1
Finish Uncle Tom's Cabin and turn in 500-word paper on its social and political influences when first published.	Fri., Oct. 15

Figure 3.1   An example of an assignment sheet.

articles from periodicals, paper, and pens. Ideally, your headquarters will have a desk where you can study in seclusion and shelves where you can stack all of the materials for each of your classes separately. When everything is stacked according to classes, you will be less likely to lose track of various books and papers. The stacks don't have to be neat.

You may want to keep materials for your M-W-F classes separate from your T-Th class material. This makes it easier to find what you need each morning.

If you live with other people and can't set up a desk and bookshelves at home, "headquarters" may have to be a corner of a room or even some boxes under your bed. You will keep your books and materials together there, but you will actually study in a number of other places.

If you *want* to study, you will find that you can do so almost anywhere. You need enough seclusion so that you can concentrate and feel psychologically and physically comfortable. You don't have to sit in an uncomfortable, hard chair to make yourself study.

Here is a list of possible study places. The list is deliberately varied. Check those that might be good for you.

1. A big chair in an out-of-the-way room   yes _____   no _____

2. On your bed   yes _____   no _____

3. The kitchen table   yes _____   no _____

4. The dining room table   yes _____   no _____

5. A card table set up in the least-used room of the house   yes _____   no _____

6. Your car parked on a side street or in a parking lot   yes _____   no _____

7. An out-of-the-way stairway at school   yes _____   no _____

8. A cafeteria or a restaurant while you are eating   yes _____   no _____

9. Out-of-the-way corners of the library   yes _____   no _____

10. Empty classrooms (often available in the late afternoon)   yes _____   no _____

You need to have alternate places to study so that if you start to work in one place, are interrupted, and can't concentrate, you can pick up and move before an uncomfortable amount of frustration sets in. Just be sure that wherever you study, you take along the books, notes, pens, and paper you need to get the particular job done.

There will be days when you have to study, but you don't feel like it. On such days you need a special place, completely free from diversions, where you go *only* to study and which, because of habit, always signals "study" to you. Seek out such a place and use it regularly as your retreat when you can't concentrate. Try to find a place completely free from diversion—no refrigerator, no telephone, no magazines, no television.

When you get to your place, think through the work you have to do. If there's a lot, jot down the jobs on a list and then number them in order of priority. Pick the *most pressing* item on the list and then get to work on it immediately.

LEARN TO MANAGE YOUR TIME

Effective time management is a result of both conscious effort and experience. If you have time problems while you are at college, they will probably be caused by one of the following: First, compared to high school, where you were in class more hours, it seems that you now have time to burn. You get a false sense of security, and you let time slip away without getting enough work done. Or, second, you are taking classes and labs, working, and you also have family responsibilities. It seems that there is no way to find enough time to do it all. Whichever category you fall into, your problems are real ones. Use the following suggestions to help you manage your time effectively.

1. Make a Time Analysis Worksheet.   Figures 3.2 and 3.3 are examples of a completed Time Analysis Worksheet. Fill out one of these at the beginning of each semester to help you analyze your *fixed time commitments,* which are written on the analysis sheet, and your *available study times,* which are boxed in with heavy pencil. This sheet has two purposes: (1) to help you focus on your daily time commitments and learn them, and (2) to help you find the hours when study would be possible. A blank Time Analysis Worksheet is provided in Figure 3.4. When you have written in or crossed off your fixed time commitments, count to make sure that you have twice as many hours of flexible study time as you have time in class. If you do not have enough study time, cut back on some of your other commitments or make some trade-offs so that you will create ample time for study. For example, if you have home responsibilities, ask family

	Mon.	Tues.	Wed.	Thurs.	Fri.	Sat.	Sun.
6:00	sleep	sleep	sleep	sleep	sleep	sleep	sleep
7:00	↓	↓	↓	↓	↓	↓	↓
8:00	dress eat	dress	dress eat	dress	dress eat		
9:00	Hist.	eat	Hist.	eat	Hist.	dress eat	
10:00	Eng.	Biol.	Eng.	Biol.	Eng.	Work	↓
11:00		Psych.		Psych.			eat
12:00	eat	eat	eat	eat	eat		↓
1:00		Biol. lab					
2:00	Math	Biol. lab	Math		Math		
3:00		Biol. lab					
4:00		rest				↓	
5:00	work	eat	eat	eat	eat	go out	eat
6:00							↓
7:00					go out		
8:00							
9:00	↓						movie
10:00							
11:00					↓	↓	
12:00	sleep	sleep	sleep	sleep	sleep	sleep	sleep

Figure 3.2 A Time Analysis Worksheet for a student living in a dorm or apartment who is taking four classes and working twelve hours per week.

members to help with some of them so that you can find the time you need to study.

2. Make a Time Management Worksheet. One of the most difficult aspects of time management is learning to estimate the amount of time it takes you to do different tasks. Most inexperienced college students underestimate the time they will need to complete college assignments. During your first days at college

	Mon.	Tues.	Wed.	Thurs.	Fri.	Sat.	Sun.
6:00						sleep →	
7:00	dress,	eat,	travel —			→	family
8:00	Psych	Acctng	Psych	Acctng	Psych	Work	
9:00	Math	travel	Math	Travel	Math		
10:00	travel		travel		travel		
	Work	Work	Work	Work	Work		
11:00	↓	↓	↓	↓	↓	↓	
12:00						family	
1:00	Work	Work	Work	Work	Work	chores and	↓
2:00						rec-reation	
3:00							
4:00	↓	↓	↓	↓	↓		
5:00	travel home —				→		family
6:00	← eat —				→		↓
7:00	time with family				→		↓
8:00					family and		
9:00					rec-reation		
10:00					↓		
11:00	sleep —				→		sleep
12:00	sleep —				→	↓	↓

Figure 3.3 A Time Analysis Worksheet for a student with a family and who is taking three classes and working 32 hours a week.

	Mon.	Tues.	Wed.	Thurs.	Fri.	Sat.	Sun.
6:00							
7:00							
8:00							
9:00							
10:00							
11:00							
12:00							
1:00							
2:00							
3:00							
4:00							
5:00							
6:00							
7:00							
8:00							
9:00							
10:00							
11:00							
12:00							

Figure 3.4   A blank Time Analysis Worksheet.

notice how many pages you can read in an hour in each of your textbooks, how long it takes to write a two-page paper, find materials in the library, or work a set of math problems. Armed with this information about your own time requirements, make a Time Management Worksheet like the one in Figure 3.5. Notice that this sheet is exactly like the Assignment Sheet in Figure 3.1 except that it has three more columns to help you figure out when you will complete each assignment.

a. Divide a piece of notebook paper into five columns and label them.

b. Write major, time-consuming tasks in column 1. It is not time efficient to use this worksheet for reminders, for appointments, or other tasks that do not take several hours of time.

c. Write due dates in column 2.

d. Estimate the time you think it will take you to complete the entire task and write it in column 3. If you are unsure of the time required, overestimate. This allows time for occasional interruptions.

Remember that library research always takes more time than you think it will. Estimate how long you think it will take, and add two hours.

Task	Date Due	Time Required	Start by	Completed
Read *Grapes of Wrath*.	April 25	15 hours	April 10 — Read an hour a day 10-11 p.m.	
Write paper on *Grapes of Wrath* — 500 words typed.	April 30	outline - 2 hrs. draft - 2 hrs. revise - 2 hrs. Type - 2 hrs. total - 8 hrs.	April 26 (2 hrs/day for 4 days) 1 - 3 p.m.	
Do math problems pp. 46-48.	May 1	3 hours	April 30 7-10 p.m.	
Read *Intro to Engineering* 30 pages.	May 3	4 hours	May 2 7-11 p.m.	

Figure 3.5 A Time Management Worksheet.

e. Consult your Time Analysis Worksheet for available study time. Then commit the time you will need in order to meet the due date to do the task.

f. Now use the time you have found to complete the assignment. If something interferes, find another time and commit it by writing it down.

   If you organize everything you do in a pocket calendar that you carry with you, you can write deadlines for assignments in it. Then block off the time that you will need to complete the assignment and label how you will use that time.

You do not have to become a slave to Time Analysis and Time Management worksheets. Use them when you need them: at the beginning of semesters to get off to a good start, when you feel pressured by a lot of work and need to feel reassured that you really do have time to get everything done, or during exam week.

3. *Get off to a fast start.* When you start to study, get right to work. Have your study area ready: cleared space, sharp pencils, plenty of paper and supplies. An organized work area is especially important if you are a methodical person who likes structure and systems. You may, on the other hand, like a certain amount of clutter. Some people can keep several projects going at once in what might appear to be disorganization to other people. The important thing is that you know where things are and that you create a work environment that suits your work style. Leave it the way you like it each time you finish studying so that you won't waste time getting ready to study. If you are in the middle of a project, leave it out so that you can get right back into it. When you start, you need to have decided exactly what you want to accomplish and how much time it should take you. Use some positive self-talk to remind yourself what you want to do, how long it will take, what the benefits will be, and that you *can* do it. Some students are motivated to get off to a fast start by contemplating, for a few seconds, the consequences of not doing the assignment. If it is especially hard to get started, you can always start with an easy task.

4. *Work to finish rather than to put in time.* Many successful college students never use time schedules. Instead, they figure out what needs to be done each day and then they study during every available time until they are finished. When they finish early, they enjoy their free time for the rest of the day. You may not have this much discipline immediately. You will eventually develop it, however, if you think in terms of completing assignments rather than putting in a set amount of time on each subject each week. For example, instead of sitting down to read history for two hours, mentally estimate that you have about six hours of history to read by Friday. Then use all available study time to complete the assignment as soon as possible. When you think not just in terms of putting in time but in terms of finishing jobs, you get a lot more done in a shorter period of time.

5. Make lists and set priorities.   Briefly list the things you want to accomplish each day. Number the items in order of importance, do one thing at a time, and cross them off as you complete them. Quit for the day when they are all completed. You may want to keep a week-at-a-glance appointment book so you can see what you need to do week by week as well as day by day.

6. Break big jobs into parts.   Look at the second item on the Time Management Worksheet (Figure 3.4). Notice in the "time required" column that a paper assignment has been broken down into manageable parts with time limits for each part. You will complete long and difficult assignments more effectively and with less stress if you deal with them in this way.

7. Make good use of your best time.   Some of us are most alert in the morning. Others get a surge of energy as soon as the sun goes down. Discover the times of the day when you are most alert, feel motivated, and concentrate best. Do your most difficult or most important studying at those times.

8. Make good use of class time.   Class is one of the best places and times to get a lot of your work for that day's class started. Under the stimulus of the classroom, you can usually accomplish twice as much as you could later on your own. Spend class time listening to the professor, writing notes, jotting down your own ideas, and asking questions. Keep your textbook handy to refer to it when the teacher does. Get to class five minutes early so that you can use that time to look over the notes you took at the last class.

When you make the most of the hour in class, you will become more interested. You can also often cut your outside study time in half and still do a good job. Students with outside jobs especially have to make the best possible use of all class time.

9. Make good use of odds and ends of time.   Use small amounts of time during the day for small jobs or to get started on larger assignments. A lot can be done in even fifteen minutes. Take something to read or to work on when you are waiting for an appointment, waiting to pick up family members, or at other times when there are a few minutes to use. This is especially important for busy people with tight schedules. Use free hours between classes to keep up with classes that require regular, spaced study, such as math, language, science, or shorthand.

*10. **Make good use of study time.*** Study during the times you have designated for study so that you will protect your free time. Most people work faster and with better concentration if they know that they must finish within a certain time period or else cut into free time. If you get bored or have trouble concentrating during this time, switch to another activity. If you get sleepy, walk around or do some exercises.

*11. **Set deadlines and rewards including short breaks.*** It is motivating to test your ability to work against deadlines. Use the Time Management Worksheet to help you do this. Then enjoy your time off with a clear conscience. Also, learn to take brief 3 to 5 minute breaks every hour or so if necessary. Make a cup of tea, listen to a song, play a computer game, or call a friend to agree to meet later. Make the breaks short and then get back to work.

*12. **Make time for memorizing, thinking, and review.*** Such important learning activities take time. Set aside at least fifteen or twenty minutes out of each major study period for memorizing and review. Use the times when you are most creative for free thinking time. Many people's best insights come to them when they are walking, driving home, taking a walk, or, especially, when waking up in the morning. Be prepared to make a record of your ideas. Keep a pad of paper handy. Some people talk into tape recorders while they are driving to capture their ideas.

At the Very Least . . .

This chapter has dealt with the ideal way of improving your organization. If you can't follow all of the suggestions every day, *at the very least* do this much:

1. Organize your study materials so that they are separate for each class.
2. Set up a study place that is free from external distractions.
3. Analyze how long it takes to do assignments and start allowing ample time.

SUMMARY

Your whole semester will go more smoothly and you will be able to concentrate and study better if you make some decisions and act on them before you begin attending classes. Buy separate notebooks for each class. Outfit them with paper for the first day in class. Find a place to stack books and other study materials for each class so they won't get lost. Decide where you will do your studying. Learn to manage your time so that you will meet your study responsibilities and still have time for recreation.

EXERCISES

A. Monitor Your Comprehension of This Chapter

Write quickly, in phrases rather than complete sentences, the information in this chapter that you understand and remember. Look back and add what you left out. Is anything unclear? Jot it down to ask about in class. Has reading the chapter caused you to think of new insights or examples of your own? Jot them down.

B. Class Exercises

1. **Small Groups.**   Discuss each of the twelve suggestions for time management in this chapter (pp. 29–36). Which ones could you follow as they are? Which ones would you eliminate because you don't think they would work? Which ones would you change or modify and how? What suggestions would you add? Report back to the class on your group's time management plan: what you like, what you would change, and what you would add to the list in the chapter.

2. **Whole Class.**   Brainstorm activities for *short* 3 to 5 minute study breaks, such as calling a friend or listening to a song. Discuss how you can take such breaks and then get back to work.

3. **Individual and Whole Class.**   On the Time Analysis Worksheet in Figure 3.4, write in your fixed time commitments for school, work, and other responsibilities. Box in the hours when you could study. Count the number of hours spent in class each week and the number of study hours. There should be twice as many study hours as class hours.

   Identify the members of the class who will have severe time problems either because they have too little or too much time to study. Discuss how these students can solve their time management problems. The class should work to come up with specific suggestions.

C. Application Exercises

1. Set up the system you will use to organize lecture notes and other classroom materials and be prepared to describe your system in class.

2. Make assignment sheets for each of your classes like the example on page 27 and place them in the front of your notebooks. Or set up a pocket calendar that you can carry with you.

3. Set up a study headquarters and decide on two good places to study.

D. *Topics for Your Learning Journal*

1. Write a paragraph describing the system you have set up for organizing your study materials and explain why you chose it.

2. Write a paragraph describing your study place, how you have organized it, and how you have made it pleasant for you to work there.

3. Either by yourself or as a class project, make a list of everything you can think of that interferes with your effective time management. Now make a list of everything you can think of that will help you manage your time. Finally, write a time management plan that will help you accomplish your goals in college.

4. When and where are your best times for creative and insightful thinking? How will you keep a record of your ideas?

5. Are you a methodical, organized person or do you like clutter, diversion, and several things going on at once? Describe how you organize your work and time that is compatible with your personality but that still allows you to be productive.

PART TWO

Going to Class

4 | Analyzing Your Learning Style and Adapting to Your Classes

When you have finished reading this chapter, you will know the following:

1. How you learn best.
2. How to figure out what to do to pass each class.
3. Where to seek outside help if you need it.
4. What to do if you get in a class that is too hard for you.

WHY ANALYZE YOUR CLASSES?

The purpose of carefully analyzing your classes is *to enable you to adapt to them better.* Classes and teachers are all different. When you adapt to each of them well, you learn well.

Part of adapting to classes involves analyzing how you learn best, analyzing how the class is taught, and then adjusting your style of learning to the class. Analyze, also, the organization of the class, what your responsibilities will be, and where you can get extra help if you need it.

WHAT IS YOUR BEST LEARNING STYLE?

We all have preferred ways of learning, and they are not the same for everyone. Current research suggests that most people have ways that they prefer to take in information, prefer to express themselves, and even prefer to study. Such preferences are known as *learning styles.*

It is valuable to know your preferred style so that when you have a choice of how to get information, express yourself, and study, you can select the method that is easiest and best for you. In some classes,

41

however, you will not have a choice. When you are not able to learn in your preferred style, you will often need to try harder than usual.

The exercises in this book are deliberately varied so that you will have to practice a variety of different styles. This should make it easier for you to adapt to all of your classes where different styles will be favored at different times. Now read through the following descriptions and check the ones that best describe you.

A. *How do you prefer to take in information?*

_____ 1. Some people learn best by *listening*. These people enjoy lectures, discussions, speeches, and tapes. It is not natural for them to take many lecture notes. They prefer to sit back and listen and may wonder what others are writing down. In math classes, such individuals may be able to follow the logic of a math problem by hearing it. They do not need to see it written on the blackboard to understand it.

_____ 2. Some people learn best by *seeing things written down.* These people want to see the math problems written on the board, and they want to copy them into their notes. They want to take notes on lectures so that they can see the ideas in written form. They appreciate outlines on the board, handouts circulated in class, and they like to read the textbook. Such individuals may even keep a notepad and pencil by the telephone to write down conversations because that helps them understand what they are hearing better.

_____ 3. Some people learn best from *visual* material. These people like pictures, illustrations, diagrams, graphs, maps, and outlines or diagrams of ideas. They also learn well from movies, slides, videotapes, and computer graphics. They appreciate it when the lecturer illustrates what is being said with visual material projected on a screen.

_____ 4. Some people learn best from *direct experience*. For these individuals, the best way to learn is by doing or making something. They like labs, field trips, and performance classes in art or theater. They are usually physically active people who would rather try to make a computer work, for example, instead of reading about it, looking at pictures of it, or hearing someone describe how to use it.

B. *How do you prefer to give out information?*

_____ 1. Some people like to *talk and discuss*. These people prefer oral reports and oral exams. They enjoy class discussions and small group work. When working on ideas for a paper or project, they like to talk their ideas through with someone else. *Talking* helps them think.

——— 2. Some people like to *write* their ideas. They may be shy about speaking, but they are comfortable expressing their ideas in writing. These individuals like journal writing, paper writing, and essay exams. *Writing* helps them think. These people are often the ones who volunteer to be the recorder during group work. They need to write as they listen to the group to make sense of what they hear.

——— 3. Some people like to *demonstrate* or *show* others how to do something. These people will volunteer to go to the board to draw or demonstrate a concept. Or they will push you aside to show you how to use the computer or how to do the lab experiment rather than try to explain it to you.

C. *How do you prefer to study?*

——— 1. Some people like to study by themselves. They find other people distracting, and they do not accomplish much in study groups.

——— 2. Some people like to study with one or more other people. They actively participate in study groups and learn much more than they could by themselves.

——— 3. Some people are more organized than others in their approach to study. They are systematic, they like planning ahead, and they usually have the things they need to do under control. They look for structure and organization in their classes and books, and they impose structure on their study materials. They like calendars, time management plans, organized notebooks and workplaces, and they like to start assignments early so that they will not suffer the stress that comes from procrastinating.

——— 4. Some people dislike plans and organization. They rely, instead, on flashes of insight and surges of creative energy to keep them moving along. They enjoy flexibility, novelty, and variety. They do not need to feel that everything is under control and predictable. They may put off work on a project until the last minute. They are still able to complete it successfully, however, because they have thought about it and they can summon the energy and drive to complete it in a short time. These people do not require neat workplaces. Outsiders may wonder how they can find anything. But they have their own order in what may appear to be chaos to others.

You may have found it easy to recognize yourself in some of the descriptions you just read because you have strong preferred learning styles. You may also have found that most of the descriptions are true of you at times. Remember that you will have to be flexible as college students and master more than one way of learning.

A number of commercial tests are available to help you further analyze your learning styles. Your Counseling Office should have some of these. If you are interested, you could make an appointment to take one.

WHAT IS YOUR PROFESSOR'S TEACHING STYLE? HOW CAN YOU ADAPT?

You now have some idea of your preferred learning style. Your professors also have preferred learning styles that are often reflected in the way they teach. When your style and your professor's style happen to match, you can learn relatively easily. When there is not a match, you will have to analyze and understand how the professor is teaching so that you can adapt and learn more easily.

It may not surprise you to learn that many of your professors learn best themselves by seeing things in print. They also like to write. Furthermore, when they lecture, they expect you to write notes. If reading and writing are not major features of your preferred learning style, you will need to develop expertise in these areas for success in these college classrooms. Use the information in this book to help you and also take reading and writing classes at college.

Recent research suggests that in addition to preferring print as a way of conveying information, professors may also have fairly distinctive ways of teaching.[1] Knowing what these are can help you adapt and learn. Read the following descriptions and check those that are similar to professors you have this semester.

———— 1. *Some professors are methodical and organized.* They are thorough, they go into detail, and they are exact, clear, and

[1] I am indebted to Muriel Rogie Radebaugh, Judy Nicely-Leach, Correen Morrill, William Shreeve, and Sheerie Slatton for their essay "Reading Your Professors: A Survival Skill," *Journal of Reading,* 31, January 1988, 328–332, where they describe the styles identified by Anthony F. Gregorc and suggest how students can adapt to different styles.

concise. They look for causes and explanations in the real world for the material they teach. They like to lecture, they are well-organized, and they are easy to follow.

These professors dislike messiness, procrastination, excuses, and disorganization. To be successful in their classes, you will need to get to class promptly and meet deadlines. In such classes it is best to attend always and to take lots of notes and review them regularly. The test questions will usually come from the lectures and the reading materials, so you should study both of them.

——— 2. *Some professors are theoretical and abstract.* These professors seem to have very quick minds and often make connections that you miss at times. These professors often use big, unfamiliar words to describe abstract ideas. They are good at producing new concepts and new conclusions.

To adapt to classes taught by professors of this type, you will have to study your notes and maybe even reorganize them after class to understand them. Tests will call for the ability to show how ideas relate to each other. They will also require the ability to use quotes from the books assigned in class to back up the new ideas that have been developed. Include these types of information on your study sheets (see Chapter 11) when you prepare for the exams. These professors may also assign research papers and expect you to come up with new insights and conclusions of your own as you write them. Write down all original ideas when they occur to you throughout the semester and use them in your papers.

——— 3. *Some professors want students to discover the ideas themselves.* These professors ask lots of questions and encourage students to think, experience for themselves, and figure out the main points from discussion or small group work. These professors do not usually lecture. They are more likely to set tasks and activities and to summarize and interpret what has transpired at the end of class.

These professors value and reward student participation, so go out of your way to participate. They expect you to take notes on discussions and especially to remember insights and original ideas. Make certain your notes include such information. They will want to see these ideas appear in papers and on exams, so study them and include them. For these professors the student's intellectual and

personal growth are extremely important. They may be
more lenient with deadlines than other professors because
they believe that a student may need extra time to do the
creative thinking necessary to complete a project. You
should ask for extra time, however only when there is an
emergency.

———— 4. *Some professors are creative and original, and they work out
their creative ideas as they teach.* These professors move
mentally from fact to theory very rapidly. Furthermore,
they do not always explain all of the logical steps in between. They like to describe processes and applications.
They are often dramatic. They are also sometimes hard to
understand.

To adapt to such classes, you will need to be willing to
risk thinking about new ideas and trying new methods.
Such activities will encourage you to see new applications
for ideas. You will need to be creative in these classes as
you work with your own original ideas.

You may have professors who strongly resemble these types or
who are a mixture of them. Furthermore, a single professor may
change from one style to another depending upon the subject, the
size of the class, or the educational level of the class.

The main point of all this is that you cannot expect every professor to teach in exactly the same way. You cannot expect to be able
to learn in exactly the same way in every class either. Adaptability
and flexibility can save you a great deal of frustration. They can help
you meet the challenges of learning in different ways in different
classes.

HOW IS THE CLASS ORGANIZED?

Besides analyzing your own learning style and the professor's teaching style, it is also useful to analyze how the class has been organized. The best explanation of the organization of a class is usually
the *syllabus,* normally distributed on the first day of class. A syllabus
usually gives several important types of information such as the
course objectives, the professor's office hours, the assignments, and
a list of the topics that will be covered during the semester. It is,
in effect, a preface and a table of contents for the course. Study it
carefully and fix both the objectives and the topics in your mind.
Consult it at the beginning of each class period to see what topic will

be covered that day. Read through it now and then later to develop a sense of the progression of topics in the class.

Learn more about the organization of a course by listening carefully to the professor's *opening remarks*. Very often the first lecture will provide a verbal outline of the course.

In some classes there will be no syllabus and no verbal explanation of the course's organization. You will understand and learn the material better if you make an effort to organize it yourself as you learn it. Take notes in class even if they seem disorganized. Then, read rapidly through your lecture notes every two or three weeks in order to discover the sequence of major topics. Make a list of the topics and group them under headings that you create. In this way, you will write your own class outline when one is not provided. The course will then make more sense to you, and you will remember it better.

WHAT ARE YOUR RESPONSIBILITIES IN THE CLASS?

Besides listing the topics to be covered, the syllabus often states the student's main responsibilities in a class. Most professors will reemphasize these responsibilities in their opening remarks. One way or another find out what is expected of you in the class. Specifically, you need to get answers to eight questions:

1. What is the most important source of information in the class? Is it the textbook, the lectures, or both? Whichever it is, that is what you master first.
2. Are there other sources of information you will need to consult or study? For example, has the professor placed on a reserve shelf in the library books that you will be expected to read? Are you expected to read any journal articles in the library during the semester? Are you expected to conduct interviews, attend labs, or otherwise gain more information for your class?
3. What are the reading assignments? When is each due?
4. Are you expected to write any papers in the class? If so, how long are they to be, will they require library research, and when are they due?
5. Are there any other special projects and assignments you must complete? By when?
6. How many exams will there be, and when? Is there a final exam? Will it cover the entire semester or only the material taught after

the last midterm exam? Will these exams be the essay, objective, or short-answer type, or some combination? Will you be examined primarily on the text, the lectures, both, or on all sources of information in the course?

7. What is the attendance policy in the class? Will unexcused absences lower your grade?

8. Is part of your grade based on your participation in class discussion?

Find out at the beginning of every semester exactly what is expected of you in each class. Then watch your time and plan ahead so that you will meet all of your class responsibilities. If you must be absent, meet with the professor, preferably before the next class meeting, and ask what you need to do to catch up. This is the *least* you must do to pass a course.

It is also a good idea to get the name and telephone number of another class member during the first week of school. This is added insurance for absence. If you cannot reach the professor to find out what you have missed, you can call a classmate to find out before you return to class.

IS THERE ANY OUTSIDE HELP AVAILABLE?

Review or discussion sessions are sometimes run by graduate assistants who work with the professor. These sessions may be voluntary or compulsory. In any case, go to them.

Many universities have tutoring services and learning labs. These services may include both individual tutoring in a particular subject and catch-up help if you have forgotten or have never learned some of the basic skills necessary to do well in college. Find out if your school has such a service, and use it. When you study with a tutor, you have to think and explain. Consequently, you learn more than when you passively sit in class. Most professors will set up office hours when they are available to discuss your points of confusion. This time is set aside for *you.* You may either make an appointment with your professor or simply show up during office hours. Come right to the point and describe what is confusing or troubling you so that your professor can help you. Professors also supply other types of help. They may prepare bibliographies to guide your outside reading and research. They may further help you by placing the important books for the class on reserve in the library.

Some professors make old exams available either in their office or in the library to help you prepare for exams.

WHAT IF A CLASS IS TOO DIFFICULT FOR YOU?

Classes usually seem too difficult when you lack the background or learning skills necessary to do well in them. Calculus will be too hard if you've forgotten or have never had trigonometry; chemistry and other college science classes will be too hard if you have a weak math background. History will seem difficult if you don't know how to take lecture notes, and so on. You may be tested during the first week of classes to see if you have sufficient background and skill to understand what will be taught. More often, however, you will not be tested.

This is what you should do when you find yourself in a class that seems too difficult: (1) you can describe the problem to the professor and get recommendations; (2) you can take advantage of all the extra help available to you (help sessions, tutors, remedial help, the help of classmates, professor's office hours) and try to pass; or (3) you can drop back and take the course or courses necessary to prepare you for the hard class. The last of these solutions is the best in many cases. Then you can take the hard class again later when you are better prepared to cope with it.

At the Very Least . . .

This chapter has dealt with the ideal way of analyzing and adapting to your classes. If you can't follow all of the suggestions every day, *at the very least* do this much:

1. Practice different learning strategies in different classes.
2. Figure out exactly what you must produce in each class.
3. Get help when you need it.

SUMMARY

All classes and professors are different. In order to adapt to each class and successfully complete it, you need to develop different learning styles. It is also useful to analyze the professor's teaching style in order to adapt to your classes successfully. You will understand a class and remember it better if you can see how it has been organized. You should, as soon as possible, determine all of your responsibilities in each class so that you won't leave important jobs undone. Finally, if a class is too hard, you need to seek help or drop back a level to a course you can handle.

EXERCISES

A. Monitor Your Comprehension of This Chapter

Write quickly, in phrases rather than complete sentences, the information in this chapter that you understand and remember. Look back and add what you left out. Is anything unclear? Jot it down to ask about in class. Has reading the chapter caused you to think of new insights or examples of your own? Jot them down.

B. Class Exercises

1. *Groups.* Create four groups in the class that are organized according to the four learning styles identified in this chapter. One group will be composed of students who identified themselves as *print* learners, one as *listeners,* one as *visual* learners, and one as *direct experience* learners. Each group should form answers to the following questions and report back to the class.
   a. What do you do and how do you feel in large lectures? If you take notes, how many pages of notes do you take per hour?
   b. How do you read textbook assignments? How do you feel about them?
   c. Do you prefer group study or studying alone?
   d. Are you good at library research? How do you feel about it?
   e. Are you good at using computers? How do you feel about them?
   f. Where do you learn best: in class or in your study place?
   g. Would you describe yourself as organized, organized in the midst of clutter, or disorganized?
   h. How do you prefer to communicate with others: writing, speaking, or demonstrating?

2. *Groups.* After the class has listened to all four group reports, students should get back in their groups and make a list of eight or more suggestions that would help members of that group learn to learn in the other three styles. Report these suggestions to the class.

3. *Whole Class.* In class discussion, identify classes that are taught according to the four teaching styles identified in this chapter. Discuss what students need to know about each of these classes. Include information about the organization of the class, the professor's expectations, and the student's responsibilities.

4. *Whole Class.* Discuss what to do if you must be absent from a class, turn in your homework late, miss an exam, or otherwise neglect to meet a major class responsibility.

5. *Whole Class.*   Discuss what to do if a class seems too hard for you. Use specific examples of difficult classes and identify specific coping strategies.

6. *Class Reports on Student Resources.*   Each student should select one campus resource on the Questionnaire on Campus Resources (Exercise C2, pages 52–54), visit the resource, and bring back a brochure or other information. Then each student should make a one-minute report on:
   a. The name and location of the resource
   b. One reason a student might go there
   c. The procedure for using it
   d. One striking feature that would motivate students to use this resource.

C. *Application of Skills*

1. *Class Analysis Sheet.*   Analyze your responsibilities in this class by completing the following sheet. Then answer the same questions for all of your other classes on separate sheets of paper.

   1. Class _____

   2. Professor _____

   3. Office Hours _____   4. Phone _____

   5. Other sources of help available _____

   _____

   6. What organizes the class, the lectures or the textbook? _____

   _____

   7. What are the major sources of information in the class? _____

   _____

   8. Describe the assignments (include reading, writing, special projects and

   due dates). _____

   _____

   9. How important is it for you to participate in class discussion? _____

   _____

   10. What is the attendance policy? _____

   _____

11. What is the policy on late homework? _____

_____

12. What is the policy on missed homework? _____

_____

13. How many exams are planned and when will they be given? _____

_____

14. Will the final cover only the material presented after the last midterm,

or will it cover the entire semester? _____

_____

15. What is the purpose of the course? _____

_____

16. What do I want to get out of this course? _____

_____

_____

17. What is the name and phone number of a classmate? _____

_____

2. *Questionnaire on Campus Resources.*   Check all the helping resources
that are available on your campus. Check also whether or not you have or
might use them.
a. Resources to help with studying and learning:

Resource	Available on Your Campus?		Will You or Have You Used?	
	Yes	*No*	*Yes*	*No*
1. Professor's office hours	_____	_____	_____	_____
2. Professor's review or help sessions	_____	_____	_____	_____
3. Teaching assistant's office hours	_____	_____	_____	_____
4. Teaching assistant's review or help sessions	_____	_____	_____	_____
5. Tutoring program	_____	_____	_____	_____

Resource	Available on Your Campus?		Will You or Have You Used?	
	Yes	No	Yes	No
6. Writing center	——	——	——	——
7. Learning assistance center	——	——	——	——
8. Reading lab	——	——	——	——
9. Math lab	——	——	——	——
10. Computer lab	——	——	——	——
11. Organized study groups	——	——	——	——
12. Supplemental instruction group	——	——	——	——
13. Study skills classes	——	——	——	——
14. Study skills workshops	——	——	——	——
15. Study skills counseling	——	——	——	——
16. Reading classes	——	——	——	——
17. Remedial math classes	——	——	——	——
18. Remedial English classes	——	——	——	——
19. Exam files	——	——	——	——
20. Reserve shelf in library	——	——	——	——
21. Organized study program in residence halls	——	——	——	——
22. Other: ———————	——	——	——	——

b. Resources to help you grow personally as well as solve the problems that could interfere with studying and learning.

Resource	Available on Your Campus?		Will You or Have You Used?	
	Yes	No	Yes	No
1. Academic advising office	——	——	——	——
2. Continuing orientation program	——	——	——	——
3. Financial aid office	——	——	——	——
4. Health service	——	——	——	——
5. Personal counseling office	——	——	——	——
6. Career counseling office	——	——	——	——
7. Job placement office, including part-time jobs	——	——	——	——
8. Peer counseling program	——	——	——	——
9. Self-development classes and workshops	——	——	——	——
10. Leadership program	——	——	——	——
11. Recreational or intramural program	——	——	——	——
12. Cultural programs: films, lectures, concerts	——	——	——	——

Resource	Available on Your Campus?		Will You or Have You Used?	
	Yes	No	Yes	No
13. Clubs and organizations	_____	_____	_____	_____
14. Support centers for special groups	_____	_____	_____	_____
a. Women	_____	_____	_____	_____
b. Blacks	_____	_____	_____	_____
c. Hispanics	_____	_____	_____	_____
d. Returning students	_____	_____	_____	_____
e. International students	_____	_____	_____	_____
f. Students in your major	_____	_____	_____	_____
15. Other: _____	_____	_____	_____	_____

D. Topics for Your Learning Journal

1. Describe a learning situation that would be ideal for you and one that would be difficult.

2. Which is your most difficult class? Why is it difficult? What can you do to learn more effectively in it? Consider the material, your learning style, and the professor's teaching style.

3. Which is your easiest class? Why is it easy? Consider the material, your learning style, and the professor's teaching style.

5 | Taking Lecture Notes and Learning How to Study Them

When you have finished reading this chapter, you will know the following:

1. Why it is important to take lecture notes.
2. How to take good lecture notes in all types of classes.
3. How to study your notes when you have finished taking them.
4. How to remember your notes.

WHY TAKE LECTURE NOTES?

Much information that you are expected to learn in college is given in the form of lectures, and lecture note taking is one of the first learning activities that you will practice during the first weeks of school. Lectures contain material the professor has worked up, and is often not readily available in books or anywhere else. If you do not listen well and record what you hear, you will not know this material. If you try to remember it without taking notes, you will forget it.

Many students believe that if they sit back and listen and think during a lecture, they will be able weeks later to remember what was said. That doesn't work. People forget at least half of what they learn within twenty-four hours of learning it. What is forgotten can be gradually relearned, however, if you have a record of it. The easiest and best way to get such a record is by taking good lecture notes.

Most students learn how to take some sort of notes in college by the trial-and-error method. Students who have had no instruction in note taking make two common errors: (1) their notes are so disorganized and poorly written that they are often impossible to read, and (2) the notes are skimpy and incomplete, offering insufficient information to study for an exam.

HOW TO TAKE WELL-ORGANIZED NOTES

Outlined notes are easier to study because you can see the separate parts of a lecture. It is easier to learn parts first and then later to see how the parts fit together to form a whole lecture.

The usual outline symbols in your notes do not have to be perfectly done. When you are trying to get down a lot of material in a hurry, you cannot always remember whether to write a *1* or an *A*. Just put all main ideas, which are the most important ideas and items of information, close to the margin and indent all material about each idea under it. If there are several items of information about a main idea, you can either number the separate items or put a dash in front of each. Figure 5.1 shows you how to set up an outline for taking lecture notes.

How do you recognize the main ideas in a lecture so that you can write them by the margin? There are various ways in which professors make their main ideas stand out. Sometimes they tell you in their introductory remarks, as in: "Our subject today is immigration to the United States in the seventeenth and eighteenth centuries. We shall be looking particularly at German, Scotch-Irish, and French immigration." You immediately have a title for your notes—*Immigration to U.S. in 17th and 18th Centuries*—and the three main divisions—*German, Scotch-Irish,* and *French.* During the lecture you will listen for details about these three groups of immigrants.

Professors also emphasize their main ideas by stating them slowly and then by repeating them in the same or slightly different words. Many professors also emphasize main ideas by writing them on the blackboard.

Another way to locate the main ideas in a lecture is to listen for certain phrases that speakers use to emphasize their main points.

Title of the Lecture

   I. First important idea or item of information
      – Information about that idea or item
        – examples
  II. Second important idea or item of information
      – List of information about that idea or item
        – examples
      – More information

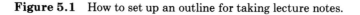

Figure 5.1   How to set up an outline for taking lecture notes.

Examples of such phrases are, "Today I want to talk about . . .";
"Now we will turn to . . ."; "Next, let's take a look at . . ."; "I'm
going to point out three . . . ; The first is . . . ; The second is . . .";
"The next point I want to make is . . ."; or "The first (or next, or last)
point I want to discuss is as follows." These verbal clues tell you that
the subject is being changed. You should indicate the change in your
notes by starting a new block of material by the left-hand margin or, if
the points are being numbered, by starting a new item in a list with
each new number.

   Some lecturers do not emphasize their main ideas in the ways
mentioned above. When you can't outline your notes easily, at least
skip a line whenever there is a change of subject. Later, read through
your notes and impose an organization on them by writing labels and
numbering sections. When a list of items is given (for example, "three
ways to take reading notes"), list the three ways down the page with
the title ("ways to take reading notes") at the top. Never write lists
across the page with two or three items on one line. They are too hard
to study that way.

HOW TO TAKE COMPLETE NOTES

Your note-taking job is not done when you have written down the main
ideas in a lecture. You need details, examples, explanations, and diagrams in your notes, too. Then they will make sense to you, and you
will remember them longer.

   Write during class, and write a lot. Fill several sheets of paper. In
a fifty-minute lecture you can usually take from three to eight pages
of notes. Get down as much as possible. This is important even if you
are not a print learner. People forget at the same rate regardless of
their learning style. Weeks later, when it is time to study for an exam,
you will be glad that you took a lot of notes.

   Try to take notes in complete thoughts rather than in isolated
words or brief phrases. Look, for example, at the history notes about
"The Lost Generation" on page 65. Note that the author of these notes
has avoided writing isolated words and phrases that would be difficult
to understand later. Instead, the ideas are expressed completely
enough so that anyone can read and make sense of them. When you
take complete notes, you then study in complete thoughts, and it is
later easier to write in complete thoughts when you take the examination. In order to do this successfully you will have to learn to abbreviate and to leave out words that are not essential to the meaning of what
is said. Make up your own abbreviations. For example, *Engl.* can stand

for *English*, *M.A.* for *Middle Ages, bio.* for *biology.* When the professor introduces a term that will be used frequently in a lecture, write it once at the top of the page along with the abbreviation you will use for it. For example write *bt = behavior therapy* at the top of the page and use *bt* in your notes to save writing the whole term repeatedly. You could write the sentence "Behavior therapy employs several methods to help clients learn more desirable behavior patterns" as "bt uses methods to change behavior." Or, if you were taking notes on an entire lecture about Mencken, you could write M = Mencken once at the beginning of your notes. Then, you could write the sentence "Mencken's solution for the moral problems of the period was to legalize prostitution" as "M—solution to moral prob—legalize prostitution." You have recorded enough so that when you study, you will form a complete thought in your mind even though you have not written every word.

TEN OTHER SUGGESTIONS FOR GOOD NOTE TAKING

Besides outlining your notes and taking complete notes, there are other ways you can improve the quality of your lecture notes.

1. Label your notes at the top of the page with your professor's name, the course, the date, and the title of the lecture. Think of your notes as chapters in a book, each with its own title. Later, when you study your notes, the titles will immediately help focus your mind on the subject of the lecture.

2. Make your notes legible. Notes taken in ink on one side of the paper can be read more easily and for a longer period of time than pencil notes. If you cannot read your own handwriting very well, analyze it. Usually you can improve legibility by changing the way you write only five or six letters. If your writing runs into the lines above or below it, skip lines to improve legibility.

3. Be an aggressive note taker. Regard note taking as hard work. Sit as close as you can to your professors so that you will be able to hear them without straining. While you are taking notes, maintain an alert physical attitude. Then your mind will usually stay alert also.

4. Start taking notes when the professor starts talking. Don't sit back during a lecture and wait for something to strike you. Remember that your professors are likely to examine you on any of the material they present in their lectures. Writing down the title of the day's lecture and taking a note or two on the introductory remarks will usually get you well started so that you won't miss important points.

5. Ignore all distractions that might interfere with your concentration. Don't think about what your professors are wearing, the other students in class, the good weather outside, or anything else but the business at hand. Instead, concentrate on getting as many notes as possible during the class period.

6. Isolate the specialized vocabulary for each course as early as possible and learn it so that you and the professor will be talking the same language. In order to talk about a subject your professor will use the language of that subject, though not always taking the time to define each term that is unfamiliar to you. Circle difficult words, draw a line from them out to the margin, and label them there with a circled *V* for *vocabulary*. This is a quick note to yourself that you must find out more about these words. Until you do, the lecture won't make complete sense.

7. Learn to differentiate fact from opinion in lectures. Get the facts straight and learn them; keep them separate from the professor's opinions. Label your professor's opinions as such if you wish. It is also a good idea to insert your own opinions, questions, ideas, and reflections into your notes as they occur to you. Separate your ideas from the material presented by your professor by placing them in square brackets, thus: [   ].

When your notes are sprinkled liberally with your own reactions in square brackets, they are more interesting to study later. Such reactions also make it easier for you to come up with topics for papers and to answer those exam questions that demand original thought. Figure 5.2 shows a fragment of notes that contain fact, professor's opinion, and student's opinion.

8. Develop your own set of symbols to identify or emphasize various items in your notes. A circled *V* in the margin can identify an unfamiliar term and square brackets can be used to set off your own ideas. In addition, a circled *A* in the margin can identify an assignment slipped in without warning at the end of a lecture. A circled *B* in the margin can identify books mentioned in the lecture. A circled *P* in the margin can identify a possible paper topic that you thought of during a lecture.

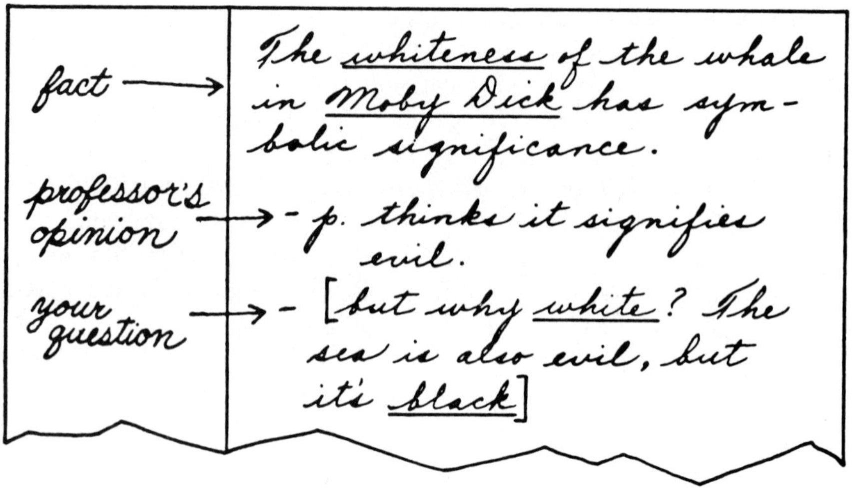

Figure 5.2   Fact and opinion in lecture notes.

Questions in your own mind can be jotted down, labeled in the margin with a *Q,* and asked at the end of class. Cross-references to passages in the textbook can be indicated in your lecture notes as "see Text, p. 231."

Finally, emphasize main ideas in your notes by underlining them, and write a star next to material that is likely to be on an exam.

9. Always take notes on discussion. Good discussion leaders come into class with a list of points that they want to make. Rather than presenting them in the form of a lecture, they draw the information from the class by asking questions. It is your responsibility in a discussion, just as it is in a lecture, to try to discover what points are being made and to record them so that you will not forget them. If you cannot outline the discussion, at least skip a line each time the subject is changed. In discussions in which you participate heavily, you probably will not have time to take notes. In such cases it is important to take summary notes on the discussion as soon as possible afterwards and certainly within twenty-four hours. In writing your summary, answer the question "What was the discussion about?" to help you isolate topics and then the question "What was said about it?" to help you get down some details.

10. Get in the habit of always attending classes. You will be less tempted to cut classes if you think of each class as a chapter in a book you are reading. If you cut a class, you miss a chapter and that interferes with comprehension.

WHAT TO DO WITH YOUR NOTES AFTER YOU HAVE TAKEN THEM: THREE STEPS

Step 1. Read and Revise Your Notes within 24 hours. If you follow the suggestions made so far for getting complete and well-organized notes, you should end up with a potentially useful set of notes. They are only potentially useful, however, until you have spent at least a few minutes with them *after* class.

At the very least you should *read and revise* the notes you have taken within twenty-four hours. During that time the class will still be fresh in your mind, and you can make certain everything in your notes makes sense to you. Remember that you will forget over half of what went on in class during the first twenty-four-hour period. If you wait for more than a day, your notes will begin to look like someone else took them. Psychologists have discovered, however, that if you go over the new material and make an attempt to set it in your mind before the first rapid forgetting has taken place, you can keep the new material in your mind for a longer period of time and you can later relearn it quickly and easily.

As you read and revise your notes, be extremely critical of your understanding. If you read a couple of lines that make no sense to you, stop and try to figure out what should be there. If necessary, find out from a classmate, or even the professor, what was said and meant at that point in the lecture. Don't leave the confusing passage as it is. It will discourage and slow you down later when you are studying your notes for an exam.

Right after class you should also attempt to straighten out the organization of your notes. If you missed some of the main heads, especially those that are the general headings for lists of items, put them in now. Underline all headings and main points that you did not have time to underline in class. If your list does not look like a list, draw a box around it, or bracket it to indicate that those points go together. Don't recopy or type your notes. This, like tape-recording notes, can be a mechanical process that does not engage your thoughts. Reading, rethinking, revising to make certain everything makes sense, and reorganizing by numbering, putting in labels, and underlining demand more mental activity. As a consequence, you understand and remember what is there better. Figure 5.3 is an example of notes that were taken in class. Figure 5.4 shows how these notes were later revised and reorganized.

Step 2. Use a method to learn your notes. At this point you can vary the way you learn your notes, if you wish, to take advantage of your preferred learning style.

Biology 3106

Chrapliwy

Evidence of Evolution from Comp. Anat.

Vestiges - Vestigial Structures

1. Def. - ves - structures reduced in size and usually in function when cf. to some ancestor.

- over 100 human vestiges - suggest ancestors

body hair - sparse now - originally dense - human "naked ape"

? - in animals - turn ear to sound for survival. hum. don't work

plica semiluminarrs (sp?)

⟩⟨   Latin semi-lunar - folds in eye. nicitating membrane.

Wisdom teeth - 3rd molars — age 20-30 — get from ancestors. no function

veriform (sp?) appendix
   vermi - worm, worm like colon. In herbivorous

cows, horses — caecum - pouch - like - for digestion   omnivors don't need it

cocix (sp?) Internal tail 3-5 bones. Dogs, cats, lizards

Figure 5.3   Original notes taken in class.

Biology 3106

Chrapliwy

Evidence of Evolution from Comp. Anat.

Vestiges = Vestigial Structures   (ves.)

1. Def. - ves - structures reduced in size and usually in function when cf. to some ancestor. [things animals have that we also have — only ours are smaller or don't function]

  2. - over 100 human vestiges - suggest ancestors [suggest we descended from animal ancestors]

3. Six examples of Human Vestiges

① body hair - sparse now - originally dense - human "naked ape"

② ear muscles   ? - in animals - turn ear to sound for survival. ~~toun.~~
        Humans have but don't work
        [Survives in ear wigglers.]

③ plica ~~semiluminarrs (sp?)~~ semiluminaris

            >< Latin semi- lunar = folds in
              eye. Nicitating membrane. that
   This is a (half)-(moon) covers the eye when an
                      animals blinks is like plica Semilum-
④ Wisdom teeth - 3rd molars - age 20-30 - get inaris in
    from ancestors - no function   humans.
  vermiform
⑤ ~~veriform (sp?)~~ appendix :   Located in
    vermi - worm, worm like. /colon₀ In herbivorous
  animals like
    cows, horses - caecum - pouch - like - for
  digestion   omnivors don't need it looks like
  Coccyx -   9/ in colon.
⑥ ~~coccix (sp?)~~ Internal tail 3-5 bones. Dogs, cats, lizards
  use for balance, locomotion, removing insects. Examples of
  human infants with tails 6 in. long. Human embryos and
  adults have internal tails.

Summary: vestiges are evidence of evolution - in man they
are small & don't function. They come from animals. over
100 ves. 6 exs: body hair, ear muscles, plica semiluminaris
(corner of the eyes), wisdom teeth, vermiform appendix, coccyx.

Figure 5.4 Original notes taken in class with revisions supplied later shown as screened type.

Method 1 favors print learners.   When you have revised and re-organized your notes, go through them quickly and write in the left-hand margin (1) *labels of the contents of your notes,* (2) *briefer notes on your notes,* and/or (3) *brief questions that will force you to reproduce the ideas in your notes as you mentally answer these questions.* Then, (4) *write a brief summary, in phrases only, at the end of the notes.*

Many students like to use notebook paper that has a wide three-inch left-hand margin. Such paper can be found in most college book-stores. The large margin provides plenty of room for labels, symbols, references to the textbook, and insights that occur to you as you study your notes. Changing the color of ink for your marginal notes and summary (red, for example) will make them stand out from your class notes. Figure 5.5 shows an excerpt from some history notes that have been marked with briefer notes and questions in the margin. Notice, especially, the use of marginal symbols and the final summary at the end.

As soon as you have written your brief labels and questions, fold your paper over so that only the left-hand margin is exposed. Then, on the basis of such a label as "Def. of lost generation" *see if you can recite, without looking,* the particulars about the origin of that term. If you can't remember, peek at your notes, cover them up, and try again. Spend a few minutes covering your notes and reciting their contents as soon as you have put in the labels. You will find relearning the material later for an exam will be relatively quick and easy.

Use your summaries occasionally for a quick review of the course from the first day to the present. This will help you see the progression of ideas in the course so that it will make better sense to you. When you get to class early, read the summary of your last set of notes for that class. This will refresh your memory of what was said last time, and it will prepare you for the lecture to come. Finally, brief summaries of lecture notes will help you prepare for exams. You can check them when you study to make sure you don't omit anything important.

Method 2 favors hearing learners.   When you have revised and reorganized your notes, get together with another member of your class and take turns reciting them aloud to each other until both of you can repeat them from memory. Discuss the contents of the notes until they make complete sense to you. If you cannot find a classmate, study by yourself, but make certain that you do it aloud. To make it easier to study later for an exam, dictate a summary of these notes, along with the ideas they have generated in your own mind, into a tape recorder. You will listen to these taped notes later at exam time. Blind students who work with study partners dictate the labels and questions   class, professor, date

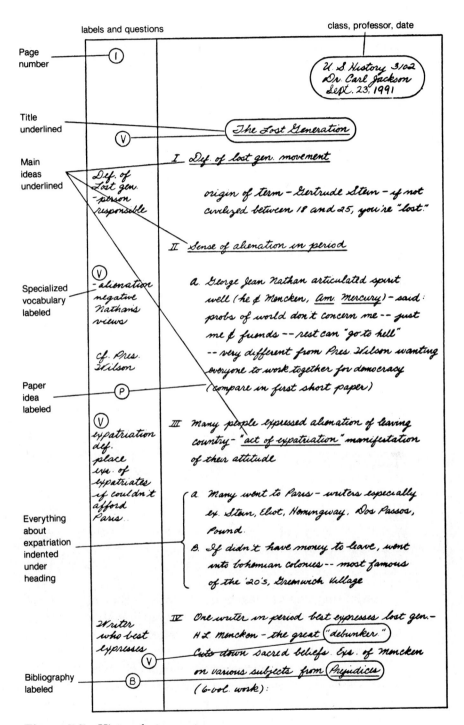

Page number .... ①

.... *U.S. History 3102*
.... *Dr. Carl Jackson*
.... *Sept. 23, 1991*

Title underlined ....

.... Ⓥ *The Lost Generation*

Main ideas underlined .... *I Def. of lost gen. movement*

Def. of Lost gen. -person responsible

.... *origin of term - Gertrude Stein - if not*
.... *civilized between 18 and 25, you're "lost."*

.... *II Sense of alienation in period*

Specialized vocabulary labeled .... Ⓥ *-alienation negative Nathan's views*

.... *a. George Jean Nathan articulated spirit*
.... *well (he & Mencken, Am. Mercury) - said :*
.... *probs of world don't concern me -- just*
.... *me & friends -- rest can "go to hell"*

cf. Pres. Wilson

.... *-- very different from Pres. Wilson wanting*
.... *everyone to work together for democracy*

Paper idea labeled .... Ⓟ

.... *(compare in first short paper)*

Ⓥ *expatriation def. place exs. of expatriates if couldn't afford Paris.*

.... *III Many people expressed alienation of leaving*
.... *country - "act of expatriation" manifestation*
.... *of their attitude*

.... *a. Many went to Paris - writers especially*
.... *ex. Stein, Eliot, Hemingway. Dos Passos,*
.... *Pound.*

Everything about expatriation indented under heading

.... *B. If didn't have money to leave, went*
.... *into bohemian colonies -- most famous*
.... *of the '20's, Greenwich Village*

Writer who best expresses

.... *IV One writer in period best expresses lost gen.-*
.... *H L Mencken - the great "debunker."*

.... Ⓥ *Cuts down sacred beliefs. Exs. of Mencken*
.... *on various subjects from Prejudices*

Bibliography labeled .... Ⓑ

.... *(6-vol. work):*

Figure 5.5   History lecture notes.

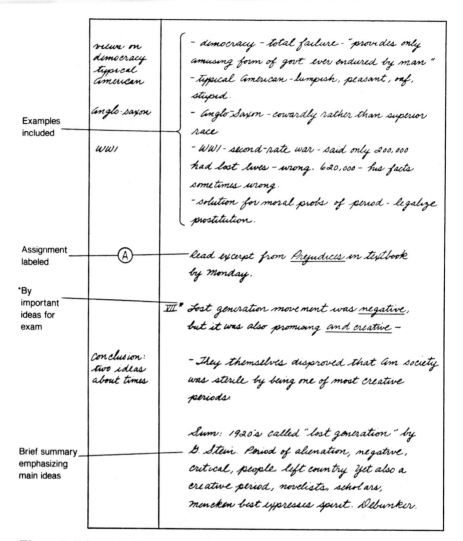

Examples included

views on democracy typical American

anglo-saxon

WWI

- democracy - total failure - "provides only amusing form of govt ever endured by man"
- typical American - lumpish, peasant, oaf, stupid.
- Anglo-Saxon - cowardly rather than superior race.
- WWI - second-rate war - said only 200,000 had lost lives - wrong. 620,000 - has facts sometimes wrong.
- solution for moral probs of period - legalize prostitution.

Assignment labeled

(A)

Read excerpt from *Prejudices* in textbook by Monday.

*By important ideas for exam

VII* Lost generation movement was negative, but it was also promising and creative -

conclusion: two ideas about times

- They themselves disproved that Am society was sterile by being one of most creative periods.

Brief summary emphasizing main ideas

Sum: 1920's called "lost generation" by G. Stein. Period of alienation, negative, critical, people left country. Yet also a creative period, novelists, scholars, Mencken best expresses spirit. Debunker.

Figure 5.5 (cont.)   History lecture notes.

material they want to learn into tape recorders all the time and then listen to it later. They are usually very successful students. Try their method if you favor speaking and listening to reading and writing as a method for learning.

Method 3 favors visual and concrete experience learners.   When you have revised and reorganized your notes, map them so that you will be able to see the ideas and how they relate to each other. One type of map is the spider map. Draw a spider body and write the title in it. Write the main ideas on the spider legs. Write examples on the hairs that attach to the legs. Figure 5.6 is an example of a spider map

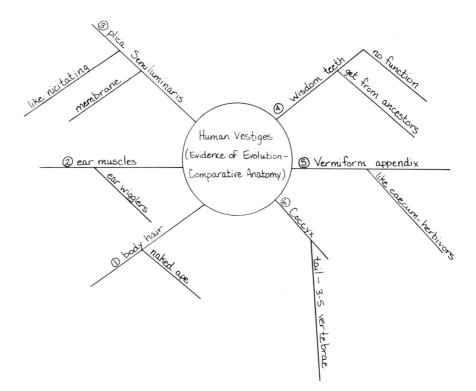

Figure 5.6   A map of the ideas in the lecture notes in Figure 5.4.

of the ideas in the lecture notes about human vestiges in **Figure 5.4.**
Other formats for creating maps appear on pages 166–167. You can
use your visual imagination and draw other types of pictures and
diagrams to help you remember your notes also. You may find it
useful to think of concrete examples. It might help you to remember
the vestigial organs on the map in Figure 5.6 if you were to locate all
of them on your own body. The final step in this study method, like
the others, is to look away, visualize your map in your mind's eye,
and recite its contents from memory. Or, you may prefer to re-draw
it from memory.

The *best* way, then, to treat your lecture notes after you have
taken them is (1) go over your notes, revise, reorganize, underline
main points, and make certain they make sense and then either
(2) write labels and brief questions in the margins, write a summary
at the end, and cover your notes and recite them to yourself until
you know them or (3) recite your notes aloud to a classmate until you
understand and can repeat them from memory, and then dictate
a summary of them into a tape recorder to study later, or (4) make a

map of the notes and either visualize or re-draw it until you can do so from memory. Follow these suggestions as soon as possible after you have taken your notes, certainly within twenty-four hours. You may want to use all of these suggestions at different times. They all work.

The worst way to deal with your lecture notes is to put them aside after class and not look at them until you are studying for an exam. By this time your notes are "cold," and it is too late to clarify confusing passages, straighten out organization, and generally make things easier to understand and study.

Step 3. Review your notes.   Three or four times during the semester read through all of the notes that you have taken to date. This will help fix them in your mind, give you a sense of the progression of ideas in the course, and make it much easier to learn them quickly when it is time to prepare for an exam.

TAKING NOTES IN MATH AND SCIENCE CLASSES

You may have to modify your lecture note-taking techniques in math classes and in science classes that require problem solving. In such classes you will either be learning how to do a mathematical problem or you will be applying math to solve word problems such as those found in chemistry and physics classes. The biggest mistake most students make in taking notes in such classes is, when writing down the problems the professor puts on the board, to omit the verbal explanations that go with them. Here are six quick tips for taking notes in math and problem-solving science courses.

1. Get down what's on the board.
2. Get down the explanation that goes with what's on the board, like "factor out the y." Write out a reason for each step of the problem as it was done on the board.
3. If your professor moves so fast that you can't get both the board material and the explanation, leave large blank spaces in your notes. Then, within twenty-four hours, write additional explanations for each step of a problem so that you will be able to understand it when you study for exams. Number and list all the steps in each problem or process so that you can understand and learn them quickly.
4. Be careful with symbols. Ones you use in other classes to separate points, such as the dash, turn into math symbols in math classes. The best way to change the subject and separate topics in math

Math 3121
Dr. B. Prater
January 15, 1991

Define
Rules of
Hierarchy | <u>Rules of Hierarchy (Order) for Doing Arithmetic</u>

Rules | I. <u>Four Rules of Hierarchy</u>
1. _____ | 1. Do what's in parentheses first
     ex. $4 \times (3 + 2)$
     add what's in ( ) first, <u>then</u> multiply
      $4 \times 5 = 20$

(V)

2. _____
  or | 2. Raise to a power or (take a root.)
     ex. $2^2 = 2 \cdot 2$
_____ | $3 + 2^2$ first raise $2^2 = 4$
      Then $3 + 4 = 7$

3. _____
  or | 3. Multiply or Divide
_____

4. _____ | 4. Add or Subtract
  or
_____

| II. Apply to problems

     ex. $3 + 4 \cdot 7$ (multiply first, then add)
      $3 + 28 = 31$
     if should want to add first, have to put
Other | addition in parentheses.
rules | $(3 + 4) \cdot 7 = 7 \cdot 7 = 49$ (note change
     in answer)

work with
_____ num-
bers at | ex. $3 - 2 - 7$ two subtractions can <u>only</u>
one time | work with two numbers at a time:
      $3 - 2 = 1$, then $1 - 7 = -6$

work from
_____ to | Use the <u>left-to-right rule</u>. Work left to
_____ | right within each order.
     Use rule also when choice between $\times$ or $\div$,
     or between $+$ or $-$.

Figure 5.7 Math lecture notes.

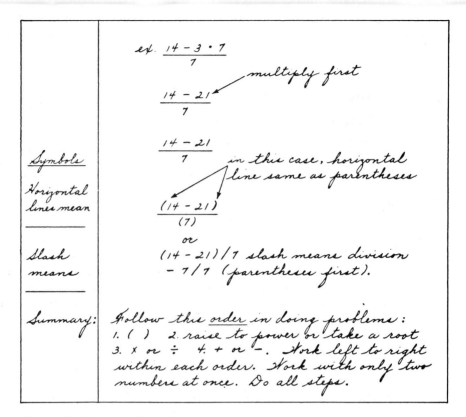

Figure 5.7 (cont.)   Math lecture notes.

notes is to draw a line clear across the paper from one margin to the other.

5. Label math and science notes in the left-hand column and write summaries just as you would notes from any other class or, go over your notes with classmates. Then recite until you know them.

6. Students report that in some math and science classes they are able to copy examples and models on the board right into their textbooks. Less writing then needs to be done since the explanations are in the textbook itself. You will, of course, have to read the textbook assignment carefully before class to make this method work.

Figure 5.7 demonstrates that the note-taking system described in this chapter works as well for math classes as it does for other classes.

At the Very Least . . .

This chapter has dealt with the ideal way of taking lecture notes. If you can't follow all of the suggestions every day, *at the very least* do this much:

1. Get complete notes in class.
2. Indicate the main topics or divisions in your notes.
3. Go through your notes after class, even if you have to do so hastily.

SUMMARY

Good lecture notes provide a record of the material your professor presents in class, material that might not be readily available in any other form. Take notes that are easy to read and easy to study. Notes should be outlined, complete, written in ink on one side of the paper only, labeled with the course title, professor's name, date, and subject of the lecture. Learn to abbreviate words and to use your own symbols to tag various types of material in your notes. Be an aggressive note taker—sit close to the professor, and don't allow distractions to interfere with note taking. Think while you listen, identify unfamiliar words and write down your ideas and questions. Within twenty-four hours following class, revise and reorganize your notes, label their contents in the left-hand margin, and cover your notes and recite their contents until you can say them from memory. Finally, write a brief summary, in phrases only, at the end of your notes. Alternate study methods include reciting your notes to a classmate, dictating summaries into a tape recorder, and mapping your notes. Use most of these same suggestions to take notes in math and science classes.

EXERCISES

A. Monitor Your Comprehension of This Chapter.

Write quickly, in phrases rather than complete sentences, the information in this chapter that you understand and remember. Look back through your marginal notes and summaries and add what you left out. Is anything in the chapter unclear? Jot it down to ask about in class. Has reading the chapter caused you to think of new insights or examples of your own? Jot them down.

B. Class Exercises.

1. *Small Groups.* Brainstorm a list of abbreviations that you can or do use in taking lecture notes. Report them to the class.

2. *Whole Class.*

a. A lecture that was delivered to new students is reproduced below. Listen to it, and take complete, well-organized notes. This lecture should be read aloud to you by either your instructor or someone else. Whoever reads it should read it slowly, as though actually delivering the lecture. That will take about ten minutes. Listen for the verbal clues that will help you identify the title and perceive the organization. If you outline this lecture accurately, your notes will take the form indicated in Figure 5.8.

Orientation Lecture[1]

There are several differences between the student who makes it in college and the student who doesn't. One major difference, and probably the most important difference, is how much the student understands about what goes on in a university learning situation. How much academic know-how does the student have? So, today, I want to look at this factor of academic know-how. I want to do what I can to provide some insight into how a student gets on at a university.

I'm going to begin by pointing out three things that the college instructor assumes about students. The first thing the college instructor assumes is that the student knows what he's doing. The college instructor assumes that the student is capable of deciding what courses he wants to take, capable of deciding whether he wants to attend class, whether he wants to do assignments. Now the instructor is going to point out certain things which should be done—certain standards in the class. He assumes that the student is capable of deciding whether he's going to do those things or not. If the student doesn't do them, he fails the course. But very few college instructors will bother the student about doing these various assignments, attending class, or anything else. That's the student's business, whether he wants to or not. It's the student's business whether he wants to stay in college or not. That's the first assumption. The student knows what he's doing.

The second assumption that the college instructor makes is that he, the instructor, is there to present material and the student is there to learn. He assumes that the student will meet him halfway. Most college instructors try to make their lectures, their courses, at least listenable, at least bearable, but they, the instructors, do not assume that they have to pound something into the student's mind. The instructor does not assume that he is going to have to make things exciting and jazzy. He does not assume that he is concerned with the student's personal behavior in class. In fact, discipline problems, in this sense, simply do not exist at the college level.

Okay, the student is there to learn. The third assumption the college instructor makes is that the student has to show some evidence of learning, some consistent performance of assignments in order to pass the course, even with a "D." The student will have to produce.

[1] From a lecture delivered to entering freshmen by James A. Wood.

LABEL CONTENTS	TITLE:_____

	Introduction: _____
	_____
	  I. _____
	     1. _____
	       _____
	     2. _____
	       _____
	     3. _____
	       _____
	  II. _____
	     1. _____
	       _____
	     2. _____
	       _____
	     3. _____
	       _____
	     4. _____
	       _____
	     5. _____
	       _____
	  III. _____
	     1. _____
	       _____
	     2. _____
	       _____
	     3. _____
	       _____
	Conclusion: _____
	WRITE
	BRIEF
	SUMMARY

Figure 5.8

Now if you stop and think for a minute, you'll realize that what the college instructor is really assuming is that this student himself is mature enough to know what he's about, mature enough to make his own decisions, mature enough to know why he's in college. And the college instructor is there to provide a service. He's there to provide the information, he's there to distinguish between those who are understanding it and those who are not understanding it and not comprehending it.

I'm going to be negative for a moment, and I'm going to look at the major causes of student failure. I'm going to get down to a very practical level here. I'm not dealing with educational theory, or motivational theory, or any other theory. I'm dealing with the instructor who looks out at a group of freshman students, observes what's going on, and notices why some students fail. And this is going to be a kind of negative view of things.

I've singled out five of these basic, simple reasons why students seem to fail out of college in this first semester, this first year.

The first reason I've noticed is that a student will wait to be warned by someone that he's in trouble. He'll wait for the instructor to say, "You've been cutting a lot of classes. That's pretty bad." Or he'll wait for an instructor to say, "You haven't been turning in your assignments. I think we ought to look into that." As a matter of fact, in most college courses no one will ever warn the student. The wise student knows that he's going to have to perform, do well in class, and he doesn't wait for somebody to tell him that he's not doing well.

The second of these reasons why students seem to fail is that the student will put off working during the semester. In many courses there's not a great deal of day-to-day or even week-to-week work. The instructor will assign readings. He will assume that the student is doing the reading and is coming to class and comprehending the material. The student, on the other hand, puts things off, until suddenly around midterm time he's faced with an impossible amount of reading, papers to write, exams and problems that he has to work out. Sometimes it hits in the middle of the semester, sometimes it doesn't really hit until the end of the semester. Then it's often too late. The student realizes that he can't get all of it done. Therefore, facing this impossible task, he will give up.

A third reason for student failure is that a student will miss an occasional assignment and figure it will make no real difference. Let me explain something to you about grading policy in college. Very seldom will an instructor give an assignment and put a grade on it without counting that grade in your final work. And in most instructors' grading systems undone assignments do not count merely as an "F," they count as a zero. You cannot miss an occasional assignment because you don't feel like doing it. Do every assignment, even though some of it may be done relatively poorly. Be sure you do them, and do them on time.

The fourth of these mechanical causes for failure is the student doesn't really understand assignments. He doesn't take notes on assignments, and doesn't read the assignment in the syllabus. I am not talking about the student who doesn't understand the reading material and the reading assignment. I'm talking about the student who doesn't understand what the instructor is talking about when the instructor makes an assignment. An instructor will often have assignments specified in a syllabus or course schedule and he may mention them in class. If you don't understand what he is driving at, you have to ask him. An instructor may make an assignment for a major paper and it may not be due for two months. The student will not take any notes on the assignment. He'll think, "Yeah, I'll remember that." A month later, when he starts working on his paper, he doesn't know what the assignment is all about. So he does the wrong thing. In most university courses, if you write a brilliant paper on the wrong subject, it's worth exactly zero. The instructor does not want the assignment done on something that you thought he might like better than what he assigned.

The fifth and last of these mechanical causes of failure, and I suppose the most obvious, is the student who starts cutting classes. Now as I said, very few instructors will call your attention to whether you are cutting classes or not. They don't have time. They are there to teach, not to see if people come to class. Some instructors will tell you that they don't take roll, they are not interested in whether you are there or not. Now beware of this. In most of these situations where the instructor tells you that he doesn't care if you come to class, he is leaving it up to you whether you want to come or not. But he is still going to be very much aware of who is there and who isn't. Later, in a close decision on a grade, your attendance will help him decide which grade to give you.

The last section of material that I'm going to deal with is to make three very simple positive suggestions which mark the good student. I'm talking now about the student who is working pretty near his capacity, that is, his capacity in terms of the energy and intelligence that he has. The student, in other words, is a professional: he knows what he's about, and he operates efficiently in an academic situation.

I'm going to make a few simple suggestions that are basic for academic success. The first of these suggestions is to take complete lecture notes. Take lots of notes on lectures and class discussions. In many courses most of the material you'll be expected to know is given to you in these lectures. There are lots of specific techniques for taking lecture notes. The basic point that I'm making here is you can't know that material when you prepare for an examination unless you've got it in your notes to begin with. I see freshmen, sometimes half the students or more in a freshman class, who will sit and wait for me to say, "Now this is absolutely important." Sometimes even when I tell them, "I'm going to test you on this," they still don't take notes.

The professional student, on a condensed lecture, will take, on regular-size notebook paper, three or four pages of notes per class period. It's hard work. But that's where you get much of your material.

The second suggestion, positive suggestion, I'm going to make is to keep up with reading assignments. And don't just read the material passively. Try to understand what is in these reading assignments. Read the assignments, or at least scan them before they are discussed or lectured on in class, because this is usually the most efficient way to get the most out of both the lectures and the readings. The good student, the conscientious student, the person who's going to make it, is the person who will at least scan a reading assignment before going into the class; then this student will read that reading assignment afterwards.

The third suggestion I'm going to make for the good student is to review occasionally your reading notes and your lecture notes. Go back over the material you have read and your lecture notes. That will fix it in your mind. It will cause you to think about it, become a little bit involved and interested in it, and it will make the continuity in a course much easier.

Okay, these are three basic positive suggestions—take complete lecture notes, keep up with the reading, review and think about the material. I'll conclude by saying that learning is the name of the game. Really learning material is what the college academic experience is all about. I think if you try it, try to apply some of these things I've said, you'll discover that your freshman year can be really successful.

b. Now read through your notes and label them in the left-hand column as in Figure 5.5. Write a brief summary at the end. Cover the contents of your notes by doubling the paper over so that only the margin is exposed. Using your labels to trigger your memory, recite the contents of your notes until you can do so perfectly without looking. Or, with a classmate, recite the notes until you can do so from memory. Then write a summary. Or, with a classmate, map the notes, summarize them, and recite them. This should all take only ten or fifteen minutes.

c. Recite the contents of the notes aloud as a class.

3. *Whole Class.*   Ask for class members to volunteer to tape record, with their professors' permission, 15 to 20 minute segments of lectures from other classes. These should be lectures that are not too technical. Everyone in the class should be able to understand them. Play these lectures in class as practice note taking exercises. Classmates should then trade lecture notes and evaluate them by using the following Evaluation Guide. Read the Guide to get a sense of the quality of notes at the different levels. Then read the notes and score them with a number from 0 to 4 that indicates how they match the descriptions on the guide. Discuss the strengths and weaknesses of the notes with the person who took them.

Evaluation Guide for Lecture Notes

4   These are excellent lecture notes. The major topics are well-separated, underlined, and stand out clearly. The details are indented under each major topic in a list format. Unnecessary words are omitted throughout, but each statement still makes sense. Abbreviations are used where possible. If appropriate, there are marginal notes to indicate references, vocabulary words, questions, and so on. While the handwriting may not be neat, it is legible. The notes are in pen on a single side of the paper.

3   These are good lecture notes. The major topics are separated, but they are not readily apparent, and one or more topics might be overlooked during a quick review. Details are indented but might not be listed. Some unnecessary words might be omitted, but not all information is expressed in complete thoughts. There may be some simple abbreviations, but they may not be used consistently. There are no marginal notes where they might be appropriate. The handwriting appears legible, but the notes are either in pencil or on both sides of the page.

2   These lecture notes can be improved. While the major topics are separated, some may be overlooked in a quick review. There are few details, and it is unclear where details end and new major topics begin. There are many unnecessary words, and many thoughts are incomplete and unconnected. Some words which obviously could be abbreviated are spelled out. There are no marginal notes where they would be obviously appropriate. The handwriting may be legible, but the notes are written in pencil or on both sides of the paper.

1   These lecture notes need considerable work. There is no separation of major topics, and what details there are have been written in paragraphs. Many unnecessary words are included, and no attempt has been made to abbreviate. There are no marginal notes where they would be appropriate. The handwriting is barely legible. The notes are in pencil and written on both sides of the paper.

0   These notes are not responsive to the assignment or show little or no effort.

C. Application Exercises

1. Practice listening and writing at the same time by taking notes on the news on television or radio two or three times. Jot down the subject and underline it for each separate news item. Then speed write to get down as many details as possible under each item. Skip a line each time the subject is changed.

2. Use the suggestions in this chapter to take notes in one of your other classes.

Revise your notes, then label the contents of your notes in the left-hand margin or map them, and write a brief summary at the end. Bring your notes to class to trade with another classmate for evaluation. Use the Evaluation Guide on page 77 to help you assign a score to the notes. Discuss what is good about the notes and what needs improvement.

D. Topics for Your Learning Journal

1. Look through a set of lecture notes from one of your most difficult classes. Make a list of everything that could be improved in these notes. Write a paragraph describing how you will take notes in that class next time you attend.

2. Make a list of ways to keep your mind from wandering during a class. Write your own plan for improving your concentration in classes.

3. List some examples of facts from recent classes. List some examples of opinions. How did you decide which items were facts and which were opinions?

4. Of the three options for learning notes presented in this chapter—marginal notes and summaries, reciting with a classmate and using a tape recorder, and drawing maps—which do you prefer and why? How will you use your preferred method or methods in your other classes?

6 | Learning Specialized and General Vocabulary

When you have finished reading this chapter, you will know the following:

1. Why it is important to improve both specialized and general vocabulary.
2. How to use context clues to interpret a word's meaning.
3. How to use the dictionary or thesaurus.
4. Some additional ways to improve your present vocabulary.

IMPROVE BOTH SPECIALIZED AND GENERAL VOCABULARY

During the four years or so that you are in college you will be expected to learn more about more different subjects than you probably ever will again in any similar length of time in your life. Every one of these new subjects will have its own *specialized vocabulary* (also called *key terms*) that you will have to learn in order to talk and write about it and to understand the professor and the textbook. For example, your biology teacher will talk about *homeostasis* and *microbiota*. You will probably hear or see the specialized vocabulary for biology almost exclusively in biology classes, in biological discussions among professors and students, and in books and articles about biology. The same will be true of your other subjects. You may never or rarely hear or see specialized vocabulary outside of the context of the course.

It will be easier for you to deal with the specialized vocabulary for each course if you differentiate in your mind between this *specialized vocabulary* and a *general vocabulary*, which is not associated with a particular subject. Your history professor, for example, may talk about *progressivism, garrulous* old men, and *rapacious* landlords during the lecture. The *specialized* term in this list is *progressivism. Garrulous* and *rapacious* could be heard in any classroom or encountered in an article in *Time.* You need to work on both your general vocabulary and the specialized vocabulary for each of your courses while you are in college. A larger vocabulary of both types makes it possible for you to think better (you think with words), to understand more, and to express yourself better both in school and after graduation.

LEARN BOTH WORDS AND CONCEPTS

Sometimes a quick dictionary definition is all you need to help you learn a word. For example, if you encountered the word *euphoric* in your reading, you could look it up and find the word *elation* to help you understand it. A synonym, or word that is close in meaning, along with perhaps a brief explanation or example is all you need. Most general vocabulary can be learned this easily. In fact, very often the words you select to learn are ones you half know already.

The major *concepts* that are developed in your classes will require much more of your time and attention to learn. For example, in chemistry class you can look up the term *ionic bonds* to get a basic idea of its meaning, but to learn all you need to know about this term will require that you read a chapter, listen to a lecture, and even perhaps perform some lab experiments. The same is true for concepts like *mental set* in psychology, *human vestiges* in biology, or *data input* in computer science. Much of the specialized vocabulary that you encounter in your classes will need to be learned as concepts over the course of a semester.

Another problem is created when the meanings of specialized vocabulary vary from professor to professor and subject to subject. Study each new specialized word in the context in which you find it (for example, *realism* may have somewhat different meanings in art, literature, and drama courses). Finally, some specialized vocabulary may be obviously technical jargon or, to confuse you more, it may be everyday language used in a special way in a particular context (for example, *work* and *force* in physics or *spread effect* in political science). Don't trust your common sense or past experience to give you the definitions of such words. Learn their new meanings in the new contexts in which you find them. These contexts include both class lectures and the textbook.

SEVEN SUGGESTIONS FOR LEARNING BOTH KINDS OF VOCABULARY

1. Use Context Clues

When you encounter a new word or specialized term, read or listen to the context or surrounding material in which it occurs first to get clues to its meaning. Some words are defined directly in the sentence. Here is an example:

> We may define *memory* as the process by which learning is maintained over the passage of time.[1]

Other words are defined with synonyms or words of similar meaning in the sentence. For example, in describing rats' ability to find their way through a maze, a psychology textbook author explains the term *latent* as follows.

> But this learning might be hidden, or *latent,* until they were motivated to follow the rapid routes for food goals.[2]

At other times an author will indirectly give clues to the meaning of a word through an extended explanation. You will need to read the explanation to help you infer or guess at the meaning of the word. Read the following material and infer the meaning for the term *cognitive maps.*

> Psychologists in the United States soon demonstrated that not even the behavior of rats was as mechanical as most behaviorists suggested. E.C. Tolman, a University of California psychologist, showed that rats behaved as if they had acquired *cognitive maps* of mazes. Although they would learn many paths to a food goal, they would typically choose the shortest. But if the shortest path was blocked, they would quickly switch to another. The behavior of the rats suggested that they learned places in which reinforcement was available, not a series of mechanical motor responses.[3]

In this example, the author uses an entire paragraph to explain *cognitive maps.* Context clues may be found in one sentence, several sentences, or several paragraphs. At times you will need to read an entire essay or chapter with its extended explanations and multiple examples to understand a word or term.

---

[1] Spencer A. Rathus, *Essentials of Psychology,* 2nd ed. (Fort Worth: Holt, Rinehart and Winston, 1989), 145.
[2] Rathus, 165.
[3] Rathus, 164.

2. Notice How Words Have Been Formed

It is useful to know the meanings of a few Latin and Greek prefixes, suffixes, and roots. Over 100,000 English words have bits and pieces of Latin and Greek in them. You can often get a pretty good idea of what a word means without looking it up if you know the meaning of its Latin or Greek components and if you also study the context in which you find it.

It is especially useful when studying science to know a little Latin and Greek. Scientists draw on these languages when they need new names for things. Figure 6.1 provides some examples.

Latin Element	Meaning	Scientific Term
bi-	two	bipodal
epi-	upon	epidermis
inter-	between	intermolecular
intra-	among	intramolecular
per-	through	permeable
peri-	around	periderm
poly-	many	polyvalent
semi-	half	semipermeable
sub-	under, less	subacute
super-	above, in addition	supersaturated
trans-	across, through	transpiration
aqua-	water	aqueous
homo-	man	homo sapiens
pater-	father	paternal
-ped, -pod	foot	biped
spir-	breathe	transpiration

Greek Element	Meaning	Scientific Term
anthropo-	man	anthropoid
astro-	star	astrocyte
auto-	self	autogamy
bio-	life	biology
chromo-	color	chromosome
chrono-	time	chronograph
cyto-	cell	cytology
eu-	well, true	euchromosome
gen-	origin, people	genotype

Figure 6.1   Latin and Greek and modern scientific terminology.

Latin Element	Meaning	Scientific Term
homo-	same	homoiothermic
hydro-	water	hydrophyte
hyper-	too many	hyperplasia
iso-	same	isomeric
-logy	study of	geology
lumin-	light	bioluminescence
macro-	very large	macrocosm
micro-	very small	microbe
mono-	one	monopod
-onomy	science	astronomy
pathos	suffering	pathology
-philous	having an affinity for	acidophilous
phyll-	leaf	phylloid
-plasia/plasy	development, formation	homoplasy
-plasm	formative material	plasma
pseudo-	false	pseudomonad
-stasis	slowing, stable	hemostasis
thermo-	heat	thermocline

Greek Numerals
(important in the metric system as well as in scientific terminology)

Greek	Meaning	Scientific Term
mono-, uni-	one	monopodial, unicellular
di-, bi-	two	dicarboxylic, biceps
tri-	three	triceps
tetr-, quadr-	four	tetrapods, quadriceps
pent-	five	pentaploid
hex-	six	hexachloride
hept-	seven	heptose
oct-, octa-	eight	octandrious
nona-	nine	nonagon
dica-, deci-	ten	decimeter
centi-	hundred	centimeter
kilo-, milli-	thousand	kilometer, millimeter
hemi-	half	hemichordate
multi-	many	multicellular

Figure 6.1   *(Continued)*

If some of the terms you have to know for your science courses "look like Greek" to you, it is because they are. Memorizing the meanings of the Greek and Latin elements in Figure 6.1 will give you clues to the meanings of many of these otherwise difficult-to-remember terms. The list is not exhaustive. When you get into your first science courses, you will add to it.

3. Study Your Dictionary or Thesaurus

When you still do not understand the meaning of a word even after you have studied it in context and analyzed its word parts, you will then need to look it up. In fact, one of the first books you should buy your freshman year is a dictionary. If you can't afford a hardback, buy a cheaper paperback edition. You will find them in your college bookstore.

When you have bought your dictionary, take a half hour to examine the front matter (that which comes before the A–Z listings) and the back matter (that which follows the listings). These pages will explain how you can make the best use of your new dictionary.

A dictionary, you will see, does much more than define words. When you have found out what information yours contains, then keep it handy and use it regularly. You will need it to make the remaining suggestions in this chapter work for you.

The specialized vocabulary in many of your textbooks will be printed in boldface type and defined in a glossary at the back of the book. A glossary is an abbreviated dictionary that gives meanings for words as they are used in that textbook. It can be extremely useful for studying word meanings in a particular textbook.

A thesaurus, which is a dictionary of synonyms, is another useful resource for vocabulary improvement. The Preface of *Roget's International Thesaurus* (3d ed.) makes a clear distinction between a dictionary and a thesaurus: "In a dictionary you start with a word and look for its meaning. In a thesaurus you start with the idea and find the words to express it." A thesaurus can help you find dozens of synonyms and associated words to help you define words or express ideas. Before you use a word that you have located in a thesaurus, however, consult a dictionary to check its meaning. Make certain that the word you have selected fits the context of your writing by saying what you want it to say.

4. Make Vocabulary Sheets

To make a vocabulary sheet, fold a piece of notebook paper lengthwise twice to form four columns. These four columns provide space for the four important activities necessary to learn vocabulary.

a. Find the word you need to learn and write it in the first column.   Set priorities in selecting words to learn. Choose *key specialized vocabulary* words and phrases that are used over and over in the course or that are the subject of an entire lecture or section in the textbook. Choose those *general vocabulary* words that are somewhat familiar to you, that interest you, or that have always bothered you because you did not know them. Even the physical act of writing them in the first column will help you begin to learn them.

b. In the second column, write the word in the context in which you first found it.   Write only enough context to show the *use* of the word, not a full explanation. Usually a phrase will do. Whenever you can, write out context that helps define the word. For example, "That the will of a popular majority should prevail in all matters is known as *populism*" tells you more about populism than "*Populism* was prevalent at the end of the nineteenth century."

c. In the third column, define the word.   Look up the meaning of a *general* vocabulary word in the dictionary. Select the part of the definition that best fits the word as it is used in the context in which you found it. Write out the definition in your own words. Don't copy a long, complicated dictionary definition that means nothing to you.

A dictionary definition may not be sufficient for the *specialized vocabulary* in a course. You may have to do some extra reading to understand some terms. Look for a more thorough explanation in the glossary in the back of your textbook, if there is one. Or, consult the index of your textbook, and read detailed information in the text. When you have read enough, write *in language you can understand and remember* exactly how the word or phrase is used in a particular course.

d. Associate the word or term with any other familiar English or foreign word, object, diagram, example, or experience; write that association in the fourth column to aid your memory.   It doesn't matter how far-fetched the association, so long as it helps you remember. Bilingual students have two languages to draw on for associations. If you know Spanish, for example, *carne,* the Spanish word for meat, will help you remember that *carnivorous* means "meat eating," or *verde* will help you remember that a *verdant* forest is green.

Figure 6.2 shows an example of a *general* vocabulary sheet made by a student whose first language was Spanish. Notice that several of the words she wrote in the fourth column are Spanish words.

Word	Phrase or Sentence	Meaning	Association for Remembering (use foreign or English words, diagrams, or examples)
pulverize	The storm pulverized the building.	to crush into small pieces	pulverizer
indefatigable	The little boy seemed indefatigable in the race.	not capable of becoming tired	infatigable
leonine	His hair gave him a leonine appearance.	of or like a lion	leo the lion
contagion	The contagion of laughter was too much for him, and he began to laugh also.	a spreading by contact	contagious
pensive	He was in a pensive mood and sat staring into space.	thoughtful or serious	pensar
nebulous	It was a nebulous idea, hard to grasp.	cloudlike, vague	nublado

Figure 6.2   General vocabulary sheet (Notice the context clues to the meanings of these words in the second column.).

Spanish is a Romance language derived from Latin. For vocabulary improvement, knowing any Romance language can be almost as useful as knowing Latin. These languages can provide you with clues to the meanings of thousands of difficult English words.

Figure 6.3 shows an example of a *specialized* vocabulary sheet for a political science course.

Word	Phrase or Sentence	Meaning	Association for Remembering (use foreign or English words, diagrams, or examples)
Spread Effect	Spread effect.... capital and managerial talent spread into the less-developed regions.	prosperity spreading into areas -- wealth coming in	California
backwash effect	The spread effect is the opposite of the backwash effect.	prosperity leaving areas -- wealth flowing out	Appalachia
populism	That the will of a popular majority should prevail in all matters is known as populism.	expert and minority opinion irrelevant. The majority opinion the only one that matters -- 19th century American politics. Lost popularity end of century	the populous, the people's opinion
gerrymander	It [the first such district] was elongated like a salamander, and Gerry's apponents called it a new monster, the gerrymander.	artificially setting up unfair voting districts in a state to favor a party or a political machine	Mr. Gerry salamander

Figure 6.3 A specialized vocabulary sheet for political science.

Word	Phrase or Sentence	Meaning	Association for Remembering (use foreign or English words, diagrams, or examples)
biolumin-escence	The biolumin-escence of the firefly.	light produced by organisms	bio -- life (biology) lumin -- light (luminarios) <u>light from life</u>
transpire	Tremendous quantities of water are transpired from the leaves.	passage of vapor from a living body through a membrane or pores	trans -- across spir -- to breathe
cytoplasm	The cytoplasm of a plant cell.	material of cell exclusive of nucleus	cyto -- cell; (all "cyto" words have to do with cells) plasm -- form-ative material plasma -- fluid in blood. <u>cell fluid</u>
pseudopodia	The extensions which form the body of the amoeba are pseudo-podia and are used in locomotion.	temporary projection of a cell. function: locomotion and ingestion	pseudo -- false, fake pod -- foot (podiatrist) <u>false foot</u>

Figure 6.4   A specialized vocabulary sheet for biology.

A specialized vocabulary sheet for biology is shown in Figure 6.4. All the words on this sheet are made up of Latin and Greek parts. Having been previously memorized by the students, these parts are now listed as aids to memory in column 4.

5. Group Words in Categories

It will help you learn specialized vocabulary if, whenever possible, you group related words in categories provided by the course itself. Or, you can group words around a Greek or Latin word part that all the words have in common. When you group, you can make either *outlines* or *diagrams,* whichever helps you most. Figure 6.5 provides two examples of words grouped according to categories, and Figure 6.6 shows two ways words can be grouped around a common Greek word part.

Diagrams such as the one in Figure 6.6, example 2, sometimes make relationships clearer than lists or outlines because each sub-

Example 1   An *outline* of related terms for geology

Ages of the Earth

1. Precambrian
2. Paleozoic
3. Mesozoic
4. Cenozoic

Example 2   A *diagram* of related words for English

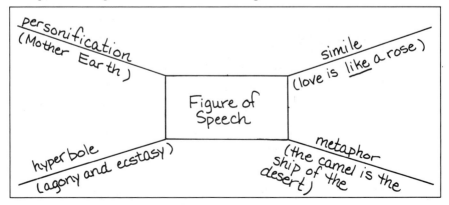

Figure 6.5   Words grouped according to categories

Example 1   A list of *plasm* words for biology

<u>Plasm</u> .... formative material

cytoplasm .... <u>cell</u> material
endoplasm .... <u>inner</u> material in cell
sarcoplasm .... <u>flesh</u> material
ectoplasm .... <u>outer</u> material in cell
protoplasm .... <u>first</u> material (in the
living nucleus)

Example 2   These same words can be grouped in the form of a diagram, which might be easier for you to study.

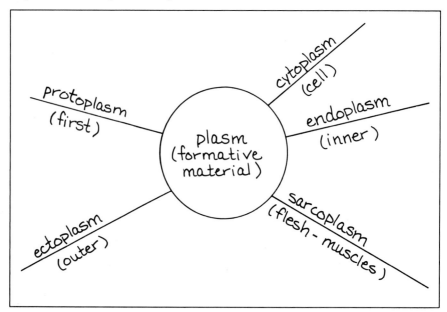

Figure 6.6   Words grouped according to a common Greek element.

item is connected to the major, organizing item by a line. The relationships among the parts are then obvious. Of course, outlines also show relationships by ordering groups of related words in lists under main topics. Use whichever is best suited for the material you are trying to learn. Either way helps you see relationships that will, in turn, help you to remember.

6. *Make Vocabulary Cards*

You may prefer to isolate and learn both specialized and general vocabulary words by putting them on three-by-five cards. Write the word and the context in which you found it on the front of the card. Using language easy to understand and remember, write a brief definition on the back of the card. Use these as flash cards to help you memorize the meanings.

7. *Use Short, Frequent Practice to Learn Vocabulary*

Many introductory courses in college are predominantly courses in specialized vocabulary. You will need to master this vocabulary quickly to pass the courses in which it is taught and, more important, to use it in upper-division courses. Short, frequent practice done out loud is by far the best way to accomplish this. You usually have to be exposed to a new word repeatedly over a period of time before it becomes a part of your active, usable vocabulary.

At the Very Least . . .

This chapter has dealt with the ideal way for improving vocabulary. If you can't follow all of the suggestions every day, *at the very least* do this much:

1. Circle specialized vocabulary in your lecture notes and textbooks and write short definitions either in the margin or above the word.
2. Label each word with a *V* in the margin.
3. At exam time transfer these words to simple two-column vocabulary sheets that you can study from at the last minute. Write the word in the left column with the briefest possible definition in the right.
4. Cover the right column and recite the meanings out loud until you know them.

SUMMARY

Every subject you study has its own specialized vocabulary. There also are general vocabulary words, not unique to a particular subject, that you will want to learn. An improved vocabulary of both types will make you better able to think, to understand others, and to express yourself. Learning the major concepts in your classes will require more time and attention than learning general vocabulary. The first steps in improving your vocabulary are studying the word in context and analyzing its parts. If you then do not understand a word, you should consult a dictionary or glossary. A thesaurus can also be useful. To make vocabulary easier to learn, you can organize the words and the information about them on four-column vocabulary sheets. Information on these sheets should include the word, some context, the meaning written in words you can easily understand, and an association with something already familiar to you. Or you can group words in categories around a common Greek or Latin word part. Short, frequent practice done out loud is the best way to learn new words. Two-column vocabulary sheets can help with your final studying for exams.

EXERCISES

A. Monitor Your Comprehension of This Chapter

Write quickly, in phrases rather than complete sentences, the information in this chapter that you understand and remember. Look back through your marginal notes and summaries and add what you left out. Is anything in the chapter unclear? Jot it down to ask about in class. Has reading the chapter caused you to think of new insights or examples of your own? Jot them down.

B. Class Exercises

1. *Small Groups.* Use context clues.
   a. Read the following explanation of the two concepts *algorithms* and *heuristics.* Get in small groups and discuss the meaning of these words. Write the meaning of each in your own words. Think of an original example of each.

   Algorithms versus heuristics. In solving problems, we sometimes turn to *algorithms* or *heuristic devices.* An **algorithm** is a specific procedure for solving a certain type of problem that will lead to the solution if it is used properly. Mathematical formulas, such as the quadratic equation, are examples of algorithms. They will yield correct answers to problems, *as long as the right formula is used.*

   Consider anagram problems, in which we try to reorganize groups of letters into words. In seeing how many words we can make from *DWARG,* we can use the algorithm of simply listing every possible letter combination, using from one to all five letters, and then checking to see whether each result is, in fact, a word. The method is plodding, but it would certainly work.

   Heuristics are rules of thumb that help us simplify and solve problems. Heuristics, in contrast to algorithms, do not guarantee a correct solution to a problem, but when they work they tend to allow for more rapid solutions. A heuristic device for solving the anagram problem would be to look for letter combinations that are found in words and then to check the remaining letters for words that include these combinations. In *DWARG,* for example, we can find the familiar combinations *dr* and *gr.* We may then quickly find *draw, drag,* and *grad.* The drawback to this method, however, is that we might miss some words.[4]

Meaning:

a. algorithm _____

_____

_____

example _____

_____

b. heuristic _____

_____

_____

example _____

_____

b. Read the following passage and use context only to figure out the meaning of the word *nurturant.*

The Revolutionary generation, therefore, became the first to define a public role for American women.

That role, logically enough in light of the persistent colonial emphasis on maternity, was as the republican mother. Revolutionary events reinforced the trends in American family life since the initial settlement of the colonies and generated a powerful image that dominated the lives of white native-born women throughout most of the nineteenth century. The ideal American woman was to be the nurturant, patriotic mother who raised her children, and especially her sons, to be good Christians, active citizens, and successful competitors in the wider arena of life.[5]

[4] Rathus, 205–206.
[5] Mary Beth Norton, "Women and the Revolution," in *The American Revolution. How Revolutionary Was It?* 4th edn. ed. by George Athan Billias (Fort Worth: Holt, Rinehart and Winston, 1990), 131.

Meaning: *nurturant* ―――――――――――――――――

―――――――――――――――――――――――――――

2. **Small Groups.** Notice how words have been formed.

Lists of Latin and Greek word parts are easier to learn if they are placed on diagrams that show how they are related. The following, for example, is a diagram or map of prefixes that mean *no,* or *not.*

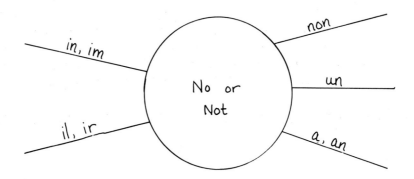

Look through the Latin and Greek elements listed in Figure 6.1 and select those that can be grouped on the following diagrams. Notice that each has been started for you. Work in groups.

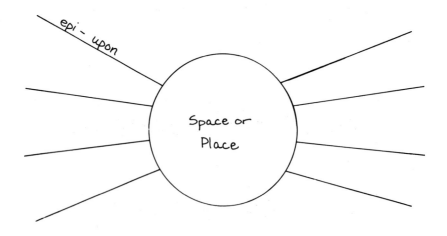

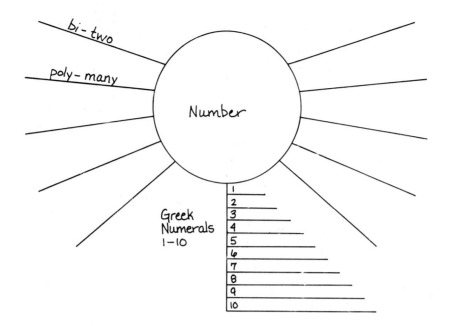

Look in the dictionary and write the meanings of the prefixes on the following graphs that refer to *direction* and *time*. Write examples of words that begin with these prefixes. Include brief meanings. The exercise has been started for you.

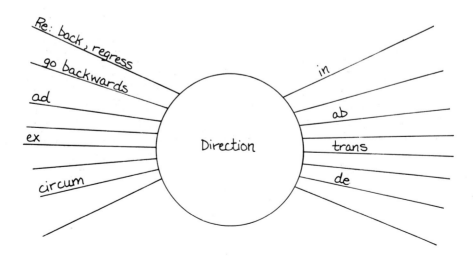

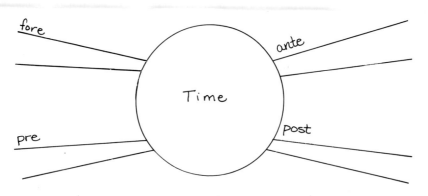

3. *Small Groups.* Combine word parts with dictionary definition.

Look up in your dictionary the meanings of the five words on the diagrams in Figure 6.6. Compare the dictionary definitions with the clues to the meanings of these words that are provided in the figure. Discuss in your group how you can use knowledge of Greek word parts along with definitions to help you analyze and remember scientific terminology.

4. *Small Groups.* Use the dictionary.
   a. Become familiar with your dictionaries by listing five types of information that your dictionary contains in the front matter (that which comes before the A–Z listings) and the back matter (that which follows the listings). Report back to the class what you have discovered and how you might use it.
   b. Look up the word *mesomorph* in your dictionaries and report back to the class four types of information given about the word.
   c. Try a dictionary speed exercise. The following general vocabulary words appear in a history textbook. Each group should look them up and write brief definitions. See which group can finish first.

Word	*Meaning*
(1) sanctimonious	_____
(2) mediatory	_____
(3) panegyric	_____
(4) sagacious	_____
(5) exculpate	_____
(6) insensate	_____
(7) intercessor	_____

(8) deprecating   _____

(9) nihilism   _____

(10) immemorial   _____

Report back to the class and discuss the meanings of these words until everyone understands them.

5. *Small Groups.* Make a vocabulary sheet.
   Make a 4-column vocabulary sheet like the example in Figure 6.2. Supply information in all four columns to help you learn the following specialized vocabulary terms that appear in the reading you have done so far in this textbook.

   1. Headquarters
   2. Positive Self-Talk
   3. External distractions
   4. Internal distractions
   5. Time analysis
   6. Learning Style

6. *Small Groups.* Group words in categories.
   a. Reorganize the information in Figure 6.5, example 1 (ages of the earth) into a diagram form. Then reorganize the information in Figure 6.5, example 2 (figures of speech) into outline form. If you can do this successfully, you have demonstrated that you understand the relationships among the pieces of information in each of these examples.
   b. To make it easier to learn, group the following material on diagrams similar to those in example 2 in Figures 6.5 and 6.6.

   Group 1
   Naturalistic (observe nature)
   Experimental (experiment)
   Three psychological approaches
   Correlational (observe specific variables)

   Group 2
   Endomorph (fat)
   Body types
   Mesomorph (average)
   Ectomorph (thin)

C. Application Exercises

1. Identify a *major concept* in each of the classes that you are taking. Write definitions for these concepts in your own words. Add examples if you can.

2. Make specialized vocabulary sheets like those in Figures 6.3 and 6.4 for each course you are taking. Remember that the easiest way to do this is to fold the paper lengthwise twice to make the four columns. Keep these sheets at the front of your notes right behind the assignment sheets. At least once a week, cover the meanings, and recite the words and meanings out loud until you know them.

D. Topics for Your Learning Journal

1. Review the different methods for improving vocabulary. Which suggestions do you like and will you use? Commit yourself to using at least one method. Describe in detail how you will use it this semester.

2. Are there other methods for vocabulary improvement that you like that are not described in this chapter? What are they? How will you use them?

7 | *Participating in Class Discussion and Group Work*

When you have finished reading this chapter, you will know how to do the following:

1. Prepare for class discussion.
2. Participate effectively in class discussion.
3. Participate effectively in group work.
4. Participate even when you are scared.

EVALUATE YOUR PRESENT LEVEL OF PARTICIPATION IN CLASS DISCUSSION

Professors often organize class discussions or group work to promote active learning and critical thinking. There are a number of reasons why you should participate in these activities. Participation allows you to interact with other people and clarify your own ideas. It also helps you think about and retain material, sometimes better than any other way. Class time goes faster and seems more interesting. You become better acquainted with the professor and the other students and, consequently, are better able to learn from them. You develop more self-confidence as you hear yourself articulate the ideas of the class. And you are able to read and listen with better comprehension and write better papers and exams as a result of your active involvement. Analyze your current level of participation in group discussion.

Self-Evaluation: Class Discussion

Do you:

	Yes	No
1. Prepare ahead of time and go into a discussion with a full mind?	_____	_____
2. Bring your textbook and refer to it when it is the subject of discussion?	_____	_____
3. Focus your mind immediately and keep it focused?	_____	_____
4. Take notes on the main points?	_____	_____
5. Stay objective and listen even when you disagree?	_____	_____
6. Think about what you hear, relate it to what you know, and anticipate what is coming next?	_____	_____
7. Stay on the subject when you speak?	_____	_____
8. Ask questions occasionally?	_____	_____
9. Contribute examples and observations?	_____	_____
10. Avoid relating long, boring personal experiences?	_____	_____
11. Avoid dominating the discussion?	_____	_____
12. Contribute something, even if only a "yes" or "no" answer, to every discussion?	_____	_____
13. Refer to what other people have said when you talk, so that they know you have heard and thought about their contributions?	_____	_____
14. Get people back on the subject when necessary by summarizing what has been said and then introduce a new point?	_____	_____
15. Say something in each class as soon as you have the opportunity and something to say?	_____	_____
16. Use the discussion techniques described in this chapter in all discussions outside of the classroom, including those with friends, on the job, or in meetings?	_____	_____

If you have marked more than two of the above as No, you need to work to improve your participation in class discussion. If you have marked all but Questions 13 and 14 as Yes, you are learning in discussion classes even if you do not say a great deal.

Now read on to get some ideas about how to improve your level of skill in discussion. Increased expertise will be valuable to you while you are in school and also after you graduate and take a job. Discussion and collaboration are important ways to make decisions and get things done in many professions.

PREPARE FOR DISCUSSIONS

If a reading assignment is to be discussed, read it before class, underline important material in it, jot main points in the margin, and bring it to class with you. Refer to Chapter 10 for more information on how to mark a textbook so that you can later find material in it easily. During the discussion keep your textbook open and refer by page number to specific passages and ideas in it that support what you say.

If you have been assigned a topic for discussion that you are to think about rather than read about, jot down some ideas about it before you go to class. Enter into every discussion with a full mind. Then your contributions will be worthwhile.

Ten Tips for Active Participation in Class Discussion

1. Tune in quickly.   Focus on and write down the topic for discussion. This is the title for your discussion notes. Continue to concentrate on it.

2. Be an active listener.   Assume an alert physical posture in order to keep mentally alert. Think about what you hear, relate it to what you already know, anticipate what is coming next. Jot down questions and observations so that you will be ready when it's your turn to speak. Maintain eye contact with the speaker.

3. Try to stay objective.   Recognize that there is room for both fact and opinion in discussion. Continue to listen, even if you disagree. Withhold judgment of another opinion until you have heard the entire argument. If you wish to speak in opposition, do so politely and logically, using evidence and examples. Do what you can to prevent other participants from indulging in emotional tirades, also, by continuing to use reason and evidence whenever you have the opportunity to speak.

4. Stay on the subject.   You should know the general subject for discussion and know exactly what point about the subject is being discussed before you start talking. When you talk, try to make all of your remarks relevant to the subject. Your remarks should be brief and to the point. Then let someone else take the floor. If you want to speak again, allow several others to contribute before you make your next remarks.

5. *Take notes on the main points.* Try to write both main points and some details either during the discussion or right after it. Skip lines or number the main points to keep them separate. See page 60 for additional suggestions about taking notes on discussion.

6. *Ask questions occasionally.* It is appropriate to ask questions that (1) call for more information, (2) clarify factual material or unclearly stated opinions, or (3) help participants discover the value in what is being discussed.

7. *Help keep the discussion clear and understandable.* You can often help clarify a vague point in a discussion by making additional observations or giving examples. This helps everyone understand what is going on better. Whenever you have an urge to relate a personal experience, make sure that it will contribute to the discussion. Then keep it brief, interesting, and to the point.

8. *Stop and summarize when necessary.* You can help maintain the flow of a discussion, especially when someone has spoken too long or is getting off the point, by interjecting a summary and then introducing a new idea. Such a contribution is not overly long, it reminds everyone of what has been said so far in the discussion, and it gives the group a new problem to talk about that will get them back on the subject. Then the discussion grows and stays organized.

9. *Don't talk too much.* If you are naturally talkative and assertive, it may also be natural for you to want to establish yourself in the group by talking, joking, or even showing off. Curb this tendency so that everyone gets an equal chance to participate. If someone else dominates the discussion day after day without contributing much, complain privately to the professor after class.

10. *Participate even when you're scared.* If you are naturally shy, it may also be natural for you to withdraw from a discussion or to appear bored or even angry that you are there. Curb these tendencies by forcing yourself to raise your hand and say something in every discussion class as soon as you can. It's always easier to speak again after you have once spoken. No one but you will know that you are nervous. Soon you will be caught up in the ideas being discussed, and you will lose your self-consciousness. You will then enjoy class more and learn more, too, because you will be actively involved in what is going on. An incidental advantage, not to be ignored, is that class time will go faster if you are involved in the discussion.

There are some students who are very shy in a class discussion. This can be particularly true if you are returning to school after being away for several years or if this is your very first semester in college. If you fall into this category, make certain you listen well, formulate your own silent contributions, and at least make brief, occasional remarks. Contribute short answers like "yes" and "no," and raise your hand when the professor asks how many agree or disagree. Ask a question occasionally. Don't worry about not contributing more than this. You will still learn from the class if you are listening and thinking. The ones who don't learn are the ones who tune out completely.

EVALUATE YOUR PRESENT LEVEL OF PARTICIPATION IN SMALL GROUP WORK

Your professors may occasionally organize a class into small groups of 2–7 students each to work together on an assignment or problem. Analyze your current level of participation in group work.

Self-Evaluation: Group Work

Do you:

	Yes	No
1. Get the instructions straight so that you know exactly what is to be accomplished?	——	——
2. Adhere to time limits and complete the work in the time allowed?	——	——
3. Actively participate?	——	——
4. Assume leadership if necessary?	——	——
5. Volunteer to write notes some of the time?	——	——
6. Volunteer to report back to the class some of the time?	——	——
7. Stay on the subject?	——	——
8. Avoid dominating the group and compromise when necessary?	——	——
9. Help to involve everyone by asking the quiet ones, "What do you think?"	——	——
10. Listen well so that you could summarize the group's work if called upon to do so?	——	——

You need to be able to answer yes to all of these questions to participate well in groups.

You can improve your level of participation by understanding the purpose of groups and how they function, and also by using a few tips to improve your participation.

THE PURPOSE OF GROUPS AND HOW THEY FUNCTION

Small group work is also sometimes referred to as collaborative or cooperative learning. Students work together to get insights and ideas, solve problems, complete assignments, or do lab and other types of projects and exercises. Research suggests that this type of learning can be beneficial to students in a variety of ways. Group work helps students learn to concentrate and think without teacher supervision, it helps improve students' motivation and attitudes, it increases their self-esteem, it helps students accept differences of opinion, and it promotes independent learning.

Groups are usually composed of two to four members. Sometimes as many as seven can be assigned to a group. More than seven is usually not productive. The group is then given a task and a time frame in which to accomplish it. Sometimes roles are assigned to group members, such as leader, reader, recorder, summarizer, or speaker. Other times students are expected to assign and assume these roles themselves as part of the group work. When the group has completed its task, the individual who has agreed to report summarizes for the rest of the class what the group has accomplished. Class discussion of the ideas that have emerged from all of the groups often concludes the class session.

There are a number of variations on this type of class activity. For example, in peer tutoring students work in pairs to tutor and teach each other. In role playing, students assume roles and act them out in order to better assume them in actual situations. In group editing sessions, students read each others' papers and make recommendations for revision. In "think alouds" students read or work on the solution to a problem but stop frequently to explain to another student how they are thinking.

Eight Tips for Active Participation in Groups.

To improve your participation in group work, follow the ten tips for active participation in class discussion and then add the following eight additional tips.

1. *Clarify the instructions for the group.* Ask, do we all understand what to do? Then repeat the instructions and ask if the rest of the

group understands them in the same way that you do. If there is disagreement, ask the instructor for clarification.

2. *Help the group complete its work on time.* Keep an eye on the clock and remind people occasionally of how many more minutes the group has to complete its work.

3. *Help the group assign roles to its members.* If the instructor has not assigned roles, help assign them by asking, for example, who wants to be the leader, who wants to be the scribe or recorder, and who wants to report.

4. *Assume leadership if no one else will.* Volunteer yourself as leader if necessary. Your responsibilities then are to assign individuals to the other roles quickly and then to move through the steps of the assignment asking people to contribute until it is completed.

5. *If you volunteer to be the scribe, you may also want to report.* The scribe sometimes jots down notes that are incomplete and difficult to read. When this is the case, report from your notes yourself. This is better than giving your illegible notes to someone else who will stumble over them and be unable to report fluently.

6. *Participate and encourage others to participate.* Ask individual members what they think. Place a value on what you know and contribute to the group and then do the same for others by acknowledging good ideas when you hear them.

7. *Be willing to compromise.* Listen to all members of the group and, when there is disagreement, ask for a vote. You are working for consensus or agreement among group members. No one group member should dominate a group.

8. *When you are the reporter, summarize quickly and clearly.* As reporter, your task will be to summarize the ideas of the group. Include ideas that the group has agreed on along with individual contributions if you can. At the same time be brief, clear, and to the point. Leave time for the other reporters in the class to give their summaries.

At the Very Least . . .

This chapter has dealt with ideal ways for participating in class discussion and group work. If you can't follow all of the suggestions every day, *at the very least* do this much:

1. Prepare for discussion and group work even if only a few minutes.
2. Listen and think.
3. Make brief contributions.
4. Stay on the subject and take some notes.

SUMMARY

Read and think about the material to be discussed before you go to class discussions. In the discussion itself begin to concentrate immediately, be an active listener, stay objective, take some notes, stay on the subject, ask some questions, give examples and observations, summarize blocks of material when you can, and keep the discussion moving. Don't dominate the discussion. Say something in each discussion class at the first opportunity. Concentrate and pay attention in discussions whether or not you continue to contribute much. When you participate in group work get the instructions straight, be willing to assume a leadership role if necessary, participate and get others to participate, and help the group accomplish its task effectively and on time.

EXERCISES

A. Monitor Your Comprehension of this Chapter.

Write quickly, in phrases rather than complete sentences, the information in this chapter that you understand and remember. Look back through your marginal notes and summaries and add what you left out. Is anything in the chapter unclear? Jot it down to ask about in class. Has reading the chapter caused you to think of new insights or examples of your own? Jot them down.

B. Class Exercises

1. Small Groups and Class Discussion

a. Form groups of four and assign each group in the class a number: Group 1, Group 2, Group 3, and so on. Assign a leader, a scribe, a reporter, and a runner for each group. The leader will read the instructions and make certain they are completed on time. The scribe will write. The reporter will read the final report. The runner will circulate the papers from one group to another.

b. *Instructions*

   (1) *5 Minutes.* Make a list of real study problems that group members have and need to solve (Examples: too noisy to study, too sleepy in afternoon to study, etc.). Select one of these as the problem that interests the group the most. Write the problem at the top of a piece of paper and hand it to another group to solve.

   (2) *5 Minutes on each problem.* Discuss solutions to the problem that has just been handed to your group. Identify the favored solution and write it under the problem. Label it with your group's number. Pass the problem to a new group. As you receive new problems, look at the solutions already written and think of additional solutions. Circulate the sheets until every group has written a solution to every problem.

Example. If there are six groups, the final sheet might look like this:

Problem: too noisy to study
Group 1—Go to library
Group 2—Study in car
Group 3—Work with others to establish study hours
Group 4—Work with others to establish a quiet study area
Group 5—Study at a friend's
Group 6—Study when others are asleep

(3) *10 Minutes.* The reporter from each group reports on the problem and the solutions that have been contributed by the other groups

(4) (Remaining time) *Class Discussion.* Assign a discussion leader who asks, which of these ideas will work? Why? Which of them might not work? Why?

C. Application of Skills

Prepare the following materials for discussion and group work for the next class meeting.

1. Read Chapter 8 and write one question to stimulate discussion about the chapter on a 3 × 5 card. Write questions that begin with *why, how, when, where, do you agree with* or *what do you think.* At the next class you will give these cards to an individual designated as discussion leader. The leader will read the questions. The group will practice using the ten tips for active participation in class discussion while discussing the questions.

2. Read Chapter 8 and learn the steps for surveying a book and a chapter before the next class. In the next class you will work in small groups and practice using the seven tips for active participation in groups.

D. Topics for Your Learning Journal

1. How do you feel when you participate in class discussion? In group work? Why?

2. Are you satisfied or dissatisfied with your present performance in class discussion and group work? Evaluate your present performance and jot down some ways you might improve.

3. State whether you agree or disagree with the following statements and say why.
   a. We all need to value who we are and what we know.
   b. We also need to understand and consider other people's ideas.

   How do your responses to these questions influence your contributions to group work and discussion?

PART THREE

Reading the Textbook

8 | *Prereading Books and Chapters*

When you have finished reading this chapter, you will know the following:

1. How understanding a book or chapter's organization can help you learn and remember material from it.
2. How to preread by surveying and using background knowledge.
3. The steps for prereading books and chapters.
4. How to preread by making predictions and asking questions.

READING AS AN INTERACTIVE PROCESS

The reading instruction in Part Three of this book has been organized as a process. This means that it describes roughly what you should do at various stages of reading and studying to help you understand and remember the material. You will prepare yourself to read with various prereading activities, you will then read for comprehension, take some notes and write some summaries, do some additional thinking, and make some special efforts to commit what you have read to memory. You will not always do these activities in this exact order. The process has been broken into chapters here to facilitate the explanation.

Another important idea that runs through this part of the book is that reading is an interactive process. This means that in order to read well you should make a special effort to recall what you already know and believe about a subject before and as you read so that you can react, add, evaluate, and in other ways mentally interact with the author and interpret what is being said as you go along. Such mental conversation will keep you engaged with your reading and will help you think about and evaluate ideas as you read. It will also help you feel "at home" with what you read and less intimidated by it. Familiar material that you can question, react to, talk back to is always easier and more enjoyable to read than unfamiliar material. At times, of course, you will encounter reading material on totally unfamiliar topics. To read it well, you will need to seek background information either from another book or from a person. You will also need to rely on your skill in reading and comprehending the material in the first place so that you will understand what the author is saying and so that you can make accurate interpretations. The remainder of Part Three of this textbook will help you develop that ability.

PREREAD BEFORE YOU READ

This chapter explains some prereading strategies that you can use to familiarize yourself with material before you read it. They will help you concentrate, interact, and comprehend later when you actually read. These strategies include surveying, drawing on the background knowledge that you already have about the subject, making predictions, and asking some questions.

Fundamental to the use of the first of these strategies, surveying, is getting a sense of the subject, identifying the ideas that have been used to develop it, and understanding the basic organization of these ideas.

UNDERSTAND THE ORGANIZATION OF BOOKS AND CHAPTERS

Authors work out a plan for arranging the material in their books and chapters before they begin to write. If authors did not consciously arrange their materials in a logical order according to a well-thought-out plan, you would have trouble reading, understanding, and remembering their ideas. Look, for example, at the following list of ideas that have not been placed in any particular order:

Those who erase the blackboard too soon
Those who use big words
No pictures or examples
Problems students face
Difficult textbooks
Five or six steps, none of which are clear
Not enough time to do them well

Assignments
Some professors
Long paragraphs

    This list is not only confusing; it would also be difficult to remember if you had to memorize it. The ideas, presented as they are, do not follow a logical sequence. Furthermore, there is no quickly apparent relationship between one item and the next.

    The human mind has a natural tendency to want to see relationships among items in a list of this sort. Look at the list a few minutes, and you will begin to see that some of the items on it can be grouped together under headings. Furthermore, there is one item on the list that can, in fact, be used as the title. Once you have discovered the title, the other items fall into a pattern:

Problems Students Face

  I. Difficult textbooks
    A. Long paragraphs
    B. No pictures or examples
 II. Some professors
    A. Those who use big words
    B. Those who erase the blackboard too soon
III. Assignments
    A. Five or six steps, none of which are clear
    B. Not enough time to do them well

    Compare this list with the original, jumbled list. Arranged as it now is in a logical sequence, it is easier to read, to understand, and to remember.

    When the authors of your textbooks organize their ideas in logical sequence, they are deliberately making it easier for you to understand and remember those ideas. They organize their ideas in outlines, but they do not write in outline form. It would be dull if they did. Part of the challenge and pleasure of reading is learning to discover the author's original outline.

CLUES TO DISCOVERING ORGANIZATION

    1. The table of contents.   The major clue to discovery of the outline of a book is the table of contents. It lists, in sequence, the major ideas and, sometimes, the subideas to be developed. Materials in your textbooks are usually arranged either according to topics or in chronological order. When they are arranged topically, you need to discover *what topics will be covered,* to consider *why the author has placed them in that particular order,* and to note *how much space is alloted each topic.* When they are arranged chronologically, as are history books, biographies, diaries, books of directions, and lab manuals, you need to know *how much time is covered and where the breaks in time occur.*

Take a look at the table of contents of this book. Notice that the major topics are placed in a roughly chronological order. You get started first (Part 1). Then you normally go to class (Part 2) before you read the textbook (Part 3). And you usually do both before you take exams (Part 4) and do written assignments (Part 5). Under each of these major headings are the chapter titles, which represent the topics to be developed under each of the major headings. This book, then, combines the chronological and topical patterns of organization.

2. The introduction.   Another way authors sometimes clarify the organization of their books is to insert a brief explanation of their organizational plan in the preface or introduction. This explanation, plus the outline of the book provided by the table of contents, will usually give you a pretty clear idea of the way the book has been put together. Sometimes, in fact, the table of contents doesn't really make sense to you until you have read the accompanying explanation in the introductory material.

An explanation of the organizational plan is only one type of useful information that may be found in the prefatory material. Other information, some or all of which may be found in introductions and prefaces, includes (1) the author's explanation of why he or she wrote the book; (2) a list of the topics to be developed in the book; (3) a statement of personal bias if the book takes up a controversial topic; (4) why this approach to the material was used, particularly if it is different from the traditional approach; (5) a description of the author's background and authority for writing on the subject; (6) definitions of key terminology; (7) background information to help you place the information in the book in a context; (8) useful tips on how to read the book; and (9) a description of accompanying instructional materials, such as software or workbooks, that might be available in a lab or learning center. You should ask your instructor where these materials are if they are mentioned in the preface.

Take a look now at the Preface to this book and make a list of the items of information that will help you read and use it. Be selective in your reading of any preface and skip over information, such as the acknowledgements, that will not help you with your reading of the book itself.

3. Familiar chapter organization. Authors very often clarify the organization of chapters by using familiar organizational schemes. It will help you at the outset to recognize that most chapters and many lectures and essays have three main parts: (1) an introduction, (2) a main body, and (3) a summary or conclusion:

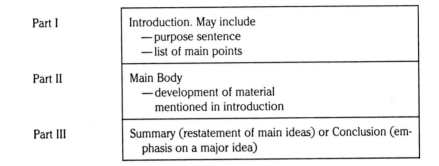

Part I	Introduction. May include —purpose sentence —list of main points
Part II	Main Body —development of material mentioned in introduction
Part III	Summary (restatement of main ideas) or Conclusion (emphasis on a major idea)

You will need to notice these three parts of the chapter when you make a survey.

WHY SURVEY BOOKS AND CHAPTERS?

The main object of surveying both books and chapters is to learn something about them immediately so that it will be easier to read later. Surveying a book provides you with an outline of its contents and overall plan as well as the purpose and slant of the author. You will, furthermore, discover additional special features that have been included in the book to help you read it.

There are other reasons why you might survey a book, however, besides simply preparing yourself to read it. You should survey any unfamiliar book before you take research material from it. For example, you wouldn't want to quote an author's opinion about capital punishment before you were sufficiently familiar with the book to know whether the author supports it or opposes it.

You might also survey a book when you are in a bookstore and are in doubt about whether or not to buy it. Fifteen minutes or less of surveying will usually yield enough information to enable you to make a decision.

There are some books that you should know something about in order to be a liberally educated person. Yet you may not want to read them all the way through. For instance, Gibbon's *Decline and Fall of the Roman Empire* is a work you have perhaps heard mentioned many times and feel you should know something about. A half hour's surveying may yield as much information as you are ever likely to need about this particular work.

There are also several reasons for surveying a chapter. First, surveying provides you with a *quick mental outline* of the main ideas. When you have such an outline in mind, you will be able to *concentrate* better when you start to read because you will know, in its broad outline, what the chapter is about. Another reason to survey is for review. After you have read an extremely complicated chapter or article, it may be a jumble in your mind. Go back and survey it to get its organization clear. Then you will be able to understand and remember the main points for a much longer period of time. You should always survey journal or magazine articles before you take research materials from them. In order to quote responsibly and intelligently you need to know something about the context of a quotation you wish to use. Finally, whenever you are about to listen to a professor lecture on a chapter, or when you are about to take a test on a book or a chapter that you have not read, survey it. Surveying, naturally, will not be as effective as reading, but it will be a lot better than not looking at the material at all.

HOW TO SURVEY A BOOK

Begin each semester by surveying your textbooks. Here is a six-step method for surveying a book in about fifteen or twenty minutes.

1. Read the title and background it.   Surveying demands intense concentration. Begin to concentrate by focusing on what the title suggests about the book's contents and the author's approach to the subject. Titles like *The Movies* or *Crystals* explicitly name the subject. *The Picture History of Astronomy* tells you both the subject *and* that the author will develop it chronologically and through pictures. The title *Art in Movement* is suggestive rather than explicit.

Background the title by making a list of eight or ten items that it calls to mind. For example, *The Picture History of Astronomy* might make you think of stars, solar system, universe, historical approach, constellations, pictures of galaxies, the planets, outer space, and so on. By making such a list in response to the title, you call up what you already know about the subject before you begin to read. This practice makes it easier to associate the new information with material that you already know. Then it is easier to concentrate, interact with the text material, and learn. If you look at a title and nothing comes to mind, you will be forewarned that the material you are about to read is unfamiliar. It will seen difficult until you develop some background knowledge about it.

2. Check the Special Features. Look to see if there is an index, glossary, or anything else included to help you read the book. An index, placed at the back of the book, gives an alphabetical listing of the topics covered in the book. It is more complete than the table of contents. Use it to find material on a specific topic or to check whether or not specific topics are covered. A glossary, also usually located at the back of the book, provides definitions of the technical terms used by the author. These definitions can also be placed in the margins or at the bottom of textbook pages. Other features might include charts, diagrams, special tables of information, illustrations, bibliographies, or exercises.

3. Read the table of contents. Look for the topics the author will cover. Notice the order in which they will be presented. Take long enough to understand, if possible, not only the order, but also the relationships among the various topics of the book and the reasons they are presented in the order they are.

4. Read all introductory and prefatory material. Move through this material rather quickly, looking for information that will help you read the book. Whenever you encounter useful information, slow down and read it carefully. By the time you have examined the introductory material and the table of contents, you should have in mind an ordered list of the topics to be developed in the book. You also want to gather as much other information as will help you do a more informed job of reading.

5. Look at the first and last chapters of the book. They are important. In the first chapter authors often introduce the subject in greater detail. In the last chapter they either summarize what has been said or present material that they particularly want to emphasize. Look at the *titles* of these chapters, read the *introductory paragraphs,* the *final paragraphs,* and look at the *headings* and *subheadings.*

6. Read the first paragraph of each of the other chapters.
This will give you a sense of the progression of ideas in the book and
will show how they are introduced in each new chapter.

Notice what you have now accomplished:

1. You know what the book is about and what major topics will be
   discussed in it.
2. You know something about the author's purpose for writing the
   book and how you should read it.
3. You know what kinds of special features have been supplied to
   make your reading easier.

HOW TO SURVEY A CHAPTER

It should take you only five to ten minutes to survey a chapter. There
are six steps involved:

1. Read the title and background it. The title tells you the
subject of the chapter. Make a list of what you know about the subject.
If the title communicates nothing (for example, "Dividends, Retained
Earnings, and Treasury Stock," a chapter title in an accounting text),
find out something about it immediately by looking up unfamiliar
terms in the glossary, a dictionary, or the index. Add what you have
just learned to the list of what you already know.

2. Read the chapter objectives and introduction. Learning
goals or objectives like those at the beginning of each chapter in this
book serve the same purpose as an introduction. Read such information carefully. These lists highlight the main ideas of each chapter
before you begin to read. If there are no objectives, read the first
paragraph and look for a purpose sentence. Underline it so that you
will know the author's main intent in the chapter. Also, look for a list
of the main points to be covered in the chapter. Get them well in mind
by underlining them and numbering them.

3. Read the summary (if there is one). A summary is a
restatement of the most important ideas in the chapter. It should be
read first as a preview of those ideas and last as a final check on your
understanding of the ideas.

Lists of terms and/or questions at the end of a chapter can
perform the same function as a summary. They can highlight the
important ideas in the chapter. Read them as a preview and as a
final check just as you would a summary. If there is no summary or

exercises, read the concluding paragraph to see which idea the author particularly emphasizes by placing it last.

4. Read the headings and subheadings.   Read all headings and subheadings, which may be set in boldface type or in italics, to help you discover the main ideas and their sequence. If there are no headings, read the first sentence in each paragraph to help you discover the main ideas in the chapter. Number and letter the headings and subheadings as in an outline, so that you can see the relative importance of ideas. Create chunks by drawing lines across the page at the end of each section. Write one or two question words next to each heading and think about how it develops the subject of the chapter. Examples of such words are *who, what, when, where, why, how much, how many, how significant,* and *what does this have to do with the subject of this chapter?* Now try to recite the main topic of each main chunk. You should be able to hold seven or eight of these topics in your short-term memory while you read. As you read, focus on the headings and questions again. They will help you keep your mind on the subject as you read.

5. Study all visual materials.   As you leaf through the chapter stop to study all tables, graphs, diagrams, pictures, and their titles or captions. Such study can help introduce you to many of the major ideas in the chapter.

6. Circle or box the important words or key terms that are in italics or bold type.   You will need to know these words in order to understand the author. Identify them now and make them stand out from the text so that your eyes will not slide over them later as you read.

Notice what you have now accomplished:

1. You have focused on the subject and recalled what you already know about it.
2. You have divided a difficult whole into manageable parts.
3. You have thought about the meaning of each part by itself and also how it relates to the whole.
4. You have in mind the main topics and the order in which they will be discussed.
5. You have a rudimentary understanding of the organization of the chapter. You are now ready to read to fill in the details and to get a fuller understanding of both the parts and the whole.

MAKE PREDICTIONS AND ASK SOME QUESTIONS

Here are two additional prereading suggestions to help you use what you already know and believe to help you interact and converse with the author.

Use the information you get from backgrounding and surveying to make some predictions about what you think the book or chapter will be about. Do this by answering the two questions: What do I know now? What do I think this will be about? You may also at this point jot down one or more questions that you would like answered as you read.

Now read to see if you have made accurate predictions. If you have not done so, stop and analyze why you are off target. Make some new predictions. Accurate predictions can help you concentrate and locate ideas quickly. Inaccurate ones can throw you off and interfere with comprehension. For example, if you predict that this chapter is about *land* surveying and then, when you begin to read, you discover that it is about *book* surveying, you will quickly want to change your predictions in order to read effectively.

Sometimes you will be able to make predictions before you begin to read because of insufficient background knowledge about the topic. When this happens, start reading and, as you read, look for familiar material. If you encounter any, relate it to what you already know and predict what you can. Check your predictions for accuracy as you read.

At the Very Least . . .

This chapter has dealt with the ideal way for prereading books and chapters. If you can't follow all of the suggestions every day, *at the very least* do this much:

1. Survey new textbooks at the beginning of each semester. At least look at the table of contents and the introduction, and examine a typical chapter to see how it is organized.
2. Before reading a chapter, at least read the title and mentally background it, look at the headings, and notice visuals, key vocabulary, and the material at the end.
3. Predict what the material is about and check for accuracy.
4. Remember that it is better to survey reading material before a class or exam than not to look at the material at all.

SUMMARY

Prereading can help you concentrate on reading. Survey to understand the organization and format of a book or chapter before you read. Background the title to discover what you already know about the subject. It is also useful to know something about the purpose and slant of the author. To survey a book, read the title and background it, study the special features, study the table of contents, read the preface or introduction, look at the first and last chapters, and read the introductions to the other chapters. To survey chapters or articles, read the title and background it, read the introduction, read the summary, read heads and subheads and jot down question words, study visual material such as pictures or graphs, and circle or box in important words and concepts. As you survey and background you should also make predictions and ask questions to help you concentrate on your reading. Change your predictions if they are inaccurate.

Surveying in Brief

These lists are intended to help you memorize the steps in surveying *books* and *chapters.* Noting the similarities and differences in the two processes will help you learn them.

Surveying Books	**Surveying Chapters or Articles**
1. Read the title and background it.	1. Read the title and background it.
2. Look for special features.	2. Read the introduction.
3. Read the table of contents.	3. Read the summary.
4. Read the preface or introduction.	4. Read the headings and sub-headings.
5. Survey the first and last chapters.	5. Study all visual materials.
6. Read the first paragraph of each of the other chapters.	6. Circle important words.

EXERCISES

A. Monitor Your Comprehension of This Chapter.

Write quickly, in phrases rather than complete sentences, the information in this chapter that you understand and remember. Look back through your marginal notes and summaries and add what you left out. Is anything in the chapter unclear? Jot it down to ask about in class. Has reading the chapter caused you to think of new insights or examples of your own? Jot them down.

B. *Class Exercises*

1. *Individuals.*

This exercise will demonstrate the amount and type of information that students can expect to get from making a quick five-minute survey of a chapter. The instructor should ask each student to turn to Chapter 11 and begin to read it sentence-by-sentence, in the usual way, for five minutes. When the instructor calls time, each student should then attempt to answer the following test questions on the chapter. The answers to this first attempt should be recorded in the first column labeled Test 1.

QUIZ ON CHAPTER 11

	Test 1	Test 2
1. What is the title of the chapter?		
2. What are four memory aids described in this chapter?		
3. How many suggestions are made in this chapter for helping you remember what you read?		
4. T or F. You should associate new information with what you already know.		
5. After taking notes on a reading assignment, the final step is to: a. organize your notes b. fill in the left-hand margin c. transfer the material to your long-term memory d. none of the above because taking notes is, itself, the final step		
6. T or F. While you study you should mentally visualize material as often as possible.		
7. T or F. One suggestion for helping you remember is to make up examples of your own.		
8. T or F. Summarizing and reviewing are basically the same activity.		
9. How many suggestions are made to help you think about new material?		
10. T or F. Monitoring your own learning helps you know when you have mastered as assignment.		

Now the instructor should ask students to review the steps for surveying a chapter. When they have finished, they should be instructed to turn again to Chapter 11 and survey it for five minutes, following the survey steps exactly.

Then students should be asked to answer the same test questions again, only this time they should place their answers in the column labeled Test 2. The answers for both tests can now be checked against the answer key.

Answer Key for Quiz on Chapter 11

1. Remembering and Thinking Critically
2. encode, organize, associate, recite, (or any of the others)
3. 10
4. T.
5. C.
6. T
7. T
8. F
9. 6
10. T

The instructor should ask for a show of hands on how many students did better on Test 2. Most readers will get more information about an entire chapter by surveying it for five minutes than they will by reading it for the same amount of time.

Note: Students may have prepared for these next two class exercises by doing the Application of Skills exercises in Chapter 7 (page 107). Students who have completed these exercises will have prepared *questions for class discussion* for Exercise 2 and will have *learned the steps for surveying* both books and chapters for Exercise 3.

2. **Whole Class Discussion.** Assign a discussion leader who will read the questions on this chapter that the group has already prepared. (If no questions have been prepared ahead of time, each student should prepare a question now. Take five minutes to write a question on Chapter 8. Begin the questions with *why, how, when, where, do you agree with,* or *what do you think*.) The class will then use these questions to practice discussion. The leader should help them employ the ten tips for active participation in group discussion.

3. **Small Groups.** Form small groups and designate a leader, a scribe, and a reporter. This is a surveying exercise that incorporates all of the prereading strategies taught in this chapter.
   a. Each group should first review "Surveying in Brief" on page 121 and also the section on predicting and asking questions on page 120. Notice the differences between surveying a book and surveying a chapter and discuss the reasons for the items on the list and the order in which they occur.
   b. Now survey this book and complete the following Survey Sheet for a Book. Group members should search for information and the scribe should write it down.

Survey Sheet for a Book

1. What is the title? _____

2. What do you already know about the subject as stated in the title?

   _____

   _____

3. Read the table of contents and list the major divisions or parts in the

   book. _____

   _____

4. Is the book organized chronologically, topically, or does it follow

   some other organizational plan? _____

   _____

5. Read the introduction and preface. Who is the author, and what do
   you now know about him or her? Mention qualifications and background, biases, unusual approach, or any other information about the

   author that you find in the introduction or preface. _____

   _____

6. List three items of useful information in the preface or introduction

   that will help you read the book. _____

   _____

7. Look at the first chapter of the book. What is its title? _____

   _____

8. Look at the last chapter of the book. What is its title? _____

   _____

   Why do you think the author decided to place it last? _____

   _____

9. Read the first paragraph of each of the other chapters. List three major ideas that are developed in the book. _____

_____

10. Look to see if there is an index, glossary, or other built-in aids to help you read the book. List these aids. _____

_____

11. Assume that you have just been asked to describe this book in fifty words or less. What would you say about it? _____

_____

12. Make three predictions about what you can expect to learn in the rest of this book.

   a.

   b.

   c.

13. Ask one question that you would like answered. _____

_____

14. Group members should now survey Chapter 10 in this book and complete the following Survey Sheet for a Chapter.

Survey Sheet for a Chapter

1. What is the title? _____

2. What do you already know about the subject as stated in the title?

_____

3. Are there chapter objectives or learning goals? Yes _____ No _____.

   If yes, what are they? _____

_____

4. Read the first paragraph. Is it an introductory paragraph? Yes _____ No _____. If yes, what information does it give about the subject and organization of the chapter? _____

_____

_____

5. Is there a summary? Yes _____ No _____. If yes, list three important items that are described in the chapter. _____

_____

6. List all other material that follows the summary. _____

_____

7. If there is no summary or other ending material, such as questions or exercises, read the last paragraph. What idea is emphasized in this final paragraph? _____

_____

8. Read the headings and subheadings or the first sentence of each paragraph. Briefly list the main ideas that are developed in the chapter. _____

_____

9. Look at all visual materials in the chapter. What ideas in the chapter do these materials illustrate? _____

_____

10. Circle or box important key words or terms and list three of them.

_____

_____

_____

11. Assume that you have just been asked to describe this chapter in fifty words or less. What would you say about it? _____

   _____

   _____

   _____

12. Make three-predictions about what you can expect to learn in this chapter.

   a.

   b.

   c.

13. Ask one question that you would like answered. _____

   _____

13. One reporter should read the *Survey Sheet for a Book* completed by the group. Other reporters may then add information that was not included in the report.

14. Another reporter should read the *Survey Sheet for a Chapter* completed by the group. Other reporters in the class may then add information if necessary.

C. Application Exercises

1. Read the introduction to one of your other textbooks and list the items of information that will help you read the book.

2. Go to the library or bookstore and survey a book that looks interesting for at least 15 minutes but no more than 30 minutes. On a sheet of notebook paper, answer the *Survey Sheet for a Book* questions on pages 124–125. Make a brief oral report to the class on what you discovered about this book by surveying it. This exercise will enable class members to become familiar with books that interest them and to share that information with the class.

3. Survey all of the textbooks that you are reading outside of this class this semester. Complete the *Survey Sheet for a Book* questions on pages 124–125 for each of them.

4. Survey the next chapter that you are assigned to read in one of your text-books outside of this class. Complete the *Survey Sheet for a Chapter* questions on page 125–127 for this chapter.

D. Topics for Your Learning Journal

1. In this chapter, you have practiced using prereading strategies: surveying, backgrounding, predicting, and asking questions. Describe the personal benefits and limitations of each of these strategies for you. How will you employ them in your reading for your other classes?

2. Consider the following advice, take a position by agreeing or disagreeing with it, and give reasons for your position.

   Students should survey all of their new textbooks during the first week of each semester.

3. Describe some ways that you interact with the material that you read while you are reading it. Do you mentally agree, disagree, think of your own examples, add what you know, or in other ways make mental contributions as you read? Give some examples of what you have done or what you might do.

9 | *Reading to Comprehend Ideas*

When you have finished reading this chapter, you will know:

1. How to recognize general and specific ideas.
2. How to recognize main ideas, subideas, supporting details, transitions, and organizational patterns.
3. How to infer main ideas when they are not directly stated.
4. How to read a difficult assignment.

READ FOR IDEAS AND KNOW WHAT TO EXPECT

In Chapter 8 you practiced prereading strategies: backgrounding, (consulting your own background before you read) surveying, predicting, and asking questions. Backgrounding helps you bring to conscious awareness what you already know about a topic. Surveying helps you to determine the author's focus on the topic. It also helps you to locate some of the ideas that are used to develop it, along with the order in which they occur. Surveying finally helps you divide a chapter of article into major idea units that makes it easier, later, to read in units. Predicting and asking questions help you think ahead and anticipate the ideas in the text. Prereading makes it easier to read and interact with the book or chapter. It improves both concentration and comprehension.

This chapter will help you improve the next phase of the reading process, reading to comprehend ideas. You will accomplish this more easily if you know what you can expect to find on the printed page and, consequently, what to look for. Then you will begin to understand *ideas* rather than *words*.

You can expect every unit of information, whether it is a sentence, paragraph, a section, or even a whole chapter, to have a subject, and to contain both general and specific ideas about that subject. You can, furthermore, expect to be able to tell the difference between the general information, or main ideas, and the specific information, or subideas, and the supporting details. You can also expect to encounter various kinds of transitional material that either explain relationships among ideas or change the subject entirely. Finally, you can expect that ideas will be organized, often according to established patterns. The rest of this chapter will heighten your awareness of the back-and-forth movement between general and specific ideas and will help you learn to recognize main ideas, subideas, supporting details, transitions, and organization in everything you read. Finally, you will be given suggestions for reading difficult material.

RECOGNIZE GENERAL AND SPECIFIC IDEAS

In all communication writers and speakers present a general idea, support that idea with specific details, and then go on to present another general idea. Figure 9.1 shows a conventional outline that visually represents such a pattern of ideas. This outline is only one version of several possible ways to develop these ideas. There is no outline form that all writers follow exactly for all writing tasks.

The most general ideas on the diagram in the figure are the main ideas. They are printed in bold face type and outlined at the Roman numeral level (I,II). Read the two main ideas. Notice that by themselves they are abstract, almost meaningless. They don't tell you much unless you already happen to know a great deal about the subject and can fill in your own details. Subideas are more specific than main ideas and are outlined at the A, B level. They tell you more about the main idea. Many paragraphs contain only a main idea and one or more subideas. When this is the case, it may be the author's judgment that no additional explanation is required. Or the author may continue development of the idea in the same or in later paragraphs with any of various types of specific supporting material. Such material is entered on an outline at levels 1, 2 or a, b.

The pattern just described can be found both in paragraphs and in longer sections of material that contain more than one paragraph. The authors of the textbook *Biology* begin a paragraph: "Adaptations may be broadly classed as anatomical, physiological or behavioral."[1] This sentence, which states the general subject of the paragraph, is

---

[1] Karen Arms and Pamela S. Camp, *Biology* (New York: Holt, Rinehart and Winston, 1979), p. 9.

The Outline	Example
I. **Main Idea (most general)**	**In college you will have to develop two types of vocabulary.**
A. Subidea (less general; more specific)	One of these is a specialized vocabulary
1. Supporting Detail (most specific)	You will need to know what your biology professor means by *D.N.A.*
B. Subidea	You will also need to develop a general vocabulary.
1. Supporting Detail	If someone calls you *ingenuous,* you will know what he means.
II. **Main Idea**	**You will need a method for developing both types of vocabulary.**
A. Subidea	A method that won't work is reading and listening to new words without looking them up.
B. Subidea	A method that will work better has four steps. Let's look at these specific steps.
1. Supporting Detail	Consciously *look* for a word you don't know.
2. Supporting Detail	Record the *context* in which you found it.
3. Supporting Detail	*Look it up* in the glossary or dictionary.
4. Supporting Detail	*Associate* it with something familiar to you.

Figure 9.1 A typical pattern of ideas.

called the topic sentence. You have, at this point in your reading, a topic in mind (three types of adaptations) that provides you with a mental focus for reading the remainder of the paragraph. You need to know more, however, before you will understand or remember the idea and terms presented in this sentence. These authors continue their paragraph with material at the subidea level: "Anatomical adaptations are those involving the physical structure of the organism." The authors are aware that the reader may still not understand what is meant by *anatomical adaptations*. Thus, the next sentence in the paragraph is an example: "For instance, a penguin's flippers are an anatomical adaptation that permits it to swim." They continue the paragraph with another subidea followed by examples. Look at the entire paragraph and notice how it moves from the general main idea in the topic sentence to the subidea level, then to the supporting detail level, and then back again to the subidea and supporting detail levels:

Adaptations may be broadly classed as anatomical, physiological, or behavioral. **Anatomical** adaptations are those involving the physical structure of the organism. For instance, a penguin's flippers are an anatomical adaptation that permits it to swim. An organism's **physiology** is all of the internal workings of its body: the biochemistry of its cells and the processes that allow it to digest food, exchange gases, excrete wastes, reproduce, move, and sense and respond to the outside world. An example of an extreme physiological adaptation to temperature is seen in the ability of the blue-green bacterium *Synechococcus* to live in hot springs at temperatures up to 80°C (175°F), which would destroy all biochemical activity in most other organisms. An example of an impressive **behavioral** adaptation is the ability of a kangaroo rat to eat the leaves of the desert saltbush. No other animal can eat this plant since its leaves are full of salt crystals. The kangaroo rat flakes off the salt-filled outer layer of the leaf with its front teeth, and then eats the salt-free inner part. This ability to prepare its food is a behavioral adaptation that allows the kangaroo rat to eat a food which is completely unavailable to other animals.[2]

Topic sentence – main idea

◄ *Subidea*
◄ *Example*

◄ *Subidea*

} *Examples*

The main ideas, subideas, and supporting details in this paragraph are stated briefly and compactly. If the authors had decided

[2] Ibid.

that more explanation was needed, they could have added further examples and explanations and divided this material into three or four paragraphs. The pattern of ideas would remain the same whether explained briefly in a paragraph or expanded into a larger section of material.

Adequate comprehension of any textbook paragraph, section, or chapter requires an understanding of both main ideas and details. As you read, both the general and specific material become interrelated in your mind until you are finally able to say or write what the chapter is about by describing both its broadest ideas and its most specific details. To help you achieve such comprehension, it is useful at this point to think separately about how to recognize *main ideas, subideas, supporting details,* and *transitions.*

RECOGNIZE MAIN IDEAS BY READING TOPIC SENTENCES

Everything you read is a fusion of main ideas and subideas, supporting details and transitions. The main idea is what most of a paragraph or longer section of material is about. Sometimes it is directly stated and sometimes it is not. When it is not, you will need to infer it or figure it out for yourself.

One way to discover the main idea in the material you are reading, is to stop at the end of a paragraph or section of material and ask yourself, "What was most of this paragraph or section about?" The answer to that question will help you discover the main idea in that unit of material.

Another way to discover main ideas is to locate topic sentences. Topic sentences are statements that introduce discussions that may go on for one or several paragraphs. They state the topic and an idea about the topic that gives control and direction to the remaining part of the discussion.

According to recent research, topic sentences are used regularly by textbook authors. They are used much less frequently by magazine and newspaper writers. Look for topic sentences, then, as you read your textbooks. They will help you focus on the major ideas and understand how they are developed.

Topic sentences are usually located at or near the beginning of a paragraph or longer section of material so that you will have an idea to which you can relate the more specific material that follows. Topic sentences may also, however, be located in the middle or at the end of a unit of material. Or, there may not be a topic sentence at all.

In this last case, you will usually be able to locate a phrase or to come up with a sentence of your own that states what most of the material is about.

Recognize Topic Sentences in Paragraphs

Read the next paragraph that comes from a sociology textbook and locate and underline the topic sentence.

> There has been a significant increase in the number of single-parent families in the United States. Today, only 68 percent of children live with both biological parents. Even more dramatic is the proportion of children who will live in a single-parent household sometime during their youth: 42 percent of white children and 86 percent of black children.[3]

You are correct if you decided that the first sentence in this paragraph is the topic sentence. It introduces the main idea that single parent families have increased in number. The rest of the paragraph explains and gives statistics to prove and clarify this idea.

Now look at another paragraph that comes from this same sociology textbook. Until you read the paragraph carefully, you might think that the first sentence is the topic sentence. But a question can never be a topic sentence because it only introduces the topic and does not state the main point that is to be made about it. Locate and underline the sentence in the paragraph that explains both the topic—social change—and the main point that the author makes about it.

> What, exactly, is social change? The best way to analyze how sociologists define social change is through example. The invention of the steam locomotive was not in itself a social change, but the acceptance of the invention and the spread of railroad transportation were. Martin Luther's indictments of the Catholic church nailed to the door of Wittenberg Cathedral in 1517 were not in themselves social change, but they helped give rise to one of the major social changes of all time, the Protestant Reformation. Adam Smith's great work *An Inquiry into the Nature and Causes of the Wealth of Nations* (first published in 1776) was not in itself social change, but it helped initiate a social change that altered the world, the Industrial Revolution. Thus, individual discoveries, actions, or works do not themselves constitute social change, but they may lead to alterations in shared values or patterns of social behavior or even to the reorganization of social relationships and institutions. When this happens, sociologists speak of social change. Hans

[3] Henry L. Tischler, *Introduction to Sociology,* 3rd ed. (Fort Worth: Holt, Rinehart and Winston, 1990), p. 372

Gerth and C. Wright Mills define social change as "whatever happens in the course of time to the roles, the institutions, or the orders comprising a social structure, their emergence, growth and decline." To put it simply, using terms we defined in Chapter 5, **social change** consists of any modification in the social organization of a society in any of its social institutions or social roles.[4]

In this paragraph the last sentence is the topic sentence. The rest of the paragraph contains supporting details—examples, and a quotation from authorities. The main idea could be stated something like this: Social change is major change in people's behavior or in the organization of society.

Recognize Topic Sentences in Sections of Material

So far you have looked at topic sentences in paragraphs. Topic sentences are also used to state the main ideas in longer sections of material that contain more than one paragraph. All of the paragraphs that make up a section will then contribute to the development of the main idea. Read the following section of material about children's roles in household purchasing. Underline the topic sentence.

The role of the children in purchasing evolves as they grow older. Children's early influence is generally centered around toys to be recommended to Santa Claus and the choice of cereal brands. Younger children are also important to marketers of fast-food restaurants. Even though the parents may decide when to eat out, the children usually select the restaurant.

As children gain maturity, they increasingly influence their clothing purchases. One study revealed that teenagers in the thirteen to fifteen age group spend an average of $12 per week. At sixteen to nineteen, their average weekly expenditures increase to $45. Teenage boys spend most of their funds on food, soft drinks, candy, gum, recreation, hobbies, movies, records, gasoline, and car accessories. Teenage girls spend most of their money on clothes and gifts.[5,6]

You are correct if you underlined the first sentence and recognized that this section is about children's purchases from childhood through the teenage years. Note, furthermore, that the first sentence

---

[4] Tischler, pp. 612–613. Used with permission. References have been removed.

[5] "Keeping Up . . . with Youth," *Parade,* December 11, 1977, p. 20. See also James U. McNeal, "Children as Consumers: A Review," *Journal of the Academy of Marketing Science,* Fall 1979, pp. 346–59; George P. Moschis and Roy L. Moore, "Decision Making among the Young: A Socialization Perspective," *Journal of Consumer Research,* September 1979, pp. 101–12; and George P. Moschis and Gilbert A. Churchill, Jr., "An Analysis of the Adolescent Consumer," *Journal of Marketing,* Summer 1979, pp. 40–48.

[6] Louis E. Boone and David L. Kurtz, *Contemporary Marketing,* 4th ed. (New York: CBS College Publishing, 1983), p. 189.

states the main idea of the section but that each of the paragraphs develops a subidea that explains more about the main idea. The section could be outlined like this:

I. Children's purchasing power evolves   *Main idea*
   A. Small children's purchases   *Subidea (paragraph 1)*
   B. Teenager's purchases   *Subidea (paragraph 2)*

This section of material is introduced with a topic sentence that identifies the subject of the entire section. In reading and studying these paragraphs, you would think of them as a unit, tracing the evolution of children's purchasing power as they grow older.

In reading a textbook chapter, you need to learn to discover the *relative* importance of ideas in the paragraphs. Determine whether each paragraph you read introduces one of the few major ideas in the chapter or whether it supports and develops one of these major ideas.

Infer Main Ideas When They Are Not Stated

When there is no topic sentence that directly states what a paragraph or longer section of material is about, you will need to look for words and phrases that, when taken together, summarize the idea in the paragraph. The next paragraph does not have a topic sentence. Read the following paragraph and underline the words and phrases that state its idea. Then in your own words, write a topic sentence for this paragraph.

> Of all symbols, words are the most important. Using the symbols of language, humans organize the world around them into labeled cognitive categories and use these labels to communicate with one another. Language, therefore, makes possible the teaching and sharing of cognitive and normative culture. It provides the principal means through which culture is transmitted and the foundation on which the complexity of human thought and experience rest.[7]

_____

_____

_____

[7] Tischler, p. 81.

Did you write a sentence that is something like the following? *Words are important because they are used to communicate and to transmit ideas.* Now try rereading the paragraph, this time inserting the new topic sentence right after the first sentence. Topic sentences make paragraphs easier to read. When authors do not supply them, think of one for yourself. Jot it, in brief form, in the margin.

Now read a second paragraph and infer the main idea. Write a topic sentence in the space below.

> All human beings have culture. It is the foundation on which all human achievements rest and is perhaps the defining characteristic of our species. But do animals have culture too? Not long ago most scholars would have said "no," but in the last two decades a variety of research has challenged this view. For example, Jane van Lawick-Goodall discovered that chimpanzees living in nature not only use tools but produce them first and then carry them to where they will use them. The chimps break twigs off trees, strip them of leaves and bark, then carry them to termite mounds where, after wetting them with spit, they poke them into tunnels and pull them out again all covered with delicious termites ready to be licked off. Sea otters search out flat pieces of rock and, while floating on their backs, place them on their stomachs and crack shellfish open against them.[8]

_____

_____

_____

Your topic sentence may be similar to this one: *There is evidence that animals, like human beings, have culture.* Notice how you had to put together several words and phrases from throughout the paragraph to create a topic sentence that states what the whole paragraph is about.

RECOGNIZE SUBIDEA AND OTHER TYPES OF PARAGRAPHS

Subidea paragraphs that support and develop major ideas very often begin with sentences that indicate those paragraphs will give further

---

[8] Tischler, pp. 83–84. References have been removed.

information about ideas that have already been introduced. Here are a few examples of sentences that occur at the beginning of subidea paragraphs.

Aside from being a pleasant daydream, this little experiment should have proved that it's possible to communicate without using words.[9]

There is a third way to deal with lawbreakers: rehabilitation.[10]

The example shows that light waves have relatively short wavelengths.[11]

Each of these sentences suggests that you look back to read what has gone before as well as to read ahead. In the first example you will want to know what "little experiment" is being described, in the second, you will want to know what the other two ways of dealing with lawbreakers are, and, in the third, you will want to go back and study the example.

Besides *main idea paragraphs* and *subidea paragraphs,* there are three other types of paragraphs that can help you locate main ideas. The *introductory paragraph,* which appears at the beginning of a chapter or major section of material, may list the main ideas that will be developed. The *summary paragraph* at the end restates the main ideas. *Transitional paragraphs* frequently summarize a main idea that has been discussed to that point and then introduce you to the next idea.

RECOGNIZE SUPPORTING DETAIL

Supporting detail is used by authors to make main ideas clear, interesting, and memorable. Sometimes it is also used to prove an idea. Supporting detail is not difficult to locate because it is usually the most interesting material that you read. It is usually familiar, close to, or even a part of the experience you bring to your reading. It is also easy to imagine, visualize, or sense.

The following is a list of types of supporting detail that authors use. When you learn to recognize supporting detail, you won't get it

[9] Ronald B. Adler, Lawrence B. Rosenfeld, and Neil Towne, *Interplay: The Process of Interpersonal Communication,* 2d ed. (New York: Holt, Rinehart and Winston, 1983), p. 112.

[10] Gerald Runkle, *Ethics: An Examination of Contemporary Moral Problems* (New York: Holt, Rinehart and Winston, 1982), p. 356.

[11] Jerry D. Wilson, *Technical College Physics* (Philadelphia: Saunders College Publishing, 1982), p. 330.

confused with main ideas and subideas, and you can better comprehend what you read.

1. *Examples* or *specific instances* may be long, brief, made-up, or real.
   Examples are concrete and usually easy to understand, visualize,
   or relate to what you know. They help make ideas clear, interesting,
   and easy to remember. Notice how the examples of animal culture
   in the paragraph on page 137 fulfill these functions.
2. *Comparisons* show how one thing is like another (Skilled college
   students are like unskilled college students in their common desire
   for a diploma).
3. *Contrasts* show how one thing differs from another (Skilled students are different from unskilled students in that they use a
   method to read a textbook). Comparisons and contrasts help you
   understand unique or unfamiliar qualities by comparing or contrasting them with the more familiar.
4. *Statistics* and other *factual material* (75 percent of the students
   who do not attend class regularly receive grades of C or worse).
   Statistics and facts are usually included to prove or make the main
   idea more believable. They also clarify.
5. *Graphs* (Statistics can be effectively illustrated by graphs.) Graphs
   condense a lot of information in a small space and allow you to see
   relationships among data. Studying them carefully can make the
   main points clearer and often more believable.
6. *Quotations* from authorities (Professor Smith admits, "I tell students they don't need to attend my class if they don't want to. I
   know, however, that if they don't come, they won't pass"). Quotations are usually used to prove and clarify a point.
7. *Vivid description* (The student took the exam from the professor's
   hand, quickly looked at the grade, gave a sigh of relief, and began
   to smile). Description is used to make ideas clear and memorable.
8. *Definition* (Transitions can be defined as words, sentences, or paragraphs that are used to help readers move from one idea to another
   and also to understand the relationship between the ideas.) Definitions are used primarily to clarify ideas.

If you do not consciously look for and recognize supporting detail as you read, it is easy to commit a very common reading (and
listening) error—you remember items of supporting detail and either
never notice or forget the main idea these items were meant to support. The reason this error is so common is that supporting detail

stands out more. When you encounter supporting detail, look to see what main idea it supports. Total and accurate comprehension requires that you locate both types of material as well as understand their relation to each other.

Read the following paragraphs about acids and bases. Locate and underline the topic sentence. Read the supporting detail.

Acids and Bases

Acids and **bases** are classifications of chemicals dating back to antiquity. The word *acid* comes from the Latin *acidus,* meaning "sour" or "tart," since water solutions of acids have a sour or tart taste. Acids in water react with metals such as zinc and magnesium to liberate hydrogen; neutralize bases to produce salt and water; and change the color of litmus, a vegetable dye, from blue to red. Citrus fruits offer a quick experience with natural acids because of their citric acid content, and any fruit with a high sugar content, such as apples, will readily ferment to produce a vinegar containing acetic acid. Bases in water, or alkaline solutions, have a bitter taste, feel slippery or soapy to the touch, change litmus from red to blue, and neutralize acids to form salt and water.

The variety of acids and bases in your life is illustrated by the following: Baking powder and baking soda are weak bases vital to cooking. Lye is a strong base often used as drain and toilet bowl cleaners. Lime, not as soluble in water as lye, is used to decrease the acidity of the soil. Antacids contain bases to neutralize excess acidity in the stomach. Acid skin tends to produce pimples. Your car battery depends on battery acid. Radiators corrode when antifreeze solutions acidify. Acid rain and acid mine drainage are major threats to our environment. Your digestion and body metabolism are critically dependent on narrow controls of acidity and alkalinity in body fluids and tissues. The list could go on and on.[12]

What types of supporting detail appear in this passage?

_____

_____

_____

Read the next paragraph, underline the topic sentence, and identify the type of supporting detail used in it.

[12] Melvin D. Joesten, David O. Johnston, John T. Netterville, and James L. Wood, *Chemistry, Impact on Society* (Philadelphia: Saunders College Publishing, 1988), p. 119.

Americans have traditionally been the marrying kind. In 1985, about 80 percent of the U.S. population age 20 to 54 had been married. Younger people, however, may be rejecting this tradition. In 1970, only 19 percent of the men and 11 percent of the women between the ages of 25 and 29 had never been married. In 1987, 42.2 percent of the men and 28.8 percent of the women that age had never been married.[13]

Type of supporting detail _____

RECOGNIZE TRANSITIONS

Authors (and speakers) use transitions to indicate that they are moving from one major section to another or from one idea to another. The word *transition* derives from the Latin word *transire,* which means *to go across.* A transition quite literally takes you from one idea "across" to the next. You might think of transitions as signposts that signal where the narrative has been and where it is going next.

Besides signaling a change of subject, transitions are also used by authors to emphasize main ideas so that they are easier for readers to spot. Sometimes transitions also state relationships between ideas (such as "These are the problems the student faced; now, how did he solve them?" or "What was the result of cutting class? Just this . . .").

The following are some examples of types of transitions used by college textbook writers and by other writers and speakers as well.

1. Heading and subheadings. Headings and subheadings fulfill two of the functions of the transition. They show you that the author is moving from one idea to another by marking a break in the text. Furthermore, they emphasize the main idea of the coming section by stating that idea.

2. Pre-outlines. Pre-outlines may be used to set out the pattern of ideas in an entire selection, or in the next two or three paragraphs. Here is an example of a pre-outline used at the beginning of a chapter about calculators. It not only states the main ideas in the chapter, it also mentions how calculators will be dealt with in future chapters.

In this chapter, we begin by looking at some of the general features of scientific calculators (Section 1.1). Then we will consider how some

---

[13] Tischler, p. 370. References have been removed.

of the simpler arithmetical operations are carried out with a calculator (Sections 1.2–1.6). This chapter concludes with a brief discussion of a few of the things that a calculator will *not* do for you. In later chapters, we will see how a calculator can be used to deal with exponential numbers (Chapter 4) or to find logarithms and antilogarithms (Chapter 5).[14]

Pre-outlining provides you with a mental outline of the material you are about to read and helps you anticipate what the author might say. Stop and number the ideas in a pre-outline (try it in the example above) and then skim ahead to see where the discussion of each of the ideas begins and ends.

3. Enumeration with or without a key phrase.   Enumeration (signaled by such words as *first, second, third; one, another; finally* or *last)* is often used to separate and emphasize items in a list of ideas. It can also be used with a key phrase to identify the subject of a list ("The first *way in which college differs from high school is . . .*"). Such transitions will help you mentally list items as you read.

4. Transitional paragraphs.   Entire paragraphs may function as transitions by separating and stating the relationship between two major sections or two chapters. The paragraphs below function as transitions from one main idea to the next. Note how previous ideas are summarized and new ideas are introduced.

From a communications textbook:

> So far we've talked about how becoming a better listener can help you to understand other people more often and more clearly. If you use the skills presented so far, you should be rewarded by communicating far more accurately with others every day. But there's another way in which listening can improve your relationships. Strange as it may sound, you can often help other people solve their own problems simply by learning to listen—actively and with concern.[15]

What ideas were discussed in previous paragraphs?_____

---

[14] William L. Masterton and Emil J. Slowinski, *Mathematical Preparation for General Chemistry,* 2d ed. (Philadelphia: Saunders College Publishing, 1982), p. 1.
[15] Ronald B. Adler, Lawrence B. Rosenfeld, and Neil Towne, *Interplay: The Process of Interpersonal Communication,* 2d ed. (New York: Holt, Rinehart and Winston, 1983), p. 159.

What ideas will be discussed? Make a prediction._____

_____

From a sociology textbook:

> We have been discussing crime statistics, the types of crimes commit-
> ted, and who commits them. But what about the victims of crime? Is
> there a pattern? Are some people more apt than others to become
> crime victims? It seems that this is true; victims of crime are not
> spread evenly across society. Although the available crime data are
> not always reliable, a pattern of victimization can be seen in the re-
> ported statistics. A person's race, sex, age, and socioeconomic status
> have a great deal to do with whether that individual will become a
> victim of serious crime.[16]

What ideas were discussed in previous paragraphs?_____

_____

What ideas will be discussed? Make a prediction._____

_____

5. *Transitional words and phrases.* By recognizing the
following words and phrases as transitional, you will follow the author's train of thought more easily.

a. *Next, soon, after, later, after a time,* or *much later* signal a change
   in time. *At another place, near, above, beneath,* or *on the other side*
   signal a change in place. When you read such transitions, move
   mentally with the author to another time or place.

b. *At the other extreme, consequently, the result of all this, by contrast,
   in comparison,* and *on the contrary* are used to separate ideas as
   well as to state the relationships between them.

c. *Let us now turn, today I want to talk about, the purpose of this
   chapter,* and *one . . . another* all signal that a new idea is about
   to be introduced and that you should shift your attention to what
   will be the new subject.

d. *For example, for instance, to quote, to illustrate,* and *to be specific*
   take you from the main idea or the subidea level to the specific
   supporting detail level in a paragraph or series of paragraphs.

[16] Tischler, p. 452.

e. *In conclusion, to summarize, finally,* or *let me end with* all signal that you are about to be presented with a concluding point or a restatement of main ideas.

6. *Paragraph linking.* Paragraph linking involves the repetition of words and phrases, usually in the topic sentences, to lead smoothly from the ideas in one paragraph to another. Here is an example from a psychology text. The repeated words and phrases that link the ideas from one paragraph to the next have been underlined. Notice how they help you keep your mind on the subject by emphasizing it:

Eustress
In an interview with Hans Selye, published in the March 1978 issue of *Psychology Today,* the man who "invented" the concept of physiological stress talks at length about ***eustress,*** or "good" stress.

According to Selye, not all stress is bad. We shouldn't try to avoid all stress, for that would be impossible. Rather, we should recognize what our typical response is to stress—and then try to adjust our lifestyles to take advantage of what that typical response is.

Selye believes that some of us are what he calls "turtles"—that is, we prefer peace, quiet, and a tranquil environment. Others of us are "racehorses," who thrive on a vigorous, fast-paced way of life. The optimum amount of stress we may require to function best is what Selye calls *eustress.* [17]

RECOGNIZE ORGANIZATIONAL PATTERNS

The ideas in a section, chapter, or article are often organized according to established and recognizable patterns of organization. These patterns reflect some of the most common ways in which people think about and develop ideas. Recognizing patterns of organization can help you locate main ideas and also help you predict and anticipate other ideas. A list of some of the most common patterns includes:

1. *Topical.* A subject can often either be divided into parts that are then described, or it can be developed with a list of related topics. This chapter follows a topical organization. Read the headings to bring into clear focus the topics that are used to develop the general subject, *read to comprehend ideas.*

---

[17] James V. McConnell, *Understanding Human Behavior,* 4th ed. (New York: Holt, Rinehart and Winston, 1982), p. 315.

2. *Chronological.* Another way to organize ideas is in the order in which they occur in time. History books, stories, and biographies are examples. Lists of instructions and recipes are also organized this way, in the order in which the reader is to perform each step. Transitional words and phrases that signal a change in time help alert readers to chronological organization.

3. *Comparison–Contrast.* A quick comparison or contrast in a paragraph functions as a supporting detail. At times, however, several paragraphs or even an entire essay or article will be organized according to ideas that are compared and contrasted throughout. An example of comparison–contrast organization appears in Exercise B6 at the end of this chapter. When you have completed this exercise, you will see how comparison and contrast can function as an organizational pattern.

4. *Cause–Effect.* You will often encounter cause–effect analysis in the material you read in college. Historians are interested in the causes and effects of historical events, psychologists are interested in the causes and effects of human behavior, sociologists and political scientists are interested in the causes and effects of social organizations and behavior, and scientists are interested in the causes and effects of physical phenomena. *Why* is the word that often prompts cause–effect analysis. When you encounter this word you can often anticipate cause–effect organization. You will often also find the words *cause* and *effect* used to identify both parts of a discussion that has been organized according to this pattern.

5. *Problem–solution.* Another way to organize a discussion is by presenting a problem and then offering solutions. Sometimes you will find the words *problem* and *solution* used to identify the major sections of material.

TWELVE CLUES TO MAIN IDEAS: A SUMMARY

The following is a list of the clues that writers use to make their main ideas more obvious and clear. All of these will not be present in everything you read. When they are present, however, they can make your reading easier. Use them to help you recognize the ideas that are central to an understanding of the material that you read.

1. *Titles, heads, and subheads.* These announce major subjects and ideas in boldface type.

2. *Purpose sentence.* Look for a sentence in the first paragraphs of a book, chapter, or article that states what the rest of the text will be about.

3. *Pre-outline.* Look for sentences that list the ideas that will be developed in the coming paragraphs.

4. *Topic sentences.* Recognize the sentences in paragraphs and sections of material that state the subject and focus of the rest of the discussion.

5. *Italics.* Sometimes main ideas appear in italics rather than boldface type to make them stand out from the rest of the text.

6. *Repetition.* Repetition of a key word or idea throughout a text is a signal that it is a major topic in the discussion.

7. *Questions.* Questions invite readers to look for answers, and the answer is often one of the major ideas that is being developed.

8. *Numbering.* Ideas that are numbered are important to notice. Either write them or make them into a mental list and put a label or title at the top.

9. *Visuals.* Pictures, graphs, diagrams, and other visual materials are often used to highlight and emphasize main ideas. Study them carefully.

10. *Details.* The use of examples, statistics, and other details always signal that a main idea is being clarified, proved, or developed. Look back or ahead and discover the idea.

11. *Organizational patterns.* The major parts of the pattern, such as the topics, the divisions in time, the two objects being compared, the cause and the effect, or the problem and the solution are the main ideas. Recognize the pattern and look for the ideas.

12. *Summary.* Summaries restate the main ideas in brief form.

WHY NOTICE CLUES TO MAIN IDEAS?

Becoming adept at spotting the clues to main ideas is one of the best ways to speed up your textbook reading and improve your comprehension. Whenever you spot one of these clues, you should slow down and read it well. It will define, map out, or summarize some of the most important ideas. You can usually then read through those ideas more rapidly. As you read, use the clues to help you form a mental outline of ideas. Then, jot those ideas in brief outline form in the margin of your book. Once you see the outline written out, you will be able to understand and remember what you have read more easily.

HOW TO READ DIFFICULT MATERIAL

Much of what you read in college will seem difficult, especially when you first begin to read it. The material itself may be difficult because the ideas are abstract, they are not explained well with supporting details, and they are not emphasized and separated with transitions. Furthermore, many ideas may be explained in a relatively short space, sentences may be long and complex, and the vocabulary may be unfamiliar.

The material will seem even more difficult if you have no background about the topic and if most of the vocabulary used to discuss it is unfamiliar to you. Use the following seven strategies to help you read material that is difficult *for you.*

Seven Strategies for Reading Difficult Material

1. *Preread.* Read the title and the first paragraph and decide whether you have sufficient *background* to begin reading. *Survey* to see how the material is organized. Make some *predictions* about what you think will be discussed. If you need more background to begin reading, get some. Talk to your professor, to the other students, or read additional material on the same subject.

2. *Look for clues to main ideas.* Use the list on pages 145–146 to help you locate the main ideas.

3. *Look up words.* Select those that are important to the meaning of entire passages and that you cannot fully understand from context. This practice increases your background knowledge and makes it easier to read the entire passage.

4. *Monitor your comprehension.* Stop and say to yourself, frequently, in your own words, what you have understood so far. Relate or connect it to what you already know as much as possible.

5. *Reread.* If you are not comprehending, go back and reread. Figure out what you cannot understand. Look up unfamiliar words. Restate difficult sentences in your own words. Try to think of your own examples.

6. *Read to the end.* Don't get discouraged and stop reading. Many ideas that are not clear at first become more clear as you continue to read. When you finish reading, survey as a review to get a sense of the whole and then reread the parts you still do not understand.

7. *Write while you read.* Underlining, making notes, writing summaries, and jotting down your own ideas help you concentrate and think while you read. The next chapter provides detailed information on ways to take reading notes.

At the Very Least . . .

This chapter has dealt with the ideal way for reading a chapter. If you can't follow all of the suggestions every day, *at the very least* do this much:

1. Look for topic sentences both in paragraphs and longer sections of material.
2. Note the repeated movement from general ideas to specific material.
3. Mentally connect supporting details to the main ideas they support.
4. Use transitions and other clues to help you locate the main ideas and understand their organization.
5. Use special strategies to read difficult material.

SUMMARY

Survey to understand the overall organization of a chapter. Then read to locate main ideas and details. As you read a textbook, your mind will constantly be switching from general statements, which mean little by themselves, to the details and explanations that accompany them. In a single chapter not all of the ideas in all of the paragraphs are of equal importance. An author usually introduces a major idea and then spends several paragraphs developing it. Your job as a reader is to discover which ideas are the major ones in the chapter, to locate where they are introduced, and to understand the kinds and purposes of the materials that are used to develop them. Learn to differentiate main ideas from subideas and supporting detail so that your focus of attention will not be diverted from the major line of thought. Learn to recognize transitions so that you will know when an author is switching the discussion from one idea to another. Learn also to recognize organizational patterns and the clues to main ideas. Recognizing these clues helps you identify the important ideas and form mental outlines of them as you read. Finally, when reading difficult material, use special strategies that help you draw on your own background, recognize what is important in the text, and monitor your understanding of what you have read.

EXERCISES

A. Monitor Your Comprehension of This Chapter.

Write quickly, in phrases rather than complete sentences, the information in this chapter that you understand and remember. Try to list the 12 clues to main ideas. Look back and add what you left out. Is anything unclear? Jot it down to ask about in class. Has reading the chapter caused you to think of new insights or examples of your own? Jot them down.

B. *Class Exercises.*

1. *Individuals or Small Groups.* There is a significant amount of specialized vocabulary in this chapter. Many of these terms represent major concepts in the chapter. Check your understanding of these terms.

2. *Individuals or Small Groups.* To better understand how writers and speakers move from the general to the specific, unscramble the items below and write them in the blanks. Write the main idea, the subideas, and the supporting details to show what you would expect if you were to read this paragraph in its original form.

— There may be four hundred other students with you in the class.
— In college you will have to take lecture notes.
— The professor will seem impersonal and far away.
— One place you will have to take these notes is in the large lecture hall.
— You will have to work hard to get good notes.

I. _____

   A. _____

      1. _____

         _____

      2. _____

         _____

   B. _____

a. Match the types of paragraphs with their descriptions.

1. _____ subidea paragraph

2. _____ main idea paragraph

3. _____ introductory paragraph

4. _____ summary paragraph

5. _____ transitional paragraph

   a. Restates the main ideas.
   b. May list the main ideas that are to be discussed.
   c. Presents a major idea and tells more about it.
   d. Supports and develops a main idea stated in a previous paragraph.
   e. Concludes the discussion of one idea and opens discussion of the next idea.

b. Which of the following are kinds of supporting detail? Circle the correct answers.

    a. examples

    b. subideas

    c. statistics

    d. main ideas

    e. quotations

    f. vivid description

    g. comparisons and contrasts

    h. pictures and graphs

c. Match the following types of transitions with descriptions of how they make main ideas more clear.

    1. —————— pre-outlines

    2. —————— heads and subheads

    3. —————— enumeration and key phrases

    4. —————— transitional paragraphs

        a. number and identify items in a list
        b. link two major sections of material
        c. set off main ideas from the text
        d. list ahead of time what is to be discussed

d. Match the organizational pattern with its description.

    1. —————— topical

    2. —————— time

    3. —————— comparison—contrast

    4. —————— cause—effect

    5. —————— problem—solution

        a. Material is arranged as it occurs in time.
        b. The question *why* prompts this pattern.

   c. The question *what can be done about it* prompts this pattern.
   d. Material is broken into parts or sub-types.
   e. Similarities and differences prompt this pattern.

3. *Individuals or Small Groups.* Before you read the following section of material from a marketing textbook, look at the title and answer these questions.

   a. What do you already know about this topic? _____

   _____

   b. What do you predict this passage will be about? _____

   _____

Read the material, mark the clues to main ideas, and answer the questions at the end.

Why Women Work

1 At the beginning of the twentieth century, only one woman in five worked outside the home. By 1985, more than 51 percent of the nation's adult female population will be part of the work force. Three of five married women work.

2 For most women, the primary motivation for working is economic. William Lazer and John E. Smallwood report that 90 percent of working mothers in sales, clerical, and blue-collar occupations and 71 percent of women employed in the professions worked for economic reasons.[18] Although unprecedented increases in the cost of living have forced the emergence of many two-income households, equal employment legislation has also played a role in stimulating increased female employment by opening job opportunities in traditionally male-dominated occupations.

3 A third factor in stimulating female employment is the social acceptability of women with careers. Women are increasingly represented in the college classroom, and account for almost half the students receiving college degrees each year. Approximately one-third of all students in the nation's Masters of Business Administration (MBA) degree programs are women. Such academic preparation helps to move well-qualified women into middle- and top-management positions.[19]

---

[18] William Lazer and John E. Smallwood, "The Changing Demographics of Women," *Journal of Marketing,* July 1977, p. 19. See also Mary Joyce, "The Professional Woman: A Potential Market Segment for Retailers," *Journal of Retailing,* Summer 1978, pp. 59–70; and Suzanne H. McCall, "Meet the 'Work-wife,'" *Journal of Marketing,* July 1977, pp. 55–65.

[19] Louis E. Boone and David L. Kurtz, *Contemporary Marketing,* 4th ed. (New York: CBS College Publishing, 1983), pp. 115–16.

c. What is this section of material about?_____

_____

d. Indicate the main idea and the subideas on the outline.

I. _____

    A. _____

    B. _____

    C. _____

e. Is there a topic sentence that states the main idea or did you have to

infer the topic after reading the section? _____

If there is a topic sentence, underline it.

f. In the column below list three supporting details.

    1. _____

    2. _____

    3. _____

g. List the three transitional words or phrases that helped you locate the
three subideas.

    1. _____

    2. _____

    3. _____

4. *Individuals or Small Groups.* Before you begin to read the following
section of material from an ethics textbook, look at the title and answer
these questions:

a. What do you already know about this topic? _____

_____

b. What do you predict this passage will be about?

Read the material, mark the clues to main ideas, and answer the questions at the end.

The Values of an Athletic Program

1   The athletic program is expected to bring publicity to the school, attract students, foster student unity, and encourage alumni giving. "The traditional American affinity for sports and reverence for education combined to form an unbeatable attraction. Every Saturday, educated sports heroes performed for an appreciative audience. Fanfare, combat, and hope of victory assured public identification and loyalty."[20] The most conspicuous function of athletic competition is to enhance the image of the institution.

2   We may want to question the appropriateness of this public relations function. Publicity is not necessarily a good thing. If this publicity is scandalous (or even negative), the school has not benefited. There is a university on the banks of the river that sponsors a "Mississippi River Festival" every summer. The "festival," for the most part, consists of rock concerts. Unfortunately, since these festivals have been plagued with violence, rape, drunkenness, drug dealing and usage, and automobile accidents, the publicity has been counter to the kind the festival was designed to produce. With respect to athletics, the public is finding out more about the universities than they would wish.

3   Does athletic fame attract students? Perhaps it does, but it would be a stupid engineering student who chose Georgia Tech over M.I.T. because of its athletic prowess. Some serious students are "turned off" by a school's athletic record. Notre Dame, which has an excellent academic program, is unjustly viewed by many as simply a sports mill. Does athletic success foster student unity? Here again, the case is not clear. Often students' enthusiasm is tepid in comparison with that of alumni and townspeople—especially when they have difficulty in getting tickets, have to pay a handsome price, or are relegated to seats in the end zone.

4   Does athletic success arouse public support? Do legislators tend to reward successful schools with more generous appropriations? They may have done so in the past, but today, with the closer scrutiny of tax dollars, there are signs that funds will be more available for activities closer to the heart of the academic mission.[21] What about alumni giving? Certainly alumni will contribute money for *athletic* purposes in the case of a few successful universities, but the overall record for alumni giving exhibits no such pattern. A careful study of 138 "big-time" schools from 1960 to 1976 yielded this conclusion: "Our statistical

[20] Christine H. B. Grant, "Institutional Autonomy and Intercollegiate Athletics," *Educational Record* (Fall 1979), p. 411.

[21] If taxpayers are now willing to reduce expenditures for athletics and other "frills" in the high schools, they may do so also for universities—even the "successful" ones.

analysis has revealed that there is simply no relationship between success or failure in football and basketball and increases and decreases in alumni giving."[22] "In the final analysis, however, the lack of any relationship between success in athletics and increased alumni giving probably matters a great deal less than the fact that so many people believe that such a relationship exists."[23, 24]

c. What is this section of material about?_____

_____

d. Indicate the main idea and the subideas on the outline.

   I. ——————————————————————————

      A. ————————————————————————

      B. ————————————————————————

      C. ————————————————————————

      D. ————————————————————————

e. Is there a topic sentence that states the main idea of this section or did you have to infer the topic after reading the section? ——————————

_____

If there is a topic sentence, underline it.

f. In the column below list four supporting details.

   1. ——————————————————————————

   2. ——————————————————————————

   3. ——————————————————————————

   4. ——————————————————————————

[22] Lee Sigelman and Robert Carter, "Win One for the Giver? Alumni Giving and Big-Time College Sports," *Social Science Quarterly,* September 1979, p. 293.

[23] Ibid. See Frederick Klein, "Bring in the Brawn: Recruiting of Athletes Intensifies as Colleges Seek Prestige, Money," *Wall Street Journal,* April 11, 1967, p. 1.

[24] Gerald Runkle, *Ethics: An Examination of Contemporary Moral Problems* (New York: Holt, Rinehart and Winston, 1982), pp. 280–81.

g. List five sentences that function as transitions.

1. _____

2. _____

3. _____

4. _____

5. _____

5. *Individuals or Small Groups.*
Before you read the following section of material from a psychology text-book, look at the title and answer these questions.

a. What do you already know about this topic? (In this case, you may know nothing. Read the section to find out more about the cerebral cortex. If you do not know enough when you have finished, seek more information.)

_____

_____

b. Ask one question that you would like to answer as you read.

_____

_____

Read the material and mark the clues to main ideas.

THE CEREBRAL CORTEX

Just where is that elusive piece of business you think of as your "mind"? Thousands of years ago it was not generally thought that the mind had a place to hang its hat within the body. It was common to assume that the body was inhabited by demons or souls that could not be explained in terms of substance at all. After all, if you look inside a human being, the biological structures you find do not look all that different in quality from those of many lower animals. So it seemed to make sense that those qualities that made us distinctly human—thinking, planning, talking, dreaming, composing—were unrelated to substances that you could actually see, feel, and weigh on a scale.

Some ancient Egyptians attributed control of the human being to a little person, or **homunculus**, who dwelled within the skull and regulated our behavior. The Greek philosopher Aristotle thought that the soul had set up living quarters in the heart. After all, serious injury to the heart could be said to cause the soul to take flight from the body. As noted by B. F. Skinner (1987), to be undecided about something in ancient Greece was to have "a divided heart." Skinner goes on to note that phrases such as the following show that modern English is still influenced by the view of the heart as the seat of will, thought, hunger, and joy: "deep in one's heart," "to know something by heart," "to look into someone's heart," and "to have a change of heart."

Through a variety of accidents and research projects, we have come to recognize that "mind," or consciousness, dwells essentially within the brain, largely in the cerebral cortex. Different sorts of body injuries have distinct effects. It has become increasingly apparent that injuries to the head can lead to impairments of consciousness and awareness, such as loss of vision and hearing, general confusion, or loss of memory. Experiments in stimulating or destroying specific areas in animal brains and human brains have also shown that certain areas of the brain are associated with specific types of sensations or activities.[25]

c. What is this section of material about?

_____

d. Indicate the main ideas and the subideas on the outline.

    I. _____

       A. _____

       B. _____

e. There is no topic sentence that describes what this section is about. Look back at your outline, and write a topic sentence of your own.

_____

_____

f. List two supporting details.

    1. _____

    2. _____

[25] Spencer A. Rathus, *Essentials of Psychology,* 2nd ed. (Fort Worth: Holt, Rinehart and Winston, Inc., 1989), p. 61.

g. What is the cerebral cortex?

_____

_____

6. *Individuals or Small Groups.*

Before you read the following section of material from a sociology textbook, look at the title and answer these questions.

a. What do you already know about this topic?

_____

_____

b. What do you predict this section will be about?

_____

_____

c. Ask one question that you would like to answer as you read?

_____

_____

Read the material and mark the clues to main ideas.

GENDER DIFFERENCES IN LONG TERM PLANNING

There are some interesting differences in how men and women think about the future. In one study researchers asked undergraduates to describe what they expected would happen to them over the next 10 years. For both male and female undergraduates today, work appears to be a universal expectation. Likewise, the kinds of jobs wanted are nearly identical. Both groups mention jobs in business, law, hospital administration, and the computer industry. Further education was anticipated by more than half of the men and women. The vast majority (94 percent) also see themselves as eventually married with a family.

Thus, at first glance there appears to be a striking similarity in men and women's future plans. They express the desire for marriage, children, and work, and the desire for higher education is equally present. However, there are significant gender differences in expectations of *how* family, work, and education will be integrated. Men and women have different assumptions and tactics for achieving the similarly desired events in their lives.

Men operate in what Maines and Hardesty call a *linear temporal world.* When they try to project what the future might hold for them they almost always define it in terms of career accomplishments—lawyer, doctor, college professor, business executive, and so on. Education is seen as something that is pursued to attain the desired career.

Men see a family as desirable and not much of an issue in terms of pursuing career goals. They see little problem in coordinating career and family demands. Many expect to have a traditional division of labor in their families that will provide a support system for their career pursuit. Mostly, the problems of family living are viewed as being resolved rather easily, and typically there is no mention of career adjustments to the wife's and children's needs.

Young women, on the other hand, operate in *contingent temporal worlds.* Work, education, and family are all seen as having to be balanced off against each other. Careers are seen as pursuits that may have to be suspended or halted at certain points. The vast majority of women envision problems in their career pursuits, and they see family responsibilities as a major issue that needs to be adjusted to. Nearly half say they will quit work for a few years as a solution to the conflict between family and work demands. Instead of a clear vision of steps needed to accomplish their career goals, women become much more tentative about their future, because they expect it to entail adjustments and compromises.

Young men seem to take their autonomy for granted. That is, they assume that they will be able to accomplish what they set out to do if they have the necessary education, skill, and good fortune. Women, on the other hand, feel much more limited in their control of their future, even with the necessary education and skill. The problems surrounding the integration of family and career lend an element of uncertainty to their ability to accomplish their future goals. Women plan to be flexible in order to adjust to career and family needs. This flexibility gives them only partial autonomy in controlling their lives.[26]

d. Underline the topic sentence.

e. What is this section of material about?_____

_____

f. What is the organizational pattern of this section?_____

_____

---

[26] Tischler, pp. 327–330. References have been removed.

g. What transitional phrase helped you identify the organizational pattern?

_____

_____

h. Indicate the main ideas and the subideas on the outline.

I. _____

   A. _____

   B. _____

   C. _____

   D. _____

i. Identify and define from context two key concepts.

1. _____

_____

2. _____

_____

j. Identify three supporting details.

1. _____

2. _____

3. _____

C. Application Exercises

1. Locate a section of material in one of your textbooks in which a major idea in the chapter is introduced in the first paragraph and developed in two, three, or more paragraphs. It may be introduced by a heading or subheading as in the class exercises above. State the main idea of this material and then list, in phrases only, five or six items of information used to develop this idea.

2. Copy a paragraph from one of your textbooks that contains a good example of a transition and underline it. Include enough context so that it will be clear why the material you have underlined is transitional. It may be a heading or subheading, preoutline, enumeration, transitional paragraph, or internal summary. Describe the function of the transition you have located. Does it emphasize and separate ideas? Which ideas? Does it state a relationship between ideas? What is it?

3. Copy a paragraph from one of your textbooks that contains supporting material and underline it. Answer the questions: What type of supporting material is it? What main idea does it support?

4. Locate an example of paragraph linking in one of your textbooks. The passage should be two or three paragraphs long. Copy the passage and underline the repeated words and phrases that link the ideas from one paragraph to the next. Write a brief outline of the ideas in the passage.

5. Examine one chapter in one of your textbooks and list the clues to main ideas in it along with examples.

D. Topics for Your Learning Journal

1. Further clarify your understanding of main ideas and supporting details by writing a paragraph or section of material yourself. Choose one of the following topic sentences, make a list of at least three supporting details to develop it, and write the paragraph or section.
   a. My neighborhood has changed (very little or a great deal) in the time I have lived there.
   b. High school, for me, was (the best or the worst) experience in my life.
   c. Returning to school after a long absence is _____.

2. Clarify your understanding of transitions by writing a short essay on a topic of your own choice in which you use three different kinds of transitions described in this chapter. Begin by making an outline of ideas. Then use transitions to make your ideas clear to your reader. Label each transition you use in the margin of your paper.
   If you have trouble thinking of a topic, use one of the following as a "starter" sentence.
   a. There are some major differences between high school and college.
   b. It is not always easy to work and go to college.
   c. It is not always easy to figure out what to do with the rest of your life.

10 | Taking Reading Notes and Writing Summaries

When you have finished reading this chapter, you will know how to do the following:

1. Mark a textbook so that you can review it quickly for a discussion or an exam.
2. Take reading notes when you do not want to write in the book.
3. Take reading notes on math textbooks and imaginative literature.
4. Write summaries.

HOW TO MARK A TEXTBOOK

The biggest problem with textbook reading is to keep your mind on it. One good way to keep your mind on it is to take reading notes. Note taking also prepares you for class. Read the textbook and take notes on it before you go to class to make the most efficient use of class time.

In Chapter 2 you were shown a method for marking a textbook. It was suggested that you follow the example in that chapter by continuing to mark this book, as well as your other textbooks, in the way demonstrated. If you have followed that advice, you should be good at marking textbooks by now.

If you have not followed that advice, this chapter will review the system presented in Chapter 2 and provide you with additional suggestions to make that system work effectively for you.

FIVE ADVANTAGES OF BUYING YOUR OWN TEXTBOOKS, MARKING THEM, AND KEEPING THEM

1. *Making notes in your own books helps you maintain a high level of concentration.* Your mind will not wander if you are actively marking ideas and summarizing them briefly in the book as you read.

2. *Making notes in your own books saves time.* When your notes are written next to the text, they can be brief—a mere reminder of what is in the text itself.

3. *Making notes in your own books helps you find important material quickly.* You often need to locate material in a book quickly as, for instance, during class discussions or open-book exams. Well-marked textbooks make looking for specific information a comparatively fast and easy process.

4. *Making notes in your own books makes them easy to review.* In an hour or less you can reread the notes you have written in your book and remember the important material better than if you had just read it. Preexam review is fast and efficient.

5. *Well-marked books are valuable reference tools in the future.* Plan to keep a well-marked textbook instead of selling it after a course is over. Such books will be valuable to refer to in future classes and after you leave college. They will refresh your memory.

TEN SUGGESTIONS FOR MARKING BOOKS

The following ten suggestions will help you mark your textbooks so that they will be of immediate and lasting value to you. Figure 10.1 illustrates a section of a textbook that has been marked according to these recommendations.

1. Read first and then underline selectively. Make conscious decisions about what to underline, and limit the amount. Too much underlining is difficult to study later and often becomes a mechanical process that requires little thought. Read a paragraph or section of material first and then go back and underline only the words and phrases that most accurately state what that chunk of material is mainly about.

2. Box transitions and number important ideas. Making transitions stand out in the text helps you locate the ideas. When you box such words as *first, second, for example, next,* or *finally,* you not

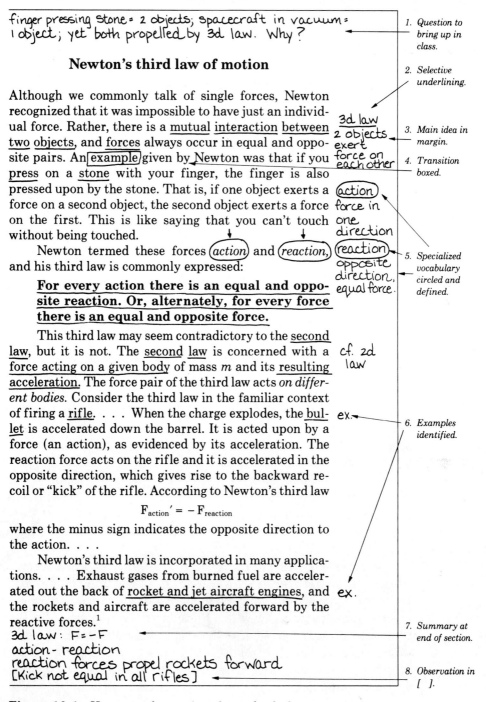

finger pressing stone = 2 objects; spacecraft in vacuum = 1 object; yet both propelled by 3d law. Why?

1. *Question to bring up in class.*

Newton's third law of motion

2. *Selective underlining.*

Although we commonly talk of single forces, Newton recognized that it was impossible to have just an individual force. Rather, there is a <u>mutual</u> <u>interaction</u> <u>between</u> <u>two</u> <u>objects</u>, and <u>forces</u> always occur in equal and opposite pairs. An example given by Newton was that if you press on a <u>stone</u> with your finger, the finger is also pressed upon by the stone. That is, if one object exerts a force on a second object, the second object exerts a force on the first. This is like saying that you can't touch without being touched.

3d law 2 objects exert force on each other

3. *Main idea in margin.*

4. *Transition boxed.*

(action) force in one direction

Newton termed these forces (*action*) and (*reaction*,) and his third law is commonly expressed:

(reaction) opposite direction, equal force.

5. *Specialized vocabulary circled and defined.*

For every action there is an equal and opposite reaction. Or, alternately, for every force there is an equal and opposite force.

This third law may seem contradictory to the <u>second</u> <u>law</u>, but it is not. The <u>second</u> law is concerned with a force <u>acting on a given body</u> of mass m and its <u>resulting</u> <u>acceleration</u>. The force pair of the third law acts *on different bodies*. Consider the third law in the familiar context of firing a <u>rifle</u>. . . . When the charge explodes, the <u>bullet</u> is accelerated down the barrel. It is acted upon by a force (an action), as evidenced by its acceleration. The reaction force acts on the rifle and it is accelerated in the opposite direction, which gives rise to the backward recoil or "kick" of the rifle. According to Newton's third law

cf. 2d law

ex.

6. *Examples identified.*

$$F_{action}' = -F_{reaction}$$

where the minus sign indicates the opposite direction to the action. . . .

Newton's third law is incorporated in many applications. . . . Exhaust gases from burned fuel are accelerated out the back of <u>rocket and jet aircraft engines</u>, and the rockets and aircraft are accelerated forward by the reactive forces.[1]

ex.

3d law: F = -F action - reaction reaction forces propel rockets forward [kick not equal in all rifles]

7. *Summary at end of section.*

8. *Observation in [ ].*

Figure 10.1 How to mark a section of a textbook chapter.

[1] Jerry D. Wilson, *Technical College Physics* (Philadelphia: Saunders College Publishing, 1982), pp. 97–99.

only locate important ideas more easily, you also see how they relate to each other.

3. *Circle specialized vocabulary.* Write brief meanings in the margin if you need to. You will need to know this vocabulary to understand the textbook, understand the instructor, and take the exams.

4. *Jot main ideas in the margin.* At the end of a paragraph, stop and ask yourself, "What was most of that paragraph about?" Write the answer in as few words as possible in the margin. This is an especially useful technique for short, dense assignments that are difficult to understand, such as those in philosophy, physics, or chemistry.

5. *Label examples.* When you encounter an example, determine what main idea it exemplifies and label it. It will help you understand the main idea when you study later.

6. *Write your own ideas in square brackets.* If you are reading actively, concentrating and understanding, you will also be thinking. Jot down the ideas that occur to you as you read either at the top or the bottom of the page and put them in [square brackets] to indicate that they are your own. Your recorded ideas will make later study more interesting and will also help you in class discussions.

7. *Write questions as you read.* Questions help you think, relate new material to what you already know, and wonder about implications and applications. All these mental activities help you learn the material in the first place and remember and use it later.

8. *Write brief summaries at the end of each section of material, and, later, at the end of chapters and the book.* Use the white space throughout the book to write summaries. Write them in brief phrases only. They should answer the questions "What was this about?" and "What did the author say about it?" Summarize after you have finished reading and in your own words as much as possible. Don't read and write at the same time, or you will end up with too many notes.

9. *Make outlines of obvious major ideas in the margins.* Outlines are a visual representation of ideas and their relation to each other. At times obvious transitions will make the ideas in a passage stand out. When you encounter such material, write brief outlines of the ideas in the margins. Look at pages 132 and 136 in the last chapter for examples of such outlines.

10. Make maps.   Outlines force you to isolate and organize important ideas so that you can visualize them and thereby understand and remember them. Writing ideas in *map form* accomplishes the same thing. You can map major sections, chapters, or even entire books. Experiment with summaries, outlines, and maps and decide which work best for you.

HOW TO MAKE A MAP

You learned how to make a spider map for lecture notes in Chapter 5. There are variations to this format. For making most maps, there are three steps.[2] First, write the subject of the material you are mapping in the middle or at the top of a piece of paper. Draw a box or a circle around it so that it stands out.

Second, locate the main ideas that support and develop the subject and write them on lines attached to the subject.

Finally, attach enough supporting details to each of these lines so that the whole map will make sense to you when you study it later.

Figure 10.2 shows an example of a map of the ideas in the section about transitions in Chapter 9 of this book. Notice that brief phrases are written on the map to help you remember the ideas and details in the chapter. Imagine, now, that you must review this part of Chapter 9 for an exam. It would be easier to study and remember this map than it would be to reread and remember the chapter.

You may make maps in any way that helps you to see the author's pattern of ideas or pattern of organization. Other mapping schemes might look like the one in Figure 10.3 that shows the pattern of ideas or like those in Figure 10.4 that show patterns of organization. The map in Figure 10.5 helps you associate the laws of motion with an object in motion. This literal visualization can make these laws even easier to remember than a more abstract map.

To make effective maps it is essential that you first read and understand the material. Do not map it until you do understand it. Sometimes you will finish reading with a clear pattern of ideas in

[2] For a more detailed explanation of mapping see the essay by M. Buckly Hanf, "Mapping: A Technique for Translating Reading into Thinking," *Journal of Reading XIV* (January 1971): 225–30. See also Patricia L. Smith and Gail E. Tompkins, "Structured Notetaking: A New Strategy for Content Area Readers," *Journal of Reading.* Vol. 32, no. 1, October 1988, pp. 46–53.

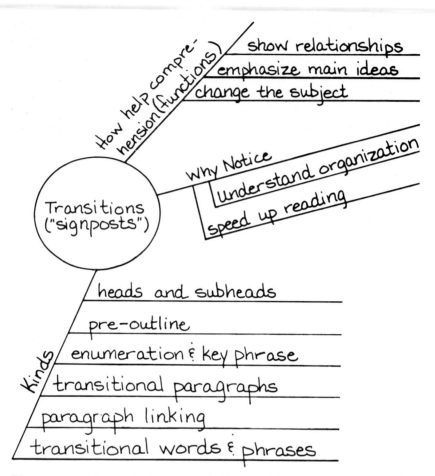

Figure 10.2   A map of ideas in the section about transitions in Chapter 8.

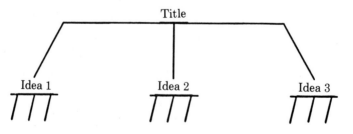

Figure 10.3   Another scheme for mapping.

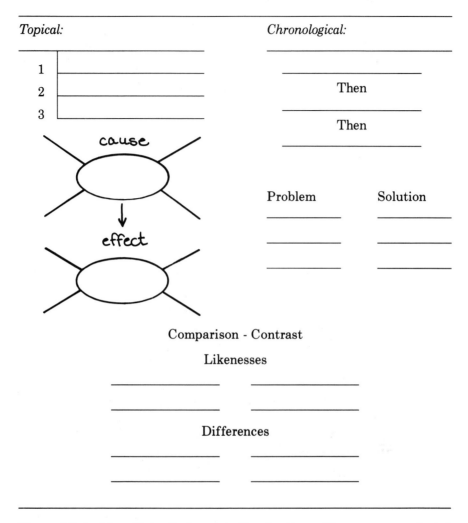

Figure 10.4   Maps that reflect organizational patterns. These maps are adapted from some of those depicted by Smith and Tompkins, op.cit., p. 49.

mind, and you will be able to map them with no trouble. Other times, especially when there are no obvious transitions and when there is no introduction or summary, it is difficult to identify the pattern of ideas. In this latter case skim back through the material and pick out six or seven ideas that seem to be main points in the material and map them with their details. Do your best to map what appears to be important. Include examples if the material is hard to understand and remember without them. Use maps to study for exams. Other types of exam study sheets will be explained later in Chapter 12.

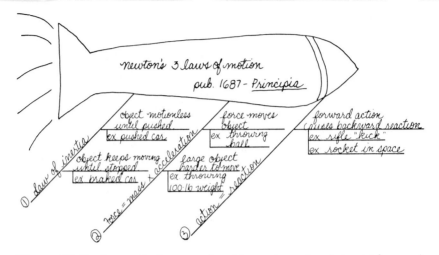

Figure 10.5   A map that uses a visual image to make abstract ideas easier to remember.

WHAT IF YOU DON'T WANT TO WRITE IN YOUR BOOKS?

Some students can't bring themselves to write in books. Either they want to resell them, or they have been so conditioned in school not to write in books that it is nearly impossible for them to do so.

If you can't or won't mark in your text, there are alternatives. Buy five-by-eight note cards, and when you finish reading the chapter, summarize or map it on the card instead of in the book itself. Take notes in your own words and phrases. Get down main ideas and a few important details. As a rough guide, spend only 10 to 20 percent of your time taking notes and 80 to 90 percent of your time reading. Then insert these cards in the book at the beginning of each chapter. Paper-clip them in if you are afraid of losing them. When you need to review or find a passage quickly, use these cards to help you. They will work nearly as well as marking in the book itself.

Another alternative to taking notes in your books is to write notes and make maps on separate sheets of paper. Keep these in folders labeled "reading notes" or in special sections of your loose leaf notebooks. Figure 10.11 provides an example of the appropriate amount of information to include in notes that you would take on cards or on separate pieces of paper.

HOW TO TAKE NOTES ON A LIBRARY BOOK

If you have been assigned library material as supplementary reading in a course, take a few notes so that you will not have to go back to the library later to reread. In taking these notes, always write the complete bibliographical source at the top of the page—author, title, publisher, place of publication, and date. Then read a section of material, stop, and take summary notes. Do not read and write simultaneously, or you will write too much. Next to the notes on a section, in the margin, write the inclusive page numbers of that section. If you copy a quote, put it in quotation marks and write in the margin the number of the page where you found it. Notes taken this way can easily be studied later. They can also be used in a research paper. You will be able to work from your notes directly without visiting the library again.

File the library reading notes for a course in a separate manilla folder or in a separate part of your notebook. Then label them as library reading for a specific course so that you will later be able to locate them easily.

HOW TO TAKE NOTES ON MATH TEXTBOOKS[3]

You will probably take more notes on math texts (and texts for other problem-solving courses, such as chemistry and physics), than you will for any other sort of textbook. Plan to take notes as you read on the following three types of material:

1. On 5×8 cards write strategies for solving problems. Some textbook authors occasionally provide such strategies that can be copied exactly (see Figure 10.6). If the author of your math text does not provide explicit strategies, you will need to construct your own. The examples are the best place to look when constructing strategies. These strategy cards need to contain a title and a list of the steps used to solve a particular type of problem. Figure 10.7, for example, shows a strategy card for solving radical equations. In most cases, the strategy card will contain a verbal description of how some particular problems are solved.
2. You will also find it useful to write math rules, laws, or theorems on *fact cards*. These facts must be learned word for word. It is

---

[3] Adapted from material prepared by William J. Dodge.

BASIC PRINCIPLES FOR SOLVING INEQUALITIES

Performing any one of the following operations on an inequality produces an inequality with the same solutions as the original inequality.

1. Add or subtract the same quantity from both sides of the inequality.
2. Multiply or divide both sides of the inequality by a *positive* quantity.
3. Multiply or divide both sides of the inequality by a *negative* quantity and *reverse the direction of the inequality.*[4]

Figure 10.6 A strategy card (Information supplied by textbook author—copy exactly).

Solving Radical Equations

1. Rewrite the eq. so that a single radical is isolated on one side of the eq.
2. If the isolated radical is $\sqrt[p]{\cdots}$, raise both sides to the pth power (to eliminate the radical)
3. Simplify the new eq. If radicals remain, go to 1; otherwise solve as usual.
4. Check answers in original equations! (critical for radical eq.)

Figure 10.7 A strategy card constructed by a student.

easier to learn them when they are on cards that you can carry around with you or tack up over your desk or some other place where you will see them frequently. Figure 10.8 shows the type of information that you might put on a card for an algebra course in which the topic is fractions.

In mathematics many theorems are stated, "If (hypothesis), then (conclusion)." To understand such a statement, carefully examine the hypothesis to see the significance of each part of it. Remember

[4] Thomas W. Hungerford, Richard Mercer, and Sybil R. Barrier, *Precalculus Mathematics* (Philadelphia: Saunders College Publishing, 1980), p. 21.

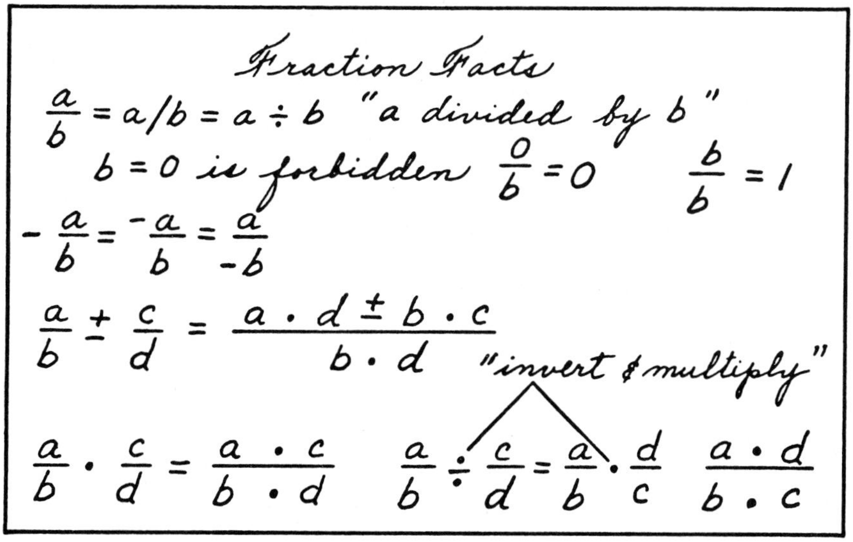

$$\mathscr{Fraction\ Facts}$$

$$\frac{a}{b} = a/b = a \div b \quad \text{"a divided by b"}$$

$$b = 0 \text{ is forbidden} \quad \frac{0}{b} = 0 \qquad \frac{b}{b} = 1$$

$$-\frac{a}{b} = \frac{-a}{b} = \frac{a}{-b}$$

$$\frac{a}{b} \pm \frac{c}{d} = \frac{a \cdot d \pm b \cdot c}{b \cdot d} \quad \text{"invert & multiply"}$$

$$\frac{a}{b} \cdot \frac{c}{d} = \frac{a \cdot c}{b \cdot d} \qquad \frac{a}{b} \div \frac{c}{d} = \frac{a}{b} \cdot \frac{d}{c} \quad \frac{a \cdot d}{b \cdot c}$$

Figure 10.8 A fact card, example 1.

that the *theorem only applies* when the *entire hypothesis is satisfied.* It may help you to understand a theorem if you rephrase it in equivalent form: "If not (conclusion), then not (hypothesis)." Figure 10.9 provides examples of fact cards using these ideas.

3. The third type of information you should extract and write out as you read your math texts are the *specialized vocabulary and*

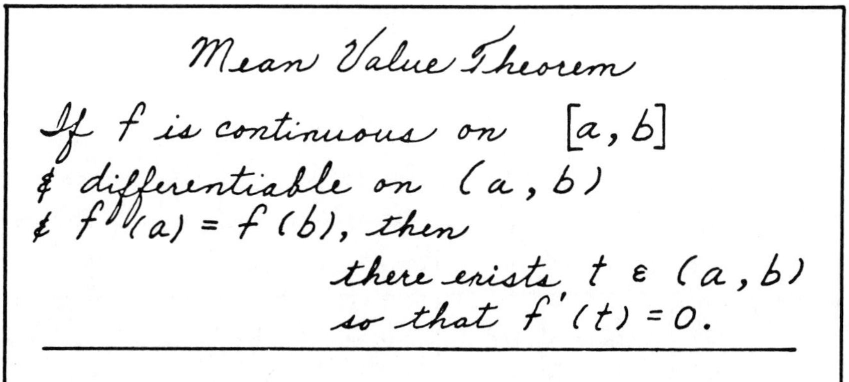

$$\mathscr{Mean\ Value\ Theorem}$$

If f is continuous on $[a, b]$
& differentiable on (a, b)
& $f'(a) = f(b)$, then

there exists $t \in (a, b)$
so that $f'(t) = 0$.

_____

If f is differentiable, then f is continuous.   or   If f is not cont., then f is not diff.

Figure 10.9 A fact card, example 2.

symbols along with their definitions. Like the theorems, these definitions must be learned exactly, word for word. You will probably find it easiest to learn these words, symbols, and definitions if you write them out on sheets of paper, as in Figure 10.10.

It will help you to understand and remember the definition in Figure 10.10 if you ask yourself what the negation or denial of the definition says: "What are nonequivalent equations or inequalities?" If you have difficulty answering this question, ask your instructor. This is a good type of question to ask during class discussion.

Now take a final look at Figure 10.10. When you have written a definition, read it to make certain that you understand every word. If you have forgotten what "solution sets" are, for example, look up that term immediately in the index or on your definition list so that the definition you have just written will make complete sense to you.

Strategy cards, fact cards, and definition lists are the permanent notes you will be taking as you read math textbooks. These do not represent the only writing you will need to do as you read math, however. Keep plenty of scratch paper handy as you read so that you can write out in detail examples of problems you encounter in the text. It is always tempting simply to read through these examples. Try writing them out, however, and you may find that you don't understand them as well as you thought. If the author says, "It is

sum	any expansion that has the form A+B (addition)
term or addend	either of A or B in the above sum
equivalent equations or inequalities	two equations or inequalities in one variable are *equivalent* if they have equal solution sets.

Figure 10.10   A definition sheet for mathematics.

clear that . . . ," make certain that it is *clear to you* and write down *why* it is clear by referring to a definition or theorem. Any questions you cannot answer about examples as you rewrite them should be brought up during class discussion. Remember that the examples are models of what you will be doing later in the exercise set. If you don't learn how to do the models first, you will have trouble working the exercises later.

When you work the exercises at the end of the chapter, you will then use all of the notes you have written out: strategy cards, fact cards, definition sheets, and the examples of the problems you have copied. All this material will help you understand how to do the final exercise set. Always do these assigned exercises whether or not they are graded each time by your instructor.

HOW TO TAKE NOTES ON NOVELS, SHORT STORIES, PLAYS, AND POEMS

You can mark up all literature you read. Summarize novels, for example, chapter by chapter. Five or six phrases jotted down at the end of each chapter to identify plot action and characters make review an easy and quick affair. If you have any major insights or ideas of your own about the novel, write them out in some detail on the flyleaves of the book. They may turn out to be good topics for future papers or points to bring up in class discussion.

You can take notes on short stories and plays, too. Mark the main characters and their identifying characteristics as they are introduced, write a plot summary at the end, and then try to write out the major themes or ideas developed.

Take more thorough notes on a poem. Go through the poem first and underline all words and allusions that you do not understand. Look them up and write in the meanings. Then read the poem again and write, in your own words, a summary of what you think it says. Take these summaries to class and listen to the professor discuss the poems. During class discussion, you may find that you have badly misread a poem; if so, change your summary on the spot so that it won't mislead you when you are studying for an exam.

HOW TO WRITE SUMMARIES

Throughout this chapter, you have been advised to write summaries. There is considerable research that indicates that summary writing is one of the best methods to help you concentrate, understand, learn, and remember the material that you read. Study after study show that students who summarize as they read comprehend much better than those who do not. Summaries require that you put reading material into *your own words* so that you understand it better, that you *reduce it in size* so that it is more manageable and easier to learn and that you *organize* it so that it is easier to remember. You can write summaries of complicated and difficult sentences, of paragraphs, of sections of material, of chapters, or of entire books. Summaries can be written in complete sentences and in paragraph form as are those at the end of the chapters in this book. Or, they can take the form of jotted notes, written in phrases only as in the example in Figure 10.11. They can be dictated into tape recorders while you read and typed later, written in books themselves, or written on separate pieces of paper. Summaries can also be made mentally, while you read.

Taking Notes & Writing Summaries
Why and How

Why Mark Books

1. helps concentrate
2. saves time
3. locate material
4. fast review
5. reference tools

How Mark

1. underline
2. Box transitions, Number ideas
3. Circle words
4. jot m.i. in margin
5. label ex.
6. [own ideas]
7. questions
8. summaries
9. outlines   } decide which best
10. maps

Make Maps

1. circle or box
2. attach m.i.
3. attach details
4. diagrams for org. patterns
5. picture of idea

Other Notes

1. cards or separate paper
2. book info on library notes
3. strategy and fact cards
   and def. sheet, math
4. notes on literature

Summaries

1. title – main statement
2. what can remember
3. fill in rest
4. check if makes sense

Figure 10.11   Example of summary of Chapter 10 in this book.

Guidelines for Writing Summaries

1. *Write or state what the material is about in its broadest sense.* Write a title or a sentence in your own words.
2. *Look back through the material and then, from memory, write in brief form as many subideas and details as you can.* Use your own words. Make lists. Leave room for more.
3. *Go back and read your marginal notes and underlining and add important material that you have overlooked.*
4. *Read your summary and revise it, if necessary, so that it is easy to understand.*

Now look at Figure 10.11, an example of a jotted note summary of this chapter. It has been written quickly, in phrases only, and it is to be used for study purposes only. Practice writing summaries of this sort as one of the comprehension monitoring activities in the A exercises at the end of each of the chapters in this book.

At the Very Least . . .

This chapter has dealt with the ideal way for taking reading notes. If you can't follow all of the suggestions every day, *at the very least* do this much:

1. Underline selectively.
2. Write brief summaries at the end of major sections or chapters.

SUMMARY

Taking reading notes will help you improve your concentration while doing reading assignments. Reading notes will also help you locate important material later in class discussion and in exam preparation or open-book exams. Underline selectively, box transitions, circle specialized vocabulary, write your own ideas and questions at the top of the page, jot down main ideas in the margin, and write summaries at the end of each section and at the end of the chapter. Finish your note-taking activities by making outlines or maps of the main points. If you do not want to write in the book, take summary notes or make maps on five-by-eight cards and insert them at the beginning of chapters or take notes on separate pieces of paper and file them. Take summary notes on library books as well. Record the page numbers on which the material was found and a complete bibliographical reference in case you ever want to use these notes in writing a research paper. Adjust your note-taking system somewhat to make it work well for mathematics textbooks and imaginative literature. Summaries should include a title and ideas jotted briefly in one's own words.

EXERCISES

A. Monitor Your Comprehension of This Chapter.

Write quickly, in phrases rather than complete sentences, all of the information in this chapter that you understand and remember. Look back and add what you left out. Is anything unclear? Jot it down to ask about in class. Has reading the chapter caused you to think of new insights or examples of your own? Jot them down.

B. Class Exercises

1. *Individuals.* Read and mark the following section of material from a marketing textbook according to the recommendations made in this chapter. This section contains obvious transitions that emphasize the main ideas. Box them. Circle specialized vocabulary. Underline selectively. Summarize the main ideas, in phrases only, in the blank space provided at the end. Remember that your summary should answer the questions "What was this passage about?" and "What did the author say about it?"

Collecting Primary Data

1 **The Survey Method.**   Some information cannot be obtained through observation. The researcher must ask questions in order to obtain information on attitudes, motives, and opinions. The most widely used approach to collecting primary data is the survey method. Three kinds of surveys exist: telephone, mail, and personal interviews.

2   **Telephone interviews** are inexpensive and fast for obtaining small quantities of relatively impersonal information. Since many firms have leased WATS services (telephone company services that allow businesses to make unlimited long-distance calls for a fixed rate per state or region), a call to the most distant state costs no more than an across-town interview.[5]

3   Telephone interviews account for an estimated 55 to 60 percent of all primary marketing research. A national survey revealed that one woman in five had been interviewed by telephone in 1980, as compared with one in seven only two years earlier. The percentage of men who had participated in telephone interviews had grown from one in ten in 1978 to one

---

[5] William Lyons and Robert F. Durant, "Interviewer Costs Associated with the Use of Random Digit Dialing in Large Area Samples," *Journal of Marketing,* Summer 1980, pp. 65–69.

in seven in 1980.[6] Telephone interviews are, however, limited to simple, clearly worded questions. Also it is extremely difficult to obtain information on respondents' personal characteristics, and the survey may be prejudiced by the omission of households without phones or with unlisted numbers.

4   One survey reported that alphabetical listings in telephone directories excluded one-third of blacks with telephones and one-fourth of large-city dwellers and that they underrepresented service workers and separated and divorced persons. In addition, the mobility of the population creates problems in choosing names from telephone directories. As a result, a number of telephone interviewers have resorted to using digits selected at random and matched to telephone prefixes in the geographic area to be sampled. This technique is designed to correct the problem of sampling those with new telephone listings and those with unlisted numbers.[7]

5   **Mail interviews** allow the marketing researcher to conduct national studies at a reasonable cost. Whereas personal interviews with a national sample may be prohibitive in cost, the researcher can contact each potential respondent for the price of a postage stamp. Costs can be misleading, however. For example, returned questionnaires for such studies may average only 40 to 50 percent, depending on the length of the questionnaire and respondent interest. Also, some mail surveys include a coin to gain the reader's attention (such as the illustration in Figure 4.4), which further increases costs.[8] Unless additional information is obtained from non-respondents, the results of mail interviews are likely to be biased, since there may be important differences in the characteristics of respondents and nonrespondents. For this reason, follow-up questionnaires are sometimes mailed to nonrespondents, or telephone interviews are used to gather additional information.[9]

6   In 1980, the U.S. Bureau of the Census conducted the largest mail survey in history when it mailed census questionnaires to 80 million households. A number of questions were raised, including the difficulties of developing an accurate population count utilizing mail questionnaires.

[6] "Marketing Research Industry Survey Finds Increase in Phone Interviewing," *Marketing News,* January 9, 1981, p. 20.

[7] Reported in A. B. Blankenship, "Listed versus Unlisted Numbers in Telephone-Survey Samples," *Journal of Advertising Research,* February 1977, pp. 39–42. See also Roger Gates, Bob Brobst, and Paul Solomon, "Random Digit Dialing: A Review of Methods," in *Proceedings of the Southern Marketing Association,* New Orleans, La., November 1978, pp. 163–65; and Donald S. Tull and Gerald S. Albaum, "Bias in Random Digit-Dialed Surveys," *Public Opinion Quarterly,* Fall 1977, pp. 389–95.

[8] Stephen W. McDaniel and C. P. Rao, "The Effect of Monetary Inducement on Mailed Questionnaire Response Quality," *Journal of Marketing Research,* May 1980, pp. 265–68; and Robert A. Hansen, "A Self-Perception Interpretation of the Effect of Monetary and Nonmonetary Incentives on Mail Survey Respondent Behavior," *Journal of Marketing Research,* February 1980, pp. 77–83.

[9] Kevin F. McCrohan and Larry S. Lowe, "A Cost/Benefit Approach to Postage Used on Mail Questionnaires," *Journal of Marketing,* Winter 1981, pp. 130–33; and Jacob Hornik, "Time Cue and Time Perception Effect on Response to Mail Surveys," *Journal of Marketing Research,* May 1981, pp. 243–48.

Another sensitive subject concerned confidentiality of answers. The 85 percent response rate was a pleasant surprise to Census Bureau officials and to researchers throughout the world who rely upon mail surveys to obtain research data.

7   **Personal interviews** are typically the best means of obtaining detailed information, since the interviewer has the opportunity to establish rapport with each respondent and can explain confusing or vague questions. Although mail questionnaires are carefully worded and often pretested to eliminate potential misunderstandings, such misunderstandings can occur anyway. When an employee of the U.S. Department of Agriculture accidentally ran into and killed a cow with his truck, an official of the department sent the farmer an apology and a form to be filled out. The form included a space for "disposition of the dead cow." The farmer responded, "Kind and gentle."[10]

8   Personal interviews are slow and are the most expensive method of collecting survey data. However, their flexibility coupled with the detailed information that can be collected often offset these limitations. The refusal to be interviewed and the increasing difficulty of hiring interviewers to call on respondents at night present additional problems in utilizing this technique.[11]

WRITE SUMMARY:

1. *Small Groups.* Map the ideas in this section of material in whatever map form you would like to use. Look back at pages 166–167 to review the possibilities. Work on the blackboard or use a large piece of newsprint and a magic marker. One person should write while others contribute material for the map. Tape the maps to the wall with masking tape and discuss what might be added, deleted, or reorganized to improve each map.

2. *Individuals.* Read and mark the following passage from a chemistry textbook according to the suggestions in this chapter. Look for clues to main ideas. Write a summary at the end.

[10] "About That Cow," *Wall Street Journal,* June 28, 1972.
[11] Louis E. Boone and David L. Kurtz, *Contemporary Marketing,* 4th ed. (Hinsdale, Ill.: The Dryden Press, 1983), pp. 93–95, 109–110.

Experimental Methods

Discoveries come about through the observation of nature or by experimentation that can be categorized as trial and error, planned research, or accidental (serendipity).

Discovery by trial and error begins when one has a problem to solve and does various experiments in the hope that something desirable will emerge. The next set of experiments then depends on the results obtained. The discovery of the Edison battery by Thomas Edison's group is an example of discovery by trial and error. Edison's group performed more than 2000 experiments, each guided by the last, before settling on the composition of Edison's battery.

Discovery by planned research comes from carrying out specific experiments to test a well-defined hypothesis. The carcinogenic nature of some compounds is determined by progressing through a set pattern of experimental tests.

Discovery by accident may be a misnomer. The investigator is usually actively involved in investigating nature through experimentation, but "accidentally" finds some phenomenon not originally imagined or conceived. Thus the "accident" has an element of serendipity and is not seen unless the investigator is a trained observer. As Pasteur said, "Chance favors the prepared mind."

The discovery of one of the leading anticancer drugs, cisplatin, is an example of an "accidental" discovery. In 1964 Barnett Rosenberg and his co-workers at Michigan State University were studying the effects of an electric current on bacterial growth. They were using an electrical apparatus with platinum electrodes to pass a small alternating current through a live culture of *Escherichia coli* bacteria. After an hour, they examined the bacterial culture under a microscope and observed that cell division was no longer taking place. After thorough analysis of the culture medium and additional experimentation, they determined that traces of several different platinum compounds were produced during electrolysis from the reaction of the platinum electrodes with chemicals in the culture medium.

Careful observation was essential, since platinum electrodes are commonly regarded as inert or unreactive, and only a few parts of platinum compounds per million parts of culture medium were present. Additional testing indicated that a compound known as cisplatin was responsible for inhibiting cell division in *E. coli*. Approximately two years after its initial discovery, the Rosenberg group had the answer to the question "What caused the inhibition of cell division in *E. coli* bacteria?" At this point they had the idea that cisplatin might inhibit cell division in rapidly growing cancer cells. The compound was tested as an anticancer drug, and in 1979 the Food and Drug Administration approved its use as such. The drug has now been proved to be effective alone or in combination with other drugs for the treatment of a variety of cancers.

Another interesting aspect of the story is that cisplatin was first prepared in 1845. Although its chemistry has been studied thoroughly since
then, the biological effects of cisplatin and its inhibition of cell division
were not discovered until "the accident" 120 years later.[12]

WRITE SUMMARY:

3. *Individuals and Small Groups.* Each individual should first read and
   mark the selection that follows according to the instructions in this chapter.
   Then students should work together in small groups to decide what should
   be in the summary. One member of the group should write while others
   contribute ideas. A member of each group should read its summary to the
   class. The summaries can be written on the blackboard or on large pieces of
   newsprint and displayed. Discuss what might be added, deleted, or reorganized to improve each summary.

CHANGES IN ATTITUDES

The Roper Organization has been asking a nationally representative
sample of men and women the same questions for the last fifteen years.
The results show that there has been a significant shift in the attitudes
and life-styles of men and women.

When the impact of the feminist movement just began to be felt
around 1970, only 38 percent of women and 40 percent of men believed
women were looked on with more respect than a decade earlier. By 1985,
after the feminist movement became a part of mainstream society, 60
percent of women and 61 percent of men believed women were respected
more than during the previous decade.

With these changes has come the realization that gender equality
benefits not only women, but men and children as well. As corporations
face a shrinking work force in the 1990s, they will be forced to respond
to the needs of workers with a variety of benefits, including child care,
unpaid maternity leaves, flexible working hours, job sharing, and part-
time work.

For the first time, the concerns of women for adequate child care and
maternity leave are being shared by men. As a result, both men and

[12] Joesten, Johnston, Netterville, Wood, pp. 5–6.

women are pressing corporations and government to respond to the needs of the family. When the DuPont Corporation surveyed 3300 male employees in 1985, they found that only 18 percent were interested in part-time work to give them more time with their children. By 1988, the percentage had jumped to 33 percent. Similarly, in 1985 only 11 percent expressed interest in a period after the birth of a child in which they could work fewer hours. Three years later the percentage climbed to 28 percent. Clearly, in those 3 years the issue of child care evolved from a female issue into a concern of both men and women (*U.S. News & World Report,* June 20, 1988).

We should not assume that economic conditions are forcing women to go to work. When women are asked if they would continue working if they were financially secure, 70 percent of women in all age groups claim that they would. This percentage is the same as it is for men when they are asked this question. Education appears to be a deciding factor in continuing to work. Women who have dropped out of high school are most likely to not work if they do not have to, whereas those with some college education are the least likely to leave the work force if they were financially secure. The least likely of all to leave the work force are women in households with the highest incomes.

The vast majority of both men and women think that marriage is the best way to live. But the type of marriage that people want is different than the marriage of the past. In 1974, about half of all men and women thought a traditional marriage where the husband worked and the wife stayed home and took care of the house and children was ideal. By 1985, only 37 percent of women and 43 percent of men wanted this type of arrangement. The majority of men and women thought the most satisfying marriage was one where husband and wife share work, housekeeping, and child care. It should also come as no surprise that younger women are the most likely to want an egalitarian life-style.

Women's employment clearly has changed the ways in which women and men define marital and parental roles. As women become less dependent and are able to buy services, marital and parental roles may become less stressful. However, some new stresses may emerge. Employed women are likely to redefine involvement in child rearing and expect more equal participation from their husbands. This situation may produce heightened marital tensions.

It appears that nontraditional gender roles produce a gain in power and control for women. Some believe that this accounts for the lower levels of depression among working women in nontraditional marriages compared to women in traditional homemaker roles. At the same time this change may produce less control for men in such marriages and the potential for higher levels of depression. At least in the short term, marital strain may be one of the costs for the current redefinitions of family roles.

Like so many other areas of American life, gender roles are undergoing rapid change. Traditional distinctions are becoming blurred and obsolete in response to new social and economic demands, but on the whole, experts expect strong family bonds to survive.[13]

WRITE SUMMARY:

D. Application Exercises

1. Bring one of your other textbooks to read and mark in class. Or, everyone in the class can read and mark one of the selections in the Appendix to this book. When everyone in the class has read and marked for half an hour, exchange your work and use the following checklist to evaluate how well the selection has been marked. Read the checklist first to see how you will be evaluated. Later, when you use the checklist to evaluate a set of notes, assign the number that best describes the notes.

Evaluation Checklist for Marking your Textbook

4   You are doing an excellent job of marking your textbook. Only the important words or phrases are underlined or highlighted. Main ideas are jotted in the margin and/or at the end of sections. You have written a concise summary of the main points covered in each section.

3   You are doing a good job of marking your textbook. While the main ideas are highlighted or underlined in the text, some less important words or phrases are underlined also. As much as half the text may be so marked, and the main ideas are getting lost. Most paragraphs have the main idea written in the margin. Most sections have been summarized, but not always in your own words.

2   You need to concentrate more on your reading in order to find the main ideas in each paragraph. Those words and phrases expressing the main idea are the only ones that should be underlined or highlighted. You are neglecting to jot the main idea in the margin, or you are writing too much in the margin so that nothing stands out. Your summaries at the end of sections do not cover all the points in that section.

---

[13] Tischler, pp. 333–336. Used with permission. References have been removed.

1 You need more practice in marking your textbook. While you are attempting to highlight the important points in each paragraph, you are neglecting to write marginal notes or section summaries. You need to review page 163 in the textbook. Look at the textbook markings of other students.

0 You are not marking your textbook at all, or you have neglected to bring your textbook to class.

2. Continue to practice notetaking in this book and in your other textbooks as well. Submit them to your instructor or exchange them with other students at least two more times. Use the Evaluation Checklist and assign a score.

C. Topics for Your Learning Journal

1. Reflect about the ideas for taking reading notes presented in this chapter and then list each class you are taking this semester along with a description of the most appropriate and useful note-taking techniques for each of them.

2. Write an explanation of how mapping helps you learn and remember textbook material. Do the same for summarizing.

11 | *Remembering and Thinking Critically*

When you have finished reading this chapter, you will know the following:

1. How to organize your reading activities into a process.
2. Ten suggestions to help you remember what you read.
3. Six suggestions to help you think critically about what you read.
4. How to monitor your own learning.

ORGANIZING THE READING PROCESS

You have been introduced to a process for reading textbooks and other materials in Part Three of this textbook. In Chapter 8 you were taught prereading activities to help you activate background knowledge, make predictions, and organize your reading through surveying. In Chapter 9 you were taught to read to comprehend ideas by learning what to expect on the printed page, such as the clues to main ideas, so that you would be able to locate them more easily. In Chapter 10 you were taught ways to underline, make notes, map, and summarize important ideas so that you could study and learn them more easily. In this chapter, you will be given suggestions to help you think about and remember the material you have read.

As you think back through this process, notice that it is not a step-by-step process like one you might follow for setting up a stereo system. Instead, all of the parts are interrelated. To make it work, you will, for example, sometimes stop to background and predict in the middle of a chapter, you will take notes while you read, you will think and try to remember while you are reading as well as after you have finished. Furthermore, you will not employ all of these suggestions all of the time. When the material is easy and you are reading for pleasure or quick information, you will just read. When the material is difficult, however, or when you must learn and remember it, you will employ many of the suggestions you have learned in these chapters. Without them, you may find yourself staring at words instead of understanding ideas. To complete the explanation of the reading process, here are some suggestions to help you *remember* what you read and also to help you *think* as you read. Both activities are important because, without them, you will forget or, worse, fail to find significance in the material that you read.

THE PROBLEM OF FORGETTING AND SOME SOLUTIONS

When you have finished reading and taking notes, you may think that you have completed a reading assignment. You haven't quite. The material you have just read, at this point, is confined to what psychologists call your short-term memory. Information in the short-term memory decays quickly or is soon replaced by newly learned material. You will forget more than half of what you have just read within twenty-four hours and most of the rest of it within a week unless you take some immediate steps to transfer it to your long-term memory. Once material becomes a part of your long-term memory, much of it can be recalled immediately and the rest of it can be relearned comparatively quickly. You will need to employ special techniques and activities to help you transfer newly learned material to your long-term memory where it will remain for the rest of your life. It is usually of some comfort to students to learn that no one, no matter how brilliant, can remember effortlessly.

You have already been provided with some solutions to the problem of forgetting. You have learned in past chapters how to produce efficient *external memory aids* such as lecture notes, vocabulary sheets, and reading notes. Since you create these aids to memory yourself, you will be able to find your way around in them easily, looking up information that you have already forgotten.

They will also be useful to you when you use *internal memory aids* to help you think about and commit to memory the information that you have written in these notes.[1] You have already been introduced to some internal memory aids that were built into the study systems presented in preceding chapters. In Chapter 4 you were introduced to a system for lecture note taking that involves *organizing* the

---

[1] I am indebted to John R. Hayes, *The Complete Problem Solver* (Philadelphia: The Franklin Institute Press, 1981), pp. 71–111, and Laird S. Cermak, *Improving Your Memory* (New York: McGraw-Hill, 1976), for some of the ideas in this chapter.

notes in the first place, *labeling* and *summarizing* their contents in your own words in the margins and at the end, and *reciting* their contents until you can do so from memory. In Chapter 5 you were given some systems for remembering vocabulary. It was suggested that you make vocabulary sheets and write an *association* for remembering the word in the fourth column of these sheets. It was further suggested that you *organize* related words in outlines and diagrams. In Chapter 9 you were shown how to *summarize* your reading notes and also how to *organize* them in outlines on maps in order to make them easier to think about and remember.

All of these activities help you think about and remember new material. You can expand your use of these, along with other major activities that can improve both thought and memory. As you read through the following suggestions, you might also consider which of them will be easiest for you to use because they fit your best learning style.

TEN SUGGESTIONS TO HELP YOU REMEMBER

1. Decide to remember.   A conscious decision to focus your attention so that you can concentrate and remember is necessary if any of the other suggestions in this chapter section are to work well. You will make this decision more easily if you generate an interest in what is to be remembered. You may have known people who can remember batting averages but can't remember the parts of speech because they were interested in baseball and not interested in grammar. When you have to remember material that is not interesting, try to think of some reasons why it is important. Ask, "What is the value of this material to me?" and come up with a positive answer. Then, think of anything else you know that might be related that could help you understand it. For example, you might generate an interest in studying chemistry by thinking of some of the chemicals used in the modern world and also what the world would be like without an understanding of chemistry.

2. Encode: Reduce and simplify.   When you have finished reading a passage, restate it in your own words so that you can understand it. Make it as brief as possible. The process of putting difficult material in your own words is called encoding. It is much like summarizing, except that encoded notes are sometimes even briefer than summary notes. For example, read the following passage and rewrite it briefly in your own words:

Primarily, the American Revolution was a political and constitutional movement and only secondarily one that was either financial, commercial, or social. At bottom the fundamental issue was the political independence of the colonies, and in the last analysis the conflict lay between the British Parliament and the Colonial Assemblies, each of which was probably more sensitive, self-conscious, and self-important than was the voting population that it represented.[2]

Did you write something like the following? *American Revolution conflict between Parliament and Colonial Assemblies over political independence.* You could further reduce this statement to "political independence" and use that phrase to help trigger all you know about the American Revolution. You can use this technique to "nutshell" sections or entire chapters. One brief sentence, word, or phrase that you have written or selected can help you recall many additional details about a topic.

Another way to reduce and simplify difficult material is to look for meaningful units or chunks in it, to label them with short phrases of your own like in the example above, and memorize the labels. The short-term memory can only hold five to nine items of information at one time. Break a long and detailed section into nine or less chunks, create simple, short labels for these chunks, and then rehearse these labels until you know them. These labels will help you recall the details through a process of association. For example, try chunking the four chapters on textbook reading. You could find and label seven chunks: (1) background and predict details; (2) survey; (3) main ideas; (4) supporting details; (5) transitions; (6) notes and summaries; (7) think and remember. As you located and labeled these chunks you would also review the details that you would use to explain them. Just before an exam or class discussion, however, you would memorize the seven brief labels. They, in turn, would help you remember the details necessary to write or speak intelligently and completely about reading textbooks.

3. *Organize the material.* Information in your long-term memory is remarkably well organized in an elaborate internal filing system. New information is efficiently sorted, filed, and stored until

[2] Charles M. Andrews, "The Imperial School," in *The American Revolution: How Revolutionary Was It?* ed. by George Athan Billias, 4th ed., (Fort Worth: Holt, Rinehart and Winston, 1990), p. 38.

you need it. You can store and retrieve new information more efficiently if you work to organize it first because material that goes into your memory already organized is easier to get back out. All of the study systems presented in this book that function as external aids to memory (lecture notes, vocabulary sheets, reading notes) stress organization as their key feature.

In organizing material that you want to learn, you can group or rearrange it according to topics, by the sequence or order in which it took place, or by some established organizational pattern such as problem-solution, cause-and-effect, or even alphabetically. You can, for example, mentally list five topics, or divide the material into three blocks of time, or note that the author listed one problem and three solutions. It will be even easier to remember if you show visually how you have grouped and rearranged the material. For this purpose use *lists, outlines, maps,* and *summaries.* Look again at Figures 10.4 and 10.11 in the last chapter to get a better idea of how material can be organized for easy study. In the next chapter, you will learn how to organize material on *study sheets* to help you prepare for exams. The process you go through to organize material to be learned forces you to select what is important, to see relationships among the bits of material, and finally, to arrange it in an order that makes sense to you. The organizing activity itself helps you to learn much of the material as you work with it.

It also helps to list and number the items you want to remember. Words, technical terms, and foreign-language vocabulary can be listed in one column with the meanings in another. Numbering the items in a list will also help you to remember them unless, of course, there are too many. You will, for example, more easily remember six steps for surveying a textbook, ten ways to remember, and six ways to improve vocabulary than you would if these items were unnumbered. Simplify such lists so that each item is represented by one word. Select ones that are easy to remember.

4. Associate the new with the old. The more you know about a subject, the easier it is to learn more. Conversely, if you know nothing at all about a subject, it is relatively difficult to get started learning it. You automatically use the information you already have in your memory to help you interpret and understand new material. One purpose of education is to fill your memory with information on a wide variety of topics to help you learn through association during the rest of your life.

Consciously use the knowledge, experiences, and ideas that you already have in your mind to help you think about and learn new material. If you are studying a subject that is brand new to you, be patient at first. Once you start learning the new material, over a period of time it will become easier to learn more about it because you will now have something in your memory with which to associate it.

Use any familiar material to help you learn the new, including ideas, knowledge, experiences, attitudes, judgments, places, occurrences, people, songs, pictures, numbers, words. It doesn't matter how far-fetched the association is, if it helps you remember. Associate a new concept in physics, like the third law of motion, with something you have observed in your life experience, like the kick of a rifle or the force of a jet engine. Or, in a history class, memorize a few important dates such as 1066 (The Battle of Hastings), 1492 (Columbus), 1603 (King James Bible), 1776 (the American Revolution), and 1861–1865 (the American Civil War). You can then remember other historical events by associating them with these familiar dates. Example: The French Revolution occurred about 10 years *after* the American Revolution, or Queen Elizabeth died a few years *before* the publication of the King James Bible.

In addition to relating new material to what is familiar to you, you can also relate it to what is important to you. What does the material have to do with you and your past or potential experience or with what you value? Make new material even more memorable by imagining yourself personally active or involved with it. For example, if you are taking a theatre class, imagine yourself on the stage, or, if you are in a computer class, imagine yourself operating a computer. Use your senses: Imagine saying, seeing, hearing, tasting, and feeling.

You can, finally, make up examples of your own. They will help you understand and remember difficult material. If you can't remember the difference between an igneous rock and a metamorphic rock, carry an example of each of them in your pocket until you can. Do whatever you can to make the abstract concrete and familiar.

5. Recite from memory. One of the best ways to improve your memory of written material is to cover it up, look away, and recite it to yourself. You will need to read and understand before you recite. Then, as you recite, think about the material you are learning. Explain it to yourself in your own words. As often as possible, visualize what you are learning either in the form of graphs and diagrams or in actual images and pictures. Effective recitation is more than just memorizing. When done well, it results in a thorough understanding of new material.

Use the active ways of studying—speaking and writing—when you recite. Reading and listening are relatively passive, and you will not learn as well if you rely on them. Here are some ways you can use speaking and writing to help you remember more:

1. As soon as you have finished reading your assignment, get together with another member of the class. Repeat and explain to that person the main points in the chapter until you can do so from memory.
2. When you study with someone else, make sure that you do at least half of the talking. The one who mainly listens doesn't learn as much.
3. When you recite the contents of your lecture notes or a textbook chapter, do it out loud. You will remember more that way than if you read silently.
4. Whenever you encounter a new word or a difficult concept, say it out loud. Hearing it will help you to understand and remember it.
5. Write any material you are trying to memorize as many times as is necessary. It is far better to write the conjugation of a foreign-language verb three times than read it in the book ten times.

Memory experts say that you should spend more than half of the time it takes to complete a reading assignment on recitation.

6. Visualize what you read and hear as often as possible. Create mental images and draw your own pictures and diagrams in the margins of your textbook (and in your lecture notes) whenever the material lends itself to such treatment. A complex diagram or graph in a textbook is always difficult. Understand and remember complicated visual material by tracing over it with a pencil or your finger. This helps you see the parts so that the whole will make better sense to you. Visualize when you are reading imaginative literature, too. Recreate in your mind the verbal pictures that authors create. Imagine some movement or action in the pictures you create and they will be even easier to remember.

For example, read the following first-hand account of the assassination of Tsar Paul of Russia in 1801. Visualize the scene. Involve all your senses. Notice color, sounds, and smells as well as action and movement.

> One of the conspirators took off his official scarf and tied it round the Emperor's throat. Paul struggled, the approach of death restoring him to strength and speech. He set free one of his hands and thrust it between the scarf and his throat, crying out for air. Just then he perceived a red uniform, which was at that time worn by the officers of the

cavalry guard, and thinking that one of the assassins was his son Constantine, who was a colonel of that regiment, he exclaimed: "Mercy, your Highness, mercy! Some air, for God's sake!" But the conspirators seized the hand with which he was striving to prolong his life, and furiously tugged at both ends of the scarf. The unhappy Emperor had already breathed his last, and yet they tightened the knot and dragged along the dead body, striking it with their hands and feet. The cowards who until then had held aloof surpassed in atrocity those who had done the deed. Just at that time General Bennigsen returned. I do not know whether he was sincerely grieved at what had happened in his absence; all he did was to stop the further desecration of the Emperor's body.

Meanwhile the cry "Paul is dead!" was heard by the other conspirators, and filled them with a joy that deprived them of all sentiment of decency and dignity. They wandered tumultuously about the corridors and rooms of the palace, boasting to each other of their prowess; many of them found means of adding to the intoxication of the supper by breaking into the wine cellars and drinking to the Emperor's death.[3]

7. Make up rhymes or sentences to help you remember. Rhymes can aid memory because they are easy to remember themselves. Think of the ones about "*I* before *e* except after *c*" and "Thirty days hath September." If you are not good at rhymes, you can compose sentences such as "Mary Visits Every Monday and Just Stays Until Noon Period" to help you remember the order of the planets: Mercury, Venus, Earth, Mars, Jupiter, Saturn, Uranus, Neptune, and Pluto. Beware of composing rhymes and sentences, however, that are more difficult to remember than the material itself.

8. Take off the first letter from each word in a list you want to remember and memorize the letters. Make words of these letters when you can. *Nec* could help you remember the naturalistic, experimental, and correlational approaches to psychology. *TISH V.W.* can help you remember the steps in surveying a chapter—title, introduction, summary, headings, visuals, words. You will find this method of remembering especially useful if you tend to panic in exams. Having a few made-up words and letters in your mind will give you something to grab quickly when you start the exam. You will feel more sure of yourself.

9. When you want to remember something in the morning, go over it just before you fall asleep at night. One reason

[3] From Memoirs of *Prince Adam Czartovyski and His Correspondence with Alexander I.* Edited by Adam Gielgud (London: Remington and Co., 1888), vol. 1, pp. 227–248, 251–255. Reprinted in *Imperial Russia,* edited by Basil Dmytryshyn (Fort Worth: Holt, Rinehart and Winston, 1990), pp. 159–160.

you forget is that other things capture your attention, interfere with what you have just learned, and cause you to forget. When you are asleep, there is less of this interference. Unless you are too drowsy, the last few minutes before you go to sleep is a prime time for fixing material to be remembered in your mind.

10. Review every week or two by reading through the summaries you have written in your lecture notes and textbooks. This review will help you see the sequence of ideas being developed in a book or series of lectures. Seeing this sequence will help you understand and learn the material. You may feel at times that you are overlearning material as you review it again and again during a semester. You should not worry about this. Reviewing to the point of overlearning will guarantee that material is imprinted in your long-term memory, ready to retrieve for a future class or an exam.

SIX SUGGESTIONS TO HELP YOU THINK ABOUT AND CRITICALLY EVALUATE NEW MATERIAL

Research suggests that rehearsing or reciting material over and over without thinking about it, as you might a telephone number until you finish dialing it, will keep it in your short-term memory for a time but will not result in permanent learning. You must do more than rote recitation to transfer new material to your long-term memory. Actively thinking about the material is required. Such mental activity can be done concurrently with reading, note taking, summarizing, and reciting. Critical thinking involves seeing the implications, making applications, and discovering exceptions to what you are learning. It also involves making inferences, creating images, making associations, thinking of your own examples, asking questions, and making final evaluative judgments about new material. It involves seeing new relationships, new combinations, or alternate solutions to problems. Here is a list of six activities that can stimulate you to think as you read.

1. Ask questions to stimulate critical thinking. There are many types of questions. Some help you understand the literal meaning of the text itself and, when answered, will help you produce a summary of the text. Questions of this type include *what* was the text about? *What* did the author say about it? *Who* was important? *When* did this happen? *How* did it happen?

Other questions invite you to go beyond the text and relate the ideas to what you already know or to see the larger implications and significance of what you have read. Examples of questions that will stimulate you to think beyond the literal meaning of the text itself include *Why* did it happen that way? What are the *causes?* What are the *effects?* How can this *problem* be *solved?* What are the *implications?* How can this be *applied* to other situations? or *What would happen* if _____? You can think of other questions of this type that will invite you to use the information you have read to think about broader issues and ideas.

2. Elaborate.   Add to the material you have read to help you understand it better. Make *comparisons,* think of *examples,* add *explanations,* add *definitions,* and *find out more information* if necessary.

Here is an example of simple, unelaborated information from a chemistry textbook:

$$\text{Avogadro's number} = 6.02 \times 10^{23}$$

It is possible to recite that number a sufficient number of times to memorize it. But you will not understand its size or its significance until you acquire some elaboration. Here, then, is the same information accompanied by elaboration.

The Mole Concept

We mentioned earlier that an organized table of relative atomic masses can be obtained by weighing equally large numbers of atoms of different elements. . . .

The specific large number used by chemists is 6.02×10^{23}. This number, known as Avogadro's number and symbolized N, can hardly be described as being merely "large." The term "large" does not begin to describe the enormity of 10^{23}. An analogy that might suggest a picture of Avogadro's number would be to try to imagine how much of the earth's surface could be covered by 6.02×10^{23} marbles. The answer is that the entire surface of our planet could be covered by Avogadro's number of marbles to a depth of more than 50 miles!

Avogadro's number of particles is called a *mole,* from the Greek word meaning "pile" or "mound." Although Amadeo Avogadro did not experimentally determine the number that bears his name, he has been so honored because his studies of gas behavior indirectly led to the finding of the number. . . .

Avogadro's number of anything may be specified as one mole; 6.02×10^{23} atoms of lead is a mole of lead atoms; 6.02×10^{23} molecules of carbon dioxide is a mole of carbon dioxide molecules; and 6.02×10^{23} sneakers (perish the thought) is a mole of sneakers. However, the *internationally recognized standard for a mole is the number of atoms in 12.000 grams of carbon-12.* This number of atoms is, of course, Avogadro's number.[4]

Notice that the author has elaborated on Avogadro's number by helping you visualize marbles to understand how large this number is, by explaining the derivation of the word *mole* to help you remember its meaning, and by inviting you to imagine a mole of sneakers. The effect of this visualizing and associating makes this abstract number more interesting and meaningful to you and, consequently, easier to remember. Such elaboration is not usually done for you, so you need to make some effort to do it for yourself.

3. *Read to generate ideas.* Part of the time you will read to understand the author, to get the meaning straight. At other times you will read to get ideas of your own. You will, in other words, use the material you read to help you think beyond the text. People who write to the newspaper editor have often read something that has triggered the ideas that they write about in their letters. React to the material that you read with ideas and insights of your own. For example, when reading about one solution to a problem, try to think of additional solutions of your own.

4. *Write to help you think.* When you get an idea from reading, write it down and elaborate on it in writing. Writing helps people think. Some people say they are not sure what they think, in fact, until they have written it down, read it, thought about it some more, and revised it. Develop the reading, thinking, writing habit early in the semester and you will have less difficulty thinking of topics and materials for discussion, essay exams, and written papers.

5. *Talk to others to clarify ideas.* It will help you think if you talk about the ideas that reading generates in your mind. Exchange of ideas with other people helps you see other viewpoints and perspectives. The purpose of class discussion, group work, and oral reports is to stimulate critical and creative thinking.

6. *Take positions but keep an open mind.* Some of what you learn in college is factual material that you can memorize. A great deal of it, however, is controversial and still open to question. Take positions on controversial issues but be able to defend your positions with facts, data, and well-reasoned opinion. Also, stay open to new

---

[4] Stanley M. Cherim and Leo E. Kallan, *Chemistry, An Introduction,* 2d ed. (Philadelphia: Saunders College Publishing, 1980), pp. 69–70.

information that could cause you to alter or change your views. In order to accomplish this, you will have to read and listen without forming a judgment until you have read or heard as much information as is available.

MONITOR YOUR OWN LEARNING

You were introduced to the idea of monitoring your reading comprehension in Chapter 2 and you have practiced it at the end of each chapter since then. This chapter recommends that you go further and monitor how well you have processed and learned material so that you can use it in your own papers, assignments, or other activities. Monitoring your own learning requires that you *insist* on understanding.

Think for a moment of some new reading material in the past that was important to you and that you had to struggle to understand. Examples might be reading the instructions for installing a car stereo, hooking up a video cassette recorder, cutting out and sewing an article of clothing, cooking a meal, filling out income tax returns, or completing your college application forms. In such cases you worked with the material, using a number of mental activities, until you finally understood it. You may have thought about it, reworded it, reorganized it, or associated it with what you already knew. You may have taken some notes, drawn pictures, traced over diagrams, or made simple lists out of the complicated ones. You might also have thought of some of your own examples, talked to yourself until you finally "got" it, or asked someone else to explain it to you. In other words, you worked with the material until you were confident that you understood it. Furthermore, your *internal monitoring system* let you know when you understood the instructions well enough to do the tasks.

You can consciously use similar processes and the same internal monitoring system when you read and learn textbook and lecture material. Consciously use a variety of learning processes, such as those described in this chapter, and then monitor your understanding of new material. You have finished studying when you know you can successfully report on it, discuss it, or take an exam on it. To do this successfully you will have to evaluate continuously what you need to learn, what you already know, and what you still have to learn. You can do this by testing yourself as you read and study. Ask questions and try to answer them, look away and recite important information, or stop and see if you can explain the implications or importance of a major concept. If you find that you cannot, stop immediately to think about and recite what you don't know. You can learn to become critical of your own memory and understanding and to improve on them when they seem inadequate. Such activity results in immediate and permanent learning and leads to the development of methods for further learning that will make you an educated person for life.

At the Very Least . . .

This chapter has presented some ideal ways of thinking about and remembering what you have read. If you can't follow all of the suggestions every day, *at the very least* do this much:

1. Find the organization in material you want to learn, or reorganize it yourself.
2. Look away and recite what you have just read from time to time.
3. Think about and elaborate on material you are learning. Discuss it with others.
4. Read through all of your notes occasionally as a review.

SUMMARY

Prereading, reading, and taking notes on a reading assignment do not finish the job. You also need to think about the new information and commit it to your long-term memory to complete the process. Improve your memory by deciding to remember, encoding, organizing, associating, reciting, visualizing, making up sentences and nonsense words, going over material to be remembered just before falling asleep, and, finally, reviewing. Improve the quantity and quality of your thinking by asking questions, elaborating, reading to generate ideas, writing to develop ideas, discussing to clarify ideas, and by taking positions while, at the same time, staying open to the possibility of new and better ideas. It is also important to learn how to monitor your own learning so that you will know when you have mastered an assignment.

EXERCISES

A. Monitor Your Comprehension of This Chapter

Write quickly, in phrases rather than complete sentences, all of the information in this chapter that you remember. Look back and add what you left out. Is anything unclear? Jot it down to ask about in class. Has reading the chapter caused you to think of new insights or examples of your own? Jot them down.

B. Class Exercises

1. *Whole Class.* Organize Material

Look at the following list for twelve seconds, one second for each item. Count "one and, two and," and so on. Now look away and write as many of these items as you can from memory.

1. working on a paper	7. studying
2. calling a friend to get an assignment	8. going to classes
3. talking to professor	9. reviewing notes
4. going to work for two hours	10. taking an exercise break
5. watching television	11. joining a study group
6. going to bed	12. going to the library

Since the short-term memory holds at the most seven to nine items, you were probably not able to remember all twelve of these. Now organize all of the items under the three time chunks in the list. List the activities in the order in which you might do them.

Morning	*Afternoon*	*Evening*
1. _____	1. _____	1. _____
2. _____	2. _____	2. _____
3. _____	3. _____	3. _____
4. _____	4. _____	4. _____

Now visualize yourself engaged in each activity. Put some action and movement into the mental images you create. Look at the reorganized list again for twelve seconds and again look away and see if you can now write these items from memory. See if one class member can reproduce them on the board from memory.

2. *Individuals or Small Groups.* Think of Examples

Think of two examples to help you remember the following information from a psychology textbook.

According to a 1980 survey made by Elizabeth and Geoffrey Loftus, most people think that Long-term Memory is much like a "video recorder," and that you can *always* recover an item if you try hard enough. As the Loftuses note, though, the experimental data don't support this viewpoint. Indeed, a large number of scientific studies suggest that most of us totally forget much of what we've experienced in the past. And, judging from the bulk of the laboratory studies on this subject, once an item is lost, it's probably gone forever.[5]

[5] James V. McConnell, *Understanding Human Behavior,* 4th ed. (New York: Holt, Rinehart and Winston, 1983), p. 376.

3. *Small Groups.* Elaborate

Elaborate on the first amendment to the Constitution to help you remember it. Explain the first amendment in your own words. Think of two examples of activities the amendment guarantees and protects. Think of one example of an activity that would be contrary to the amendment. What could happen if there were no first amendment?

> Amendment 1. Congress shall make no law respecting an establishment of religion, or prohibiting the free exercise thereof; or abridging the freedom of speech, or of the press; or the right of the people peaceably to assemble, and to petition the Government for a redress of grievances.

4. *Whole Class.* Visualize

Visualize the following descriptive material from a metallurgy textbook and draw a simple picture of it. One class member may draw on the blackboard.

Hardness Testing

Everyone is familiar with denting a piece of metal by hitting it with a hammer. The hardness of a metal is tested in a similar manner. An accurately ground steel ball or diamond point is pressed into the metal sample, under a known load (or pressure), by a hardness testing machine. Gauges then measure the size of the resultant dent in the metal sample. Hardness tests are among the most important and reliable means of testing a metal for its capability of doing a certain job. The dents made in hardness testing usually do not destroy the metal part for use. Hardness is not a true or basic property of a material but, rather, it is a measure of the material's resistance to penetration or denting.[6]

5. *Whole Class.* Recite

Recite the steps for surveying a chapter that are on page 121. Use the first letters of the words in each of the steps to help you remember:

> TISH VW (title, introduction, summary, heads, visuals, words)

Recite the steps for surveying a *book*. Think of your own nonsense word, sentence, or rhyme to help you remember these steps.

See if volunteer class members can now write these steps on the board from memory.

6. *Individuals or Small Groups.* Encode

Encode by reducing and simplifying the twelve clues to main ideas on pages 145–146. Think of *one word* to nutshell each suggestion, list and number them, and recite them until everyone in the group can say the words without looking at the list. A member of each group should reproduce the lists on the blackboard from memory.

[6] Donald V. Brown, *Metallurgy Basics* (New York: Delmar Publishers, 1983), p. 89.

7. *Individuals or Small Groups.* Encode

> *Encode* the following paragraph by reducing it to one sentence and 3 or 4 phrases that you write in your own words. *Associate* the material in this paragraph with what you already know and think of two *examples* of your own.

> At the heart of most stepfamily relationships are children who, like their parents, are casualties of divorce. In the best stepfamily relationship, all the adults work together to meet the needs of the children, realizing that all too often, no matter what they do, there will still be problems. In reality, stepfamilies are torn apart by many of the same pressures that divide intact families. Financial problems can be especially acute when parents must support children from different marriages. Resentment builds quickly when stepparents feel they have little power or authority in their own houses. The most difficult stage is the early years when stepparents want everything to go right. Once stepparents realize that relationships with stepchildren build over time and that their potential network of allies includes all the other adults in the stepfamily relationship, the adjustment for all will be faster and healthier.[7]

8. *Individuals or Small Groups.*   The following section of material presents an example of controversy. *Encode* it by locating the main points and putting them on a *map*. Add a few details to each idea to clarify them. *Explain* in your own words what the selection is about. *Associate* these ideas with your experience. On the basis of your experience and the evidence in this selection, form a *tentative opinion* of your own. Say why you have formed this opinion.

Emotional Development

> There are a number of theories concerning the development of emotions. Basically they break down into two camps. The first, proposed originally by Katherine Bridges holds that we are born with a single emotion and that other emotions become differentiated as time passes. The second, proposed by Carroll Izard, holds that all emotions are present and adequately differentiated at birth. However, they are not shown all at once. Instead, they emerge in response to the child's developing needs and maturational sequences.

> **Bridges' and Sroufe's Theory**   On the basis of her observations of babies, Bridges proposed that newborns experience one emotion— diffuse excitement. By 3 months, two other emotions have differentiated from this general state of excitement—a negative emotion (distress) and a positive emotion (delight). By 6 months, fear, disgust, and anger will have developed from distress. By 12 months elation and affection will have differentiated from delight. Jealousy develops from distress, and joy develops from delight—both during the second year.

---

[7] Tischler, p. 373.

Alan Sroufe has advanced Bridges' theory, focusing on the ways in which cognitive development may provide the basis for emotional development. Jealousy, for example, could not become differentiated without some understanding of the concept of possession. Anger usually results from situations in which our intentions are thwarted. For example, 7-month-old infants show anger when a biscuit is almost placed in their mouths and then removed. It may be that the development of concepts of intentionality (that is, the idea that people can do things "on purpose") and of rudimentary causality (the ability to perceive other people as the causes of frustration) precede the differentiation of anger.

Izard's Theory   Carroll Izard proposes that infants are born with discrete emotional states. However, the timing of their appearance is linked to the child's cognitive development and social experiences. For example, in one study, Izard and his colleagues claim that 2-month-old babies receiving inoculations showed distress, whereas older infants showed anger.

Izard's view may sound very similar to Sroufe's. After all, both are suggesting that there is an orderly unfolding of emotions such that they become more specific as time passes. However, in keeping with Izard's view, researchers have found that a number of different emotions appear to be shown by infants at ages earlier than those suggested by Bridges and Sroufe. In one study of the emotions shown by babies during the first three months, mothers reported that their babies showed the emotions of interest, joy, anger, surprise, and fear. These figures are based on mother's reports, and it is possible that the infants were actually showing more diffuse emotions. Perhaps the mothers were "reading" specific emotions "into" the babies based on their own knowledge of appropriate (adult) emotional reactions to the infant's situations.

In sum, researchers seem to agree that a handful of emotions are shown by infants during the first few months. They agree that other emotions develop in an orderly manner. They agree that emotional development is linked to cognitive development and social experience. They do not agree on exactly when specific emotions are first shown or on whether discrete emotions are present at birth.[8]

9. *Individuals or Small Groups.*   Use the following selection to help you *analyze and generate ideas of your own.*

Population Control in China

In the 1970s, the average Chinese woman of childbearing age was giving birth to six children. The Chinese government decided to take drastic action to ensure future survival.

A goal of a population of no more than 1.2 billion people by the year 2000 was set. To accomplish this goal, China instituted a nationwide campaign to convince couples to follow the government's guidelines.

[8] Rathus, pp. 260–261. Used with permission. References have been removed.

To promote acceptance of the one-child limit, the government devised a reward-punishment system that makes daily life easier and richer for those who comply and burdensome for those who do not. A nationwide campaign to promote the one-child family features the Glorious One Child Certificate, under which couples sign an agreement to limit their family to a single child in exchange for extensive benefits.

As long as they only have one child, an urban couple receives a monthly bonus of $5 (Chinese dollars, equal to $3.50 American). Because the average working family income is only $30 to $35 (Chinese dollars) a month, the bonus amounts to an extra 15 percent in income.

In China, under the Glorious One Child Certificate plan, a couple may also choose between two other types of preferential treatment. They can opt for child care at no cost at nursery schools until the child is 7 years old or for free medical care for the child until age 14. They also receive preferential treatment in living accommodations, food allowances, and work assignments.

Couples who have two children—spaced over a long period of time— are neither punished nor rewarded. They receive no extra money, no extra work points, and no free education or medical benefits for a second child. They must assume the extra cost of raising the second child themselves, with no help from the state.

Penalties are harsh for those who have a third child. Ten percent of their pay or work points will be deducted from the time of the fourth month of pregnancy until the third child is 14 years old. The same penalties are imposed on couples who have their second child in fewer than 4 years and on women who have a child out of wedlock.

An additional punishment for the three-or-more-child couple is denial of any job promotion and loss of all work bonuses for at least 3 years. This is to make sure that couples who exceed the state limit for children do so at the price of personal sacrifice. They cannot prosper by doing extra work.

Are these policies working? By 1984 the fertility rate for women of childbearing age had dropped to 1.94. This is just below the number required for the population to remain stable. By 1986, the fertility rate had started to move up again, owing to a less stringent interpretation of the one couple one child rule.[9]

a. Make a map that depicts the problem-solution organization in this selection. (Refer back to Figure 10.4 on page 167).
b. Use the following questions to help you think about what you have just read.
1. *Why* were these policies enforced?
2. What were the *causes* of the policy?
3. How was the *problem solved?*
4. What were the *effects* of the solution?

---

[9] Tischler, p. 526. Used with permission. References have been removed.

5. What are the *implications* for future generations of people in China?
6. Where else in the world might such a policy work?
7. *What would happen if* this policy were implemented in the United States?
8. *Form an opinion* of your own about the workability of this policy in the United States.
9. *Think of alternative policies* to population control.

D. Application Exercises

1. Identify examples of controversial subjects in the classes you are taking. Bring them to class, list them on the board, and discuss how to ask questions and form opinions about these subjects.

2. Practice the reading process summarized at the beginning of this chapter on a reading assignment in another class or on one of the reading selections in the Appendix of this book:
   a. Preread the material by backgrounding the title, making a list of predictions of what you think it will be about, and by surveying and dividing it into meaningful chunks. Draw lines across the page each time the subject changes.
   b. Look for main ideas, using the encoded list of clues to main ideas that you made in Exercise B6.
   c. Underline selectively as you read, and jot the important ideas in the margin. Erase the lines you drew during prereading, if necessary, and draw new lines to indicate major subject changes. Write brief summaries at the end of each section either in the margin or in white space in the book.
   d. Write a one-page summary, in phrases only, of the entire selection. Map the important ideas.
   e. Ask some questions to help you think about the material. Refer back to pages 192–193 for question words to get you started.
   f. Monitor and evaluate your reading process. What worked? What can be changed? How can you apply what you have learned in your other classes this semester?

E. Topics for Your Learning Journal

1. Describe something you have read recently that caused you to form some new ideas of your own. What were these ideas?

2. Which suggestions to help you remember and think did you like best in this chapter? How can you use them?

3. Which suggestions to help you remember and think would be difficult for you to use? Why? What will you use instead to accomplish the same goals?

PART FOUR

Taking Exams

12 | *Preparing for Exams*

When you have finished reading this chapter, you will know how to do the following:

1. Make the best use of your study time just before an exam.
2. Organize the material you have to study.
3. Make study sheets to help you prepare for an exam.
4. Use other study methods to help you prepare for an exam.

PLAN YOUR STUDY TIME

In the last chapter you learned a number of techniques and activities to help you think, learn, and remember. All will help you prepare for exams both during the semester and the final study session that precedes the exam. This chapter explains additional study activities that will help you organize and learn material during the final study session.

The activities described in this chapter will only work, however, if you provide time to use them. One difference between high school and college is the time and effort necessary for effective exam preparation. Instead of the hour or two you may have spent studying for a high school test, you will now need ten, twelve, or even twenty hours to prepare for a college examination. Make a Time Management Worksheet to help you plan your exam study time. Look back at page 33 for a reminder on how to do this. Begin by writing the times you will take the exams on the worksheet. This is especially important when you are taking several exams during a brief period of time as during midterm or final exam weeks. Then add study time. Allow ample time to study for each exam and then add a couple of hours for possible interruptions and distractions. Now, get off to a fast start and work to finish your studying within the time you have allotted.

HOW TO GET STARTED—THE MASTER STUDY SHEET

For most courses you will have accumulated a lot of information from several sources by exam time. You may have, for example, a stack of lecture notes, anywhere from 50 to 450 pages of marked-up textbook assignments, handouts from class, notes on library reading, returned papers and other written assignments, old exams the teacher has let you see, vocabulary sheets, notes on review sessions, and finally, some ideas and insights of your own. This is a lot of material. When you get it all together and take a good look at it, your first question will probably be, "Where do I start?"

First, go to the source of information that has been the basis of organization, or backbone, of the course. In some courses the textbook provides the organizational framework, and the lectures clarify and amplify the text. In other courses the lectures are central, and the textbook and other materials are assigned to give additional information and other points of view.

Using this prime source of information and organization together with the syllabus, if one is available, you can begin to study for an exam by making a Master Study Sheet that lists the topics that have been covered during the semester in the order they were presented. Making a Master Study Sheet is a simple process that should not take you more than five or ten minutes. The purpose of it is to permit you to see all the parts of a course as an organized whole. You will also be able to see exactly what has to be studied, and you will then not omit anything. You may find that the class syllabus functions as a table of contents to the course because it lists the topics and the order in which they are covered. Rewrite the syllabus as a simple, brief list. This active reprocessing of the class topics will help you get a grasp of the course far better than simply rereading the syllabus.

Examples of Master Study Sheets made by students that have proved to be effective guides for study appear as Figures 12.1, 12.2, and 12.3. Notice that all these sheets are short, containing heads and subheads only. They contain no detail. Rather, they give an overall picture of what has been presented in the course and what needs to be studied for the exam. They pave the way for the second and most important step in the final study process, the making of study sheets.

THE SECOND STEP—STUDY SHEETS

The next step in studying for an exam is to make a detailed study sheet for each item listed on your Master Study Sheet. Notice on the Master

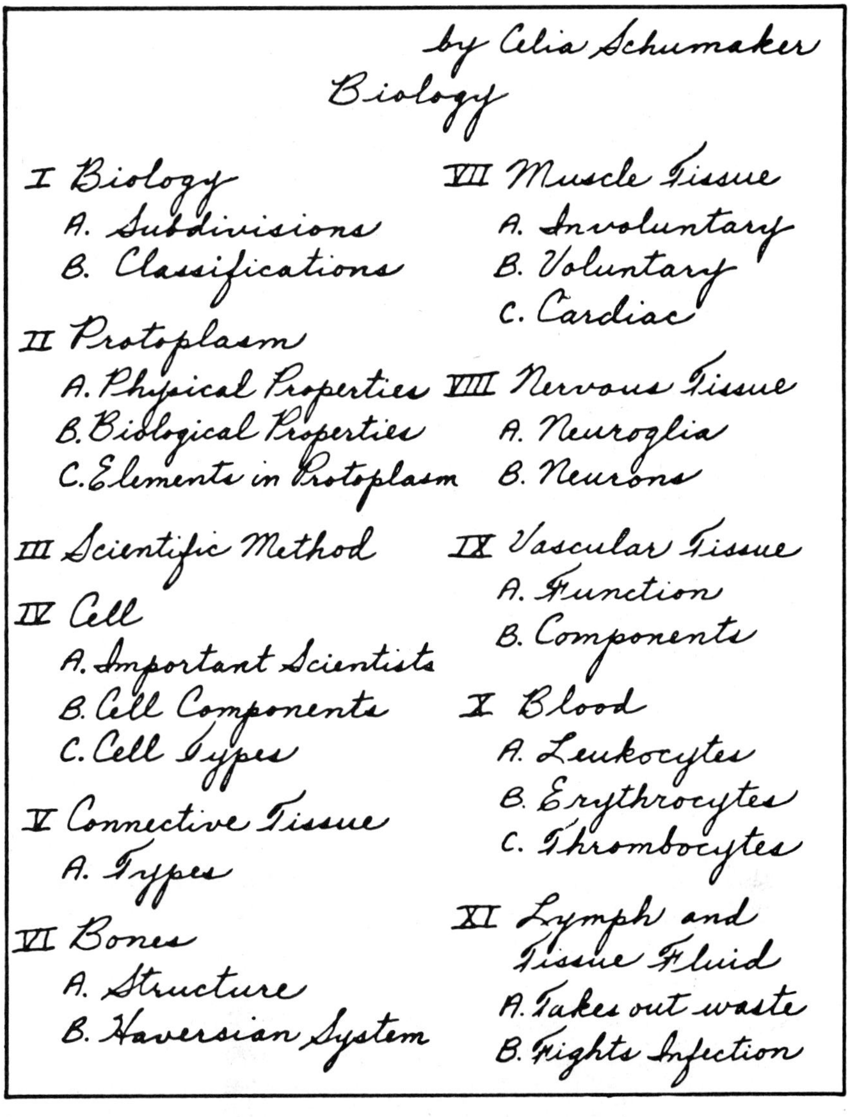

by Celia Schumaker
Biology

I Biology
  A. Subdivisions
  B. Classifications

II Protoplasm
  A. Physical Properties
  B. Biological Properties
  C. Elements in Protoplasm

III Scientific Method

IV Cell
  A. Important Scientists
  B. Cell Components
  C. Cell Types

V Connective Tissue
  A. Types

VI Bones
  A. Structure
  B. Haversian System

VII Muscle Tissue
  A. Involuntary
  B. Voluntary
  C. Cardiac

VIII Nervous Tissue
  A. Neuroglia
  B. Neurons

IX Vascular Tissue
  A. Function
  B. Components

X Blood
  A. Leukocytes
  B. Erythrocytes
  C. Thrombocytes

XI Lymph and Tissue Fluid
  A. Takes out waste
  B. Fights Infection

Figure 12.1   Example 1: Master Study Sheet for biology.

Study Sheet for biology, reproduced in Figure 12.1, that the sixth item is "Bones." Having made a quick list of the topics she wanted to study for her biology test on her Master Study Sheet, this student then made study sheets for each of the topics on her list. On her "Bones" sheet (Figure 12.4) she wrote out the material about bones that she thought she should learn for the exam. Figures 12.5 and 12.6 show two other examples of detailed study sheets. Their topics are drawn from the Master Study Sheets for history and for math, which you just looked at in Figures 12.2 and 12.3.

by Steve Garcia

History

I. The Great Awakening
   Jonathan Edwards
   George Whitfield

II. 3 Interpretations –
    Am. Rev.
    Patriotic (def.)
    Imperialistic (def.)
    Progressive (def.)

III. Loyalists (or Tories)

IV. Ben Franklin participation in Am. Rev.

V. Articles of Confederation

VI. Slavery during Rev.

VII. Religion after Rev.

VIII. Govt. after Rev.

IX. Federalists & Anti-Fed.

X. Hamilton's & Jefferson's views on how to run Govt. after Rev.

XI. French Rev.
    - Americans' view
    - Effect on U.S.

XII. Prelude to war of 1812.
     - Fall of good relations w/ Eng.

XIII. Military aspects of war of 1812.

XIV. Postwar attitude, Eng. & American
     - John Quincy Adams
     - Henry Clay

XV. America's success is not material
    - why?

Brief summary of Table of Contents: The War of 1812 proved that America could act as an independent nation. The American Government showed both weaknesses and strengths during the French Rev.

Figure 12.2   Example 2: Master Study Sheet for history.

by Gregg Keethler

Pre-Cal

I. Definition of Trigonometry
II. Directed Angles
III. Radian Measure
IV. Definition of Trigonometric Functions
V. Certain Triangles and Special Angles
VI. Acute Reference Angles and Functions
   of Acute Angles
VII. Trigonometric Functions
   A. Range
   B. Periodicity
   C. Graphs

Figure 12.3   Example 3: Master Study Sheet for preparation for calculus.

Now that you've looked at these examples, you can begin to see what characterizes good study sheets. All of the material on them is a reduced and simplified version of your lecture notes and other study materials. Notice that they contain lots of ideas, but they are all in *brief form*. Use a summary process, and write only enough so that when you glance at one of the words or phrases on the sheet, a host of related ideas and details will flood into your mind. If a phrase does not call forth a number of details, you may have to write a bit more about that subject in order to trigger your memory. One of the purposes of these sheets is to set the associative processes of your mind in motion.

Although the study sheets produced here are neat enough so that anyone can read them easily, yours need only be neat enough so that you can read them easily. Write big, write fast, and use only one side of a sheet of paper. You have to be able to read study sheets quickly.

Finally, *outline or map* your study sheets as much as possible. Make the main points stand out clearly by underlining or circling them. Write a list of items down the page and number each item. Remember that it is easier to learn and remember material when you

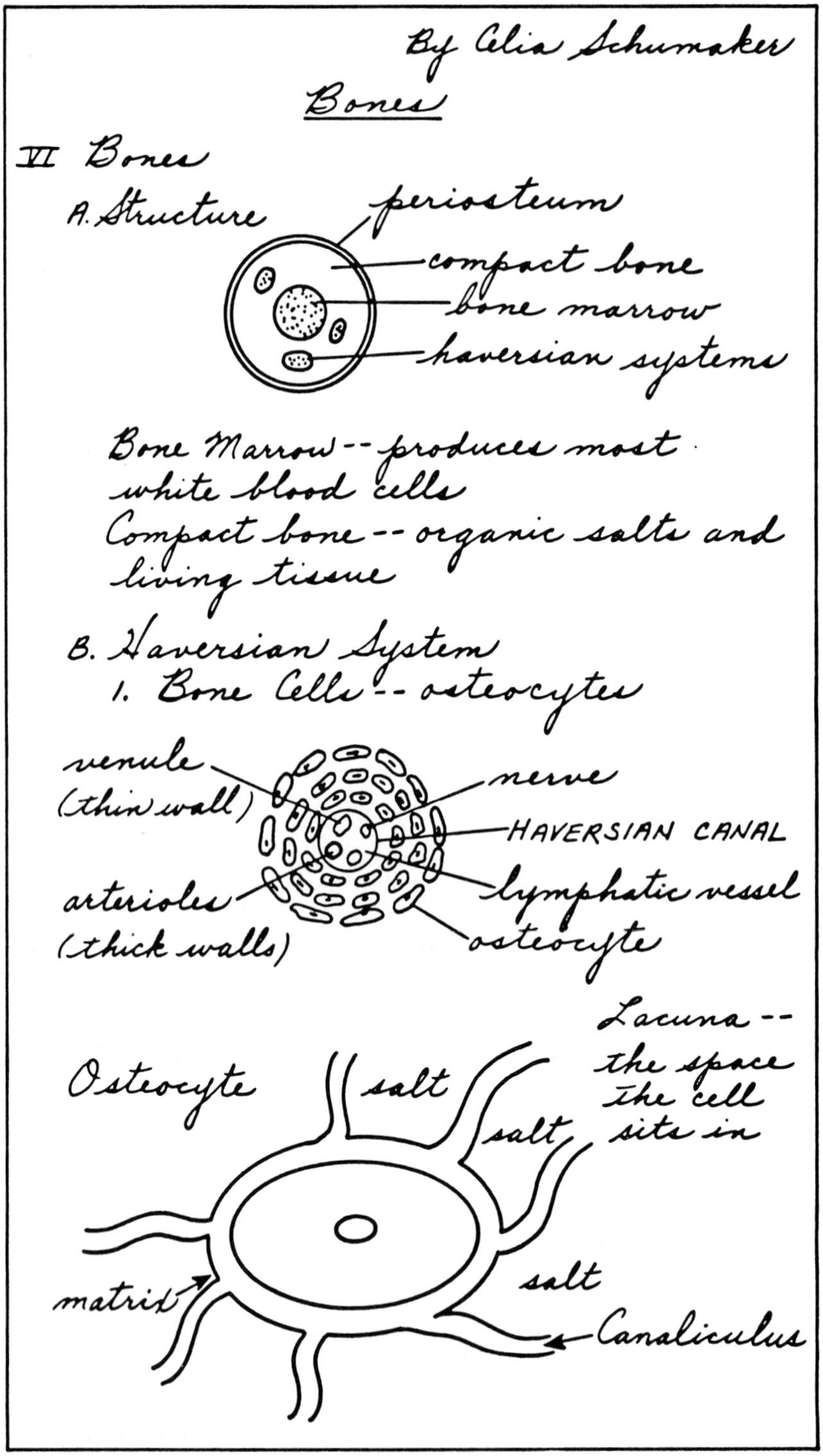

Figure 12.4 Example 1: A study sheet for biology.

by Steve Garcia

The Great Awakening

The Great Awakening

A massive religious revival, where screaming and swooning in the aisles became common. All people are damned and there is little they can do to salvage themselves.

A. Jonathan Edwards
  1. Rejected Puritans' covenant theology
  2. Established Princeton & Dartmouth, 1700's
  3. "Sinners in the hands of an angry God" -- famous sermon
  4. He was center of Rev.
  5. Sermons were against "man can save himself" theory
  6. Want a religion of the "heart & senses"

B. George Whitfield -- arrives in Phil. (1739) era.
  1. Methodism occurring in England
  2. "Willingness to resist authority of leaders brings guilt to the people" -- era of materialism
  3. Clergy was hostile toward revivalists
  4. Great Awakening leans toward democracy
  5. Revolution splits the churches
  6. Protestant churches arise in midst of Rev.
  7. Revivalists had no faith in established hierarchies.

Summary: The beginning of the American Revolution along with the Great Awakening can be considered as a radical democratic movement to the left.

Figure 12.5 Example 2: A study sheet for history.

can see it in an organized body. If it is easier for you to learn from maps than from outlines, then map sections of material on your study sheets as you learned to do in Chapter 10.

Where do you get the material for study sheets? Just as you did with your Master Study Sheet, start by drawing material from the primary organizing principle in the course—the lectures or the text-

by Gregg Keithler

<u>Acute Reference Angles and Functions of Acute Angles</u>

Definition: <u>Reference angle Ø of Θ</u> = smallest angle between terminal side of Θ and X axis.

* Theorem I: Any trig. function of an angle Θ in any quadrant is the same (except possibly for sign) as the same function of the acute reference angle Ø of Θ.

Definition of trig. functions for acute angles:

$$\sin\theta = \frac{opposite}{hypotenuse} \qquad \cos\theta = \frac{adjacent}{hypotenuse}$$

$$\tan\theta = \frac{opposite}{adjacent} \qquad \cot\theta = \frac{adjacent}{opposite}$$

$$\sec\theta = \frac{hypotenuse}{adjacent} \qquad \csc\theta = \frac{hypotenuse}{opposite}$$

Definition: If a and b are 2 angles such that
$a + b = \pi/2$,
then a and b are <u>complementary</u> angles.

Cofunctions: sine and <u>co</u>sine
tangent and <u>co</u>tangent
secant and <u>co</u>secant

Cofunction identities: For $0 < a < \frac{1}{2}\pi$

$$\sin a = \cos(\tfrac{1}{2}\pi - a) \qquad \cos a = \sin(\tfrac{1}{2}\pi - a)$$
$$\tan a = \cot(\tfrac{1}{2}\pi - a) \qquad \cot a = \tan(\tfrac{1}{2}\pi - a)$$
$$\sec a = \csc(\tfrac{1}{2}\pi - a) \qquad \csc a = \sec(\tfrac{1}{2}\pi - a)$$

Figure 12.6 Example 3: A study sheet for preparation for calculus.

book. Then turn to other sources for more information. But remember to keep everything organized according to the headings you have written at the top of your study sheets. The purpose of study sheets is to help you synthesize material from lectures, texts, and other sources such as notes on library books and articles, handout sheets, returned papers, and notes on review sessions. Finally, by all means add your own thoughts and insights in square brackets as they occur to you. Put down your own examples, your applications, comparisons, and diagrams so that you will be ready for those questions on the exam that ask you not only to reproduce the material you have learned, but also to tell what you *think* about it.

Making study sheets won't guarantee you success on every exam. You have to learn to make study sheets that are *complete* and that will supply you with the information you need to do well on an exam. Some students, especially those with sketchy lecture notes, make sketchy study sheets, and find when they take the exam that they don't know enough. Use your internal monitoring system to evaluate your study sheets as you make them. If they are sketchy or incomplete and you feel that they won't work, go back to the textbook or ask to look at a classmate's notes. Add information until you know the study sheet will help you learn what you need to know.

ADAPT STUDY SHEETS TO DIFFERENT TYPES OF EXAMS

Learn as much as possible about each exam before you take it so that you can devise special study sheets for special types of exams. Some ways to learn about an upcoming exam are to: (1) attend the classes that precede it to get exam information; (2) attend review sessions; (3) analyze old exams, if available, in exam files in the library or learning center; (4) analyze all of the exams you have taken so far in the course; and (5) ask the instructor about the nature of the exam. Instructors will usually tell students about the level of the questions. Questions can require that you reproduce information as you learned it, or they can require you to say what you think by asking you to make applications or interpretations. Study sheets can help you prepare for both types of questions. Instructors will also usually give information about the origin of the questions, that is whether they are instructor-made, departmental, or part of a test-bank that comes with the textbook.

To prepare for instructor-made exams, notice how the professor expects you to think about the material in the course. In a sense, instructors act as your guides. Make some effort to be sensitive to their approach. You will gain added insight into their approach and expectations if you analyze their favorite key direction words. Directions that ask you "to take a position and defend it," "to argue," "to evaluate," or "to judge" call for different thinking and study activities than questions that ask you "to list," "to explain," or "to define."

Departmental exams are written by several instructors and given to everyone enrolled in the various sections of a course. To prepare for departmental exams, try to get some old exams to study. If none are available, listen carefully to the information your instructor does give about the exam and attend all special review sessions.

To prepare for exams drawn from testbanks, study the textbook. Testbank questions are prepared by textbook authors rather than instructors and ask questions about the text. Make various types of study sheets, as described in this chapter, on textbook material.

Instructors will also tell you whether an exam will be objective, quantitative, or essay. Armed with this information, you can adapt your study sheets to help you prepare for specific types of exams. Here are some variations on the standard study sheet. The first two are particularly useful in preparing for objective exams. The third will help you prepare for quantitative exams, and the last three will help you prepare for essay exams.

1. Vocabulary study sheets. You will encounter questions that demand a knowledge of specialized vocabulary in virtually every exam you take. Here are some examples of such questions:

From biology: Which phylum do true bacteria belong to?
    a. cyanophyta
    b. schizophyta
    c. protista
    d. sarcodina
    e. bacillariophyceae

From chemistry: Is the conversion of chlorine to chloride an oxidation or reduction process?

From math: Explain the difference between *K-selection* and *K-combination.*

From history: What was the "Puritan ethic?"

Prepare for such questions by making vocabulary study sheets that list the specialized vocabulary in the left column and brief meanings in the opposite column. Then cover up the meanings until you can recite them. Don't go into an exam without knowing the specialized vocabulary. You are likely to have difficulty interpreting the questions let alone answering them.

In Chapter 6 you learned the difference between finding a one-word meaning for a specialized term and learning it as concept. In studying for exams, learn the specialized vocabulary as concepts. Know more than a one-word definition for these important terms.

2. *Identification study sheets.* Make identification study sheets to help you prepare for matching questions or questions that ask you to "identify." Here are examples of such questions.

From history: Identify:
The Magna Charta
Mary, Queen of Scots
The Great Awakening

From biology: Identify:
The Scientific Method
The Classification System

From literature: Identify:
Othello
Desdemona
Iago

Such questions require study sheets that are set up in the same way but that are more detailed than vocabulary study sheets. Write the important people, events, processes, or procedures in the left column and, in the right, some words and phrases that will help you later to compose short, detailed answers or to find the matching answer from a jumbled list.

3. *Quantitative study sheets.* Quantitative exams that require you to read and solve word problems and apply math skills call for different types of study sheets. Here is an example of a question from a quantitative exam:

From chemistry: Calculate the number of molecules in a 5.0 gram sample of water.

To answer such questions you should make study sheets that include units of measurement and their equivalents, formulas, equations, and practice problems. Making strategy cards, fact cards, and definition sheets as described in Chapter 10, pages 169–173, will also help you prepare for quantitative exams.

4. *Question-and-answer study sheets.* The standard study sheet, with the topic written at the top, helps you organize and learn material for both objective and essay tests. When you have finished making them, go back and write simple but comprehensive global questions for each major topic at the top of blank pieces of paper. Now, without looking at the study sheet, list in words and phrases all of the information you would use to answer these questions. When you have finished, look back at the study sheet and add information you missed. Figure 12.7 is an example of such a question along with its answer material.

Later, in the exam, no matter how a question on the topic might actually be phrased, you will be able to answer it by recalling information from your question-and-answer study sheet.

5. Comparison-and-contrast study sheets. Comparison and contrast questions are favorites of some professors. Since it is hard to come up with all the material you need for these questions in the exam itself, you should prepare ahead of time by making comparison-and-contrast study sheets. Remember that *comparison* asks you to show *similarities,* and *contrast* asks you to show *differences.* Here is an example of a question that asks you to contrast.

> *From history:* Write a brief essay contrasting the climate, geography, and economics of the three sections of English colonies in America as they developed by the eighteenth century.

Prepare for such questions by writing two or more topics that could be compared or contrasted at the top of each study sheet. Then list

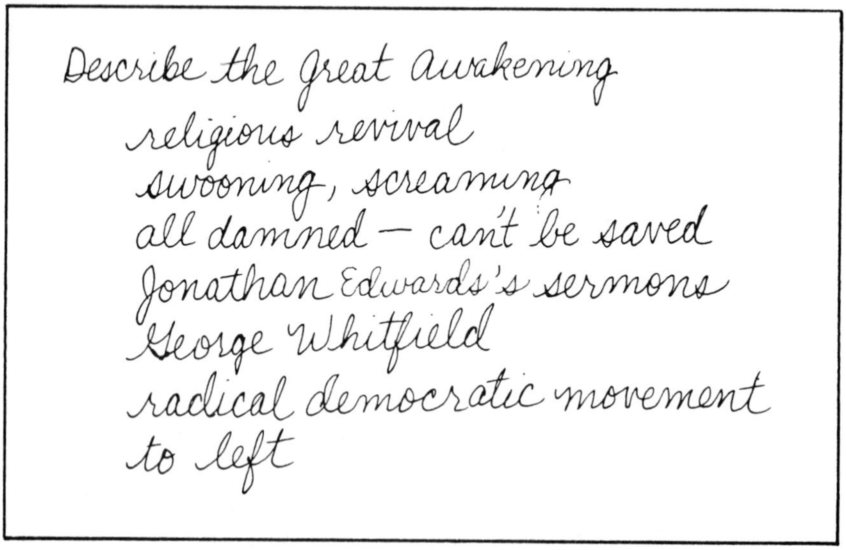

Describe the great awakening
religious revival
swooning, screaming
all damned — can't be saved
Jonathan Edwards's sermons
George Whitfield
radical democratic movement
to left

Figure 12.7   A question-and-answer study sheet about the material on the study sheet in Figure 12.5.

the similarities and differences. In listing similarities, note that only one list is necessary. Imagine putting the two items you are comparing side by side, looking for characteristics that they *both* share, and making one list. In contrasting, however, you slide the items apart and make two lists to show their differences. Reread the history question above about the English colonies. To help you anticipate and study for this question, you could have made a study sheet entitled: *3 sections of English Colonies in 18th Century*. The similarities would be a single list of the features all three sections share. The differences would require three lists, each headed by one of the three colonial sections. The three lists would show their differences in such areas as climate, geography, and economics. In the exam, you would mentally refer to this sheet while composing your answer.

6. *Mental elaboration study sheets.* Most professors like to write some questions that call for your original thoughts on various subjects. Here are some examples of such questions:

> *From philosophy:* What attitudes do you believe are essential attributes of yourself? Are these attributes the kind of things that might survive your bodily death?

> *or*

> Give a brief statement of what you think philosophy is and what some of the tasks of philosophy are. What views of philosophy would you *reject* and why would you reject them?

> *From a management course:* On the basis of the readings in class and your own opinion, do you believe that collective bargaining is or is not on the way out? Why? Should it be adversarial?

These questions call for extensive reflection, and you will be better prepared for them if you have made some mental elaboration study sheets. Label them with the major topics in the course as you would standard study sheets. Then start thinking and jot down your thoughts. Think of real-life examples and applications, of consequences or effects, of solutions, of how you personally might be influenced or changed. Associate, compare, and contrast new material with material already familiar to you. Think of arguments for and arguments against. Make value judgments. Write down your thoughts and your beliefs. All this will help you get ready for the questions that direct you to *argue, evaluate, judge, take a position, defend,* or *tell what you think* or *believe.*

HOW TO USE STUDY SHEETS

By the time you have finished making your study sheets, you will have done a considerable amount of studying. You may find that you know almost everything you have written on your sheets already. Put away all your other notes and books and finish learning what is on these sheets. The best way to do this is to use recitation. Look at a brief point on a study sheet and then, looking away, see how much additional information you can think of that has to do with that point. If there are lists to be learned, look away from the sheets and repeat to yourself the items on the list until you know them. If you repeat the material out loud, you will learn it even faster.

Go over your study sheets more than once. You learned in Chapter 11 that a particularly good time to study them is just before you go to sleep on the night before the exam because there will be no interference from other learning while you sleep. Go over them again when you wake up. Try to spend an hour with them just before the exam. If you have two exams in a row, use the time between exams, even if it's only ten minutes, to read rapidly through the second set of study sheets. You will then go into your exams with a full and orderly mind.

WHY DO STUDY SHEETS WORK?

The chairman of a chemistry department was baffled recently by a group of students scoring between 50 and 60 percent on an examination. He decided to give them another chance by giving them the exact same exam again. One week later, with plenty of warning, he gave the same students the exam they had taken the week before. The class average edged its way up to a mere 75. He said that they all could have had 100 percent simply by taking the time to look up the answers to the questions, memorize them, and write them on the exam. When he asked them how they had studied, most said that they had "read through the first exam a couple of times."

Many students think that reading something through two or three times will result in their learning the material. It doesn't, because reading is a passive way of studying. So is listening. Reading and listening involve mainly the short-term memory, and information is lost quickly. Writing and speaking, on the other hand, are the active ways of studying. In order to make study sheets, you have to write. In order to study from them, you have to speak, even if you are only mumbling to yourself. Writing and speaking are learning activities that move material from the short-term memory to the long-term memory.

Think about the other learning activities involving the long-term memory that you employ when you make study sheets. Study sheets force you to get all the different materials for a course *synthesized* and *organized* so that you can retain it in your long-term memory more easily. They force you to *elaborate* and *associate*. They also provide you with something to *visualize* during the exam itself. You visualize the study sheet that contains information about the question, and you then answer the question more easily. Finally, study sheets force you to *recite* by looking away and either writing or speaking the material to be learned until you know it.

SIX OTHER ACTIVE WAYS TO PREPARE FOR EXAMS

1. *Study in Groups.* You may decide to study with a group of other students. Group study will work for you only if you have already studied quite a bit and can be an active contributor to the group. Write study sheets and spend some time with them first. Add to them and clarify them when you meet with others. Make sure you do your share of talking. Those students in the group who write and talk learn the most. Those who listen learn the least. If you don't get a chance to talk in the group, it is better to study alone and talk to yourself.

   Group study is especially important for math and science exams. Most exams of this type require problem solving, and you can solve more problems and get the insights necessary to solve them more efficiently if you are working with a partner or a small group of students. Use old exams, lecture notes, and textbooks to locate practice problems.

2. *Write Questions and Answer Them.* Think of possible test questions, jot the ideas down for them, and actually write out answers to some of these questions. It may help you to get a tutor or a classmate to read your answers and go over them with you. They can give an opinion about what you did well and where you need to improve. If you are preparing for an oral exam, practice speaking the answers instead of writing them.

3. *Turn Your Textbook into a Reference Book for Open Book Exams.* Open book exams are given frequently in math, science, and engineering classes, but also sometimes in other classes. The usual reason is that the textbook contains large amounts of complicated material that students cannot be expected to memorize. Students *can* be expected to understand this material, however, to locate it quickly, and be able to use it to answer questions. Prepare for open book exams by locating, marking, and labeling important tables, formulas, theorems, and other material with small self-sticking notes. You can buy a pad of these in the bookstore. You can also reproduce the most important information that you will have to refer to frequently on 3×5 or 4×6 cards. When you study later with a group, you can practice using the materials you have prepared. Make certain you have identified what you need and that you can locate it quickly.

4. *Recite.* If you do not have time to make study sheets, you should still recite material until you know it. Read your lecture notes, look away, and recite the information in them until you can do so from memory. Review the marginal notes and summaries in your textbooks and recite them also. Remember that just reading material, even if you read it two or three times, will not cause it to remain in your memory. Reciting, however, does help you commit material to memory.

5. *Get Organized to Take Each Exam.* Find out exactly where each exam will be given, at what time, and what materials you will need such as examination booklets and pens. If the exam is given in the classroom where you learned the material, you are in luck. Research shows you will answer questions better in the room where you learned the material in the first place. Try to spend part of your study time in that room also. This can make you more at ease during the test itself and help recall.

6. *Use Positive Self-Talk to Improve Confidence and Motivation.* By the time you have followed the suggestions in this chapter, you deserve to feel positive about your ability to do well on the exam. Use positive self-talk as you study. Remind yourself that you *have* learned a great deal already and that you can learn the rest of it. Remind yourself of this both while you study and when you enter the exam room. Positive self-talk will help you remain confident and ready to do your best.

STANDARDIZED TESTS

You will not escape taking standardized tests. They are used more and more frequently to measure strengths, weaknesses, and special competencies of large groups of students. They are used to place students in college and, later, in special classes. They are also used as exit tests in some institutions to measure and evaluate what students have learned. You can and should prepare for these exams. Test preparation can raise scores significantly.

How should you prepare? An information bulletin is available for most standardized tests. You can get a copy, or find out where to get a copy when you register for the exam. Read it carefully as soon as you get it. These bulletins usually describe test format, the material to be tested, and provide some sample questions. They also tell you when and where the test will be held, give suggestions about how to do well on the test, and sometimes list test preparation manuals or other materials that you can study to help you prepare for the test.

You should try to get a copy of a sample test and then practice taking it under timed conditions, just as if you were taking the test itself. You should also score it. Sample tests are sometimes available in test information bulletins. They are also available in test preparation manuals, available in bookstores. If you can't find the one you need, go to your testing center to find out how to obtain specific test preparation materials. When you have scored your practice test, locate your weak areas and concentrate your test preparation there. Test preparation manuals contain practice materials that will help you review and even learn new material to help you improve in weak areas.

Plan your test preparation strategy. You can work exercises in the manuals, write material on study sheets or cards to recite later, study with a classmate, or join a test preparation class. Classes are usually taught through the Testing Office or the Learning Assistance Center. Whichever you choose, plan to spend several hours preparing for a standardized exam. This is especially important if you are taking it to get into a college or program or to place out of certain courses. You want the exam to demonstrate the best that you are capable of doing. That will only happen if you are well prepared to take it.

Complete your test preparation by taking another timed practice test. Make certain that you are familiar with the format and requirements of the test. You need to know time limits, understand the types of questions and how to answer them, and know whether or not to guess when you are not sure of the answer. At this point you also need to decide what to do if you do not make the score you hope for on the exam. Set an alternate goal plan.

At the Very Least . . .

This chapter has dealt with the ideal way of improving your exam preparation. If you can't follow all of the suggestions, *at the very least* do this much:

1. Read through your lecture notes and make some study sheets.
2. Survey the book and make additional study sheets.
3. At least one hour before the exam, stop, put away books and lecture notes, and recite from your study sheets until exam time.
4. Work with a group to prepare for math and science exams.

SUMMARY

Get yourself organized to study for an exam by first making a Time Management Worksheet and then by making a one-page Master Study Sheet on which you list the blocks of material that will be on the test. This sheet shows you exactly what you will need to study and prevents you from accidentally omitting any important material. It should take five or ten minutes to make it. The second and most important step in studying for an exam is to make study sheets for each item on the Master Study Sheet. Draw material for these sheets from lectures, textbooks, and other sources, and organize and synthesize them by topic. Outline the material as much as possible, and write it so that you can read it quickly and easily. Make variations of the standard study sheet to help you prepare for different types of exams: vocabulary, identification, quantitative, question-and-answer, comparison-and-contrast, and mental elaboration study sheets. Use active ways of study that involve the long-term memory such as speaking and writing. Other ways to prepare for exams include group study, asking and answering questions, labeling and tagging important material in your textbooks, recitation, and getting organized to take the test. You should also include some positive self-talk to improve confidence and motivation. Prepare for standardized tests by using practice tests to learn test format and by studying weak areas. Include some positive self-talk to improve confidence and motivation.

EXERCISES

A. *Monitor Your Comprehension of This Chapter*

Write quickly, in phrases rather than complete sentences, the information in this chapter that you understand and remember. Look back through your marginal notes and summaries and add what you left out. Is anything in the chapter unclear? Jot it down to ask about in class. Has reading the chapter caused you to think of new insights or examples of your own? Jot them down.

B. *Class Exercises*

1. *Small groups.* Make a Master Study Sheet for the topics and sub-topics covered so far in this book. Or, if you are using this book as supplementary material in a class, make a Master Study Sheet for the material you have studied in this book so far. Write with black markers on large pieces of newsprint, if possible, and tape up your study sheets with masking tape so all members of the class can read them.

2. *Small groups.* Make standard study sheets entitled "How to Prepare for an Exam," "How to Read a Textbook," and "How to Take Lecture Notes." Then make question-and-answer study sheets on the three topics.

3. *Small groups.* Make a comparison-and-contrast study sheet entitled "Surveying a Book and Surveying a Chapter." Each member of the group should practice reciting the steps for each process until they have committed them to memory.

4. *Individual.* Make a mental elaboration study sheet entitled "How to Think about the Material for an Exam."

C. *Application Exercises*

1. Make Master Study Sheets for the material covered so far in each of your other classes.

2. Make standard study sheets to help you prepare for the next exam you will take in one of your other classes.

D. *Topics for Your Learning Journal*

1. Write some examples of positive self-talk that would help you while preparing for an exam.

2. List the courses you are presently taking and the types of exams you expect in them. Then describe the types of study sheets that would help you prepare for each type of exam.

13 | Taking Exams: Objective, Quantitative, Essay, Standardized

When you have finished reading this chapter, you will know the following:

1. How to take objective exams.
2. How to take the quantitative exams given in math and other problem-solving classes.
3. How to plan and write an essay exam.
4. How to combat test anxiety.
5. How to avoid the most common errors students make in taking exams.

THE OBJECTIVE EXAM

The main characteristic of objective exams is that nearly all the material you will be working with is printed on the exam itself. You will not have to search your mind for all of the information needed to answer the questions, as you do with essay exams. In many instances all you have to do is recognize the correct answer. For example, in a true-or-false test you recognize which statements are true and which are false. In a multiple-choice test you recognize which of several answers is correct. In a matching test all the material is there—your job is to rearrange the presented material so that it is accurate. In a fill-in question you read the supplied context for a clue to the missing word you are being asked to supply.

Because the material is there to recognize, arrange, or complete, students often believe that objective exams are easier than essay exams—and consequently they do not need to study for an objective test. They believe that they can go in, guess, and do well enough. But guessing is never good enough. *You need to study for objective exams just as much as for other exams.* The best way to do so is to organize your ideas on study sheets, and then go over these sheets until you know the material.

Here are examples of each of the four major types of objective exam questions. They are straightforward questions with no tricky wording and with nothing to throw you off. Your chances of answering these questions correctly by guessing, however, are slim.

A True-False Question

T   F   The language spoken in England from 1150 to 1500 (the language of the *Canterbury Tales*) is called Old English.

> The answer is *false.* The language of this period is called Middle English. If you don't know this fact, you can't answer the question.

A Fill-In Question

The country in which the Renaissance had its first great expression was ————.

> The answer is *Italy.* If you have made a study sheet on the Renaissance, you will know this fact.

A Matching Question

Draw lines from the names of the people in the first column to their areas of specialization in the second column.

1. Doré   1. Social worker
2. Tolstoy   2. Engineer
3. Brunel   3. Painter
4. Engels   4. Illustrator
5. Millet   5. Novelist

> Go ahead and guess on this one and see how you do. Compare your answers to the correct ones: 1-4; 2-5; 3-2; 4-1; 5-3. Unless you already knew why these people are remembered by history, you probably didn't come out very well on your guessing.

A Multiple-Choice Question

In what century did the Protestant Reformation begin?

a. 16th   c. 18th
b. 19th   d. 17th

> The correct answer is *a.* The question is not a tricky one. You either know the answer or you don't. If you have studied from a complete study sheet on the Reformation, you will know the answer.

It is important, then, to study thoroughly for an objective exam. But sometimes, even when you study a great deal, you can still have trouble with these exams. The sample questions you have just read are simple and straightforward. Objective exam questions can, however, be confusing, tricky, require special knowledge just to read them, or be put together in an unexpected way. The following question, for example, requires knowledge of a specialized term to answer it.[1]

What is a writ of habeus corpus?
a. a requirement that suspects be read their rights
b. a court order to produce or release a person in police custody
c. an injunction, or a court order, to stop a particular activity
d. a document initiating a military court martial
e. a document requiring an official to perform some duty.

Notice that if you do not know what a writ of habeus corpus is, then all of these answers sound plausible. You must have studied to know that b is the correct answer.

Here is another multiple choice question that requires both exam preparation and careful reading of the test question.

In *Regents of the University of California v. Bakke* (1978) the Supreme Court
a. held that it is unlawful to establish racial quotas
b. held that race can be considered, along with other qualifications, as part of an admissions program
c. established the notion of a "suspect" racial classification
d. held that quotas are acceptable to rectify past discriminations
e. a and b

The answer is *e.*

Careful, thorough study is important in preparing for objective exams. When you take the exam itself, you will need some *test-taking strategies* to help you. Here are some suggestions.

1. *Read through the whole exam rapidly,* answering only the questions you know. Put a mark in the margin by all questions that you are not absolutely sure of so that you will be able to find them easily when you come back later to answer them.

2. *Go back to the unanswered questions. Read each of them with a pencil in hand, circling the key words that identify the information asked for in the question. Underline all words like* only, all, always, never, sometimes, *or* which is not. These words can have a big influence on the way you interpret the question.

[1] All of the sample objective test questions in this chapter have been drawn from college exams. The next two are from a government final.

After you have marked the question as suggested, attack it from two angles. First, look at the encircled words and think of what you know about each of them. Visualize your study sheets and your lists of key terminology. Bring your knowledge to bear on the question. Second, analyze the question for tricky wording by carefully considering the qualifying words you have underlined and how they influence the meaning of the question.

3. *If you are stuck on a multiple-choice question, read the question again, stop and think of the answer, and then look for it.* In a good multiple-choice question all of the answers are plausible. Sometimes you can read through the answers and become confused. It may help to stop and think of the correct answer, and then read through the choices again.

4. *Sometimes in answering a difficult multiple-choice question a process of elimination will help you* at least to narrow down the choices. Here is an example of how you can use this process:

Why are supporting details used by authors?

a. To move smoothly from one idea to the next.

b. To help the reader distinguish the main points.

c. To clarify a main point and make it more interesting.

d. To show the relationship between a major point and a detail.

Now, perhaps for the moment at least, you may not be able to remember why authors use supporting details and, consequently, cannot use suggestion 3 above. So you move through the choices. Answer *a* is a description of the function of a transition, so you eliminate it. Answers *b* and *d* are also functions of the transition. You are sure of that much. So, by the process of elimination, answer *c* must be correct.

5. *Don't automatically eliminate the choices "all of the above," "none of the above,"* or answers like "both a & b" or "a, b, & c." Here are examples of questions in which "all of the above" and "a, b, & c" are the correct answers.

Which of the following is an example of humanitarian reform in the 19th century?

a. Abolishment of slavery

b. Prison reform

c. Children's hospitals

d. All of the above

Which of the following are likely to be counted among Washington lobbyists?

a. former administration officials

b. former members of Congress

c. former congressional staffers

>   d. a and b
>
>   e. a, b, and c

If you use the process of elimination and can't eliminate anything, choose "all of the above" as your answer. If, on the other hand, you find that you can eliminate every answer, and "none of the above" is the last answer, choose it.

6. *Always find out if you can mark more than one choice in answering multiple-choice questions.* Students often take for granted that all multiple-choice questions have only one correct answer. Some students fail exams because they assume this when, in fact, more than one answer can be circled for each question. Instructors will usually tell you in the directions printed at the top of the exam if more than one answer can be marked. If there are no instructions, and you have reason to believe that more than one answer could be chosen, ask your professor. Here is a question in which two of the choices are correct. See if you can figure out which ones they are:

>   Which of the following are part of the process of surveying a book?
>
>   a. Read the table of contents.
>
>   b. Read the introduction.
>
>   c. Read a sample chapter from the middle of the book.
>
>   d. Quickly glance at each page.

Both *a* and *b* are correct answers.

If you have read all the questions on the test as carefully as possible, if you have circled the key words, underlined and analyzed the qualifying words, used the process of elimination to arrive at answers, and tried to think up your own examples to clarify the question—in short, if you have followed all the above suggestions and you are still stuck on a few questions, there are a few more things you can try before you resort to blind guessing.

7. *Sometimes you will read a multiple-choice question and draw a complete blank. Leave the question itself and read each of the answers separately and thoughtfully.* Sometimes one of them will give you a clue to the meaning of the question itself.

8. Another way to attack a difficult multiple-choice question is to *read the question repeatedly with each separate answer.* Sometimes one of the answers will appear to complete the thought of the question better than the others. This won't guarantee that the answer is the right one, but reading the question in this way will give you a slightly better chance at the correct answer than blind guessing.

9. If you can, without distorting the test writer's meaning, *paraphrase or restate a difficult question in your own words.* Then try to think of some examples that will make the meaning even clearer.

Go back and reread the original question and see if it is easier to answer than it was at first.

10. *Use what you have learned from the test itself* to help you answer the tough questions you have saved for the end. Actively look for information to help you answer the questions on which you are stuck.

11. *As an absolute last resort, guess on the remaining questions.* But before you guess, make sure there is no penalty for wrong answers. Some test writers subtract all the wrong answers, or at least a percentage of the wrong answers, from the right answers. If such is the case, answer only the questions you know for sure. Guessing could lower your grade by giving you more wrong answers than if you had left them blank. If there is no penalty for guessing, answer all the questions, even if you guess. Most professors count all unanswered questions as wrong.

12. *Proofread the entire test before you turn it in.* You may have learned new information from the test itself which makes it obvious that some of your answers are wrong. If so, change them. The old idea that your first impulse answer on an objective test is always the right one has now been proved a myth. Change any of your answers if you have good reason to do so. All last-minute changes, however, should be well thought out.

THE QUANTITATIVE EXAM [2]

You will encounter quantitative exams in your math, science, and other technical courses. In such exams you will be called upon to solve math problems, to read and solve word problems, and to apply math skills. Here are some *test-taking strategies* to keep in mind when you are taking exams of this type.

1. *Start with the questions you know how to do.* Carefully read and work each of them. Then go back and try the harder ones.

2. *When you go back to the unanswered questions, read each of them carefully for clues to help you answer these questions.* Here is an example:

> What is the density of an ideal gas at standard temperature and pressure in molecules per cubic centimeter?

Even if you do not know or remember what density is, this question tells you how to work the problem because it asks for the density in molecules per cubic centimeter. That means you want to divide the

---

[2] From materials supplied by Barbara Prater.

number of molecules by the volume they occupy, given in cubic centimeters.

3. *Use your time well.* Quite often the points allotted to each question are noted on the exam. If you are pressed for time, work on the problems that are worth most. Don't waste ten minutes of an hour exam on a five-point problem, unless it is the only one left.

4. *Never write just an answer. Always show all your work* so that your professor can see how you arrived at the answer. Don't skip steps or do them in your head because you think they are trivial. Skipping easy steps encourages careless mistakes. Here is an example of a problem given to a large group of college freshmen:

Given the equation $PV = nRT$, solve for n.

Fifteen percent of the students solved this problem in their heads and came up with the wrong answer: $n = RT/PV$. If they had written

$PV = nRT$ (To find n, divide both sides of the equation by RT)
$PV/RT = n \cdot RT/RT$
$n = PV/RT$,

then they would have avoided their mistake, because they'd have put in the necessary step.

5. *Remember that you are explaining to the professor what you know, so do it logically and clearly.* Always explain, preferably by equation, how you got your answer. Here is an example of a question with three answers that are labeled "bad," "fair," and "good." Accompanying each answer is an explanation that tells why they are labeled as they are.

The question: If it takes $\frac{1}{16}$ lb. of lettuce to make one taco, how many lbs. of lettuce will be required to make 100 tacos?

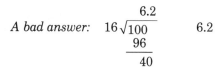

A bad answer:

This answer is bad because the professor has little idea of how the student arrived at the answer. You can often get partial credit for partially correct reasoning, if you have shown your logic. This answer, however, does not give a clear idea of the logical thought process the student used to answer this question.

A fair answer: $\frac{1}{16} \cdot 100 = 6.2$ lb.

Here the student has shown clearly the process used for finding the answer. But whether the student was thinking clearly or was just lucky is unclear.

A good answer: $^{1}/_{16}$ lb. lettuce/taco $\cdot$ 100 tacos = 6.2 lb. lettuce

Here the student has shown the entire thought process involved in calculating the correct answer.

6. *Check when you have finished to make sure that your answers are logical.* For instance, if your answer to the above problem was less than $^{1}/_{16}$ lb. of lettuce, you would know it was wrong; $^{1}/_{16}$ lb. was needed for one taco and you have 100.

Check to see if your answers are consistent with each other and if they are consistent with other information on the test. For instance, if you need 6.2 lb. of lettuce for 100 tacos, and later calculate 1 lb. will make 200 tacos, one answer is obviously wrong. Use one question to help you with another. Quite often problems are related simply because few good or easily worked problems exist.

7. *If you think you are missing a necessary piece of information,* check to see if you calculated it or if it was given in a previous problem or in a previous part of the question.

8. *Check to see if you used all of the data given.* Not often will a professor put extra or unnecessary information into a problem. If you are given a piece of information that you didn't use, you may not have worked the problem correctly. This rule is less applicable for upper-level courses.

9. *Proofread for careless errors.* If there is time, a good way of locating careless errors is to rework the problems rapidly to see if you come up with the same answers the second time. When you do not, locate the errors and correct them.

THE ESSAY EXAM

The essay exam answer is written in paragraphs. Each essay answer should begin with a starting sentence that comes right to the point. The remainder of the answer should address all parts of the question in relevant detail and reflect the writer's skill in topic development and composition. Here are some *test-taking strategies* to help you develop skill in writing answers for this type of exam.

Before you begin to write:

1. Put your name on your exam booklet and read through the entire test rapidly. Read the general instructions to determine exactly what is required. Notice point distributions for each question and make a quick estimate of how much time you should allot to answering each question. Now quickly read the questions. There may be as few as three or as many as ten. Select the easiest ones to answer first. Don't panic if there are some you don't know. Lapses of memory are normal during exams. After you have started writing, information for the other questions will often come to you. All this helps you see what you are up against before you begin to write so that later, as you write the answer to the first question, you won't be worrying about the other ones.

2. Analyze, mark, and number the parts of each question before you begin to write the answer.   Don't let haste or nervousness cause you to misread important words in the question, such as *physiological* for *psychological,* or *environmental* for *evolutional.* Underline key terminology. Circle the words that tell you what to do, such as *compare, contrast, list, describe, enumerate, critically evaluate, explain,* and then do exactly what those words direct you to do as you think through and compose your answer. You should also number the parts of the question so that you won't neglect to answer any part of it. Finally, notice, if you are asked to reproduce material from the textbook or lectures, if you are asked to give your own opinions, evaluations, examples, or if you are asked to do a combination of these things. Make sure you do exactly what you are directed to do.

Here is an example of a question that has been marked and numbered and can now be answered:

1. (Explain the difference) between specialized and general vocabulary and give an example of each. (Name and describe) three methods for learning both types of vocabulary that are taught in the textbook. (Identify the method) that works best for you, (give an example) of how you have used it, and (explain why) you prefer it to other methods.

You may find it helpful to mentally rephrase or rewrite essay questions as a series of positive statements that help you understand exactly what you must accomplish in your answer:

1. I will explain the major difference between specialized and general vocabulary.
2. I will give an example of each type.
3. I will name and describe *three* methods from the textbook for learning *both* types of vocabulary.
4. I will identify the method that works best for me.

5. I will give an example of how I have used that method.
6. I will explain why I prefer it to other methods.

Such close analysis helps you understand a question and reminds you to answer all parts of it.

3. Understand the meaning of key direction words and then do what they ask. Here is a list of some common ones:

a. *Compare* asks you to show similarities. It can also ask you to show differences. Read the question carefully to see if you are asked to do both.

b. *Contrast* asks you to show differences.

c. *List, outline,* or *enumerate* ask you to abandon usual paragraph format and to number and list items down the page.

d. *Explain* and *discuss* call for a complete explanation, written in paragraphs, with a topic sentence and plenty of supporting details from the course itself.

e. *Describe* asks for characteristics and even details that you can visualize.

f. *Critically evaluate, interpret, give your opinion about,* or *tell what you believe* invite you to include your own ideas again in paragraph form.

g. *Identify* means to name and to give information.

h. *Define* asks for the meaning of the item.

i. *Prove* or *show* asks you to persuade or convince the reader with explanations, quotations, statistics, facts, or even graphs or charts.

4. Jot ideas for each answer in the margin of the exam next to each question. Number these ideas to form an outline. Here is a question with such an outline jotted in the margin:

1. spiral
   a. together - file
   d. inserts - mix up
4. I use: 2 looseleaf
   a. everything - inserts
   d. loose items - holes tear
3. folders
   a. separate - inserts   d. flimsy - loose papers

There are at least three basic ways to organize your study materials. Name them and describe at least two advantages and disadvantages of each system. Briefly describe the method you have chosen.

If you are not allowed to write on the exam itself, you might write these jottings on a piece of scratch paper or on a page from your exam booklet. Some students who know their material well write only the initials of words. If initials aren't enough, then write words. But write as little as possible and as quickly as possible.

This writing of ideas for your answers should continue throughout the exam. For instance, if you are writing the answer to one question and you suddenly think of an idea for another question, stop and jot it down immediately so that you won't forget it.

Your brief outlines will help you in several ways. They will help you write well-organized essay answers. They will give you confidence and reduce tension because you will know that you have something to say for each question when you come to it. Furthermore, if you continue to jot down ideas as you work on the exam, your confidence will increase, and the tension you usually feel at the beginning of an exam will be channeled into productive activity. Finally, these brief outlines will help you make the mental switch from one question to the next. Most people have had the experience of concentrating so hard on the first question that when they turn to the next one they feel drained and can't think of anything to say. A brief outline helps you move from one question to the next quickly.

Depending on the length of the exam, it will take you five to ten minutes to analyze the questions and preplan your answers. Don't let it take longer than this before you begin to write, and don't be bothered by the person sitting next to you who may have filled half an examination booklet before you begin. Just remind yourself that ultimately you are saving yourself time. When you begin, you will be able to concentrate on composition and move smoothly from one question to the next rather than inefficiently groping for ideas.

As you write:

1. Manage your time. Keep glancing at your watch so you will not go over the time you have allotted for each question. Remember that if you run out of time and write only half of the exam perfectly, you will get 50 percent on the exam.

2. Answer all parts of the question. Refer back to the numbered parts of the question or to your list of positive statements about what your answer should contain. Make sure you answer every part in detail.

3. Come right to the point in the first sentence. You might begin an answer to the question above, about ways to organize study materials, like this:

> The three basic ways to organize study materials are in spiral notebooks, in looseleaf notebooks, or in folders with pockets. The advantages of spiral notebooks are . . .

4. Stick to your outline. Start a new paragraph for each new section on your outline. Give details and examples. Remember your reader who will be looking for a complete and efficient answer that is clear and easy to comprehend.

5. Be specific by using various types of supporting detail in your answer. Quotations, statistics, examples, facts, comparisons, contrasts, even graphs and diagrams are all appropriate when they make your answer clear and show that you know what you are talking about.

6. Use transitions for even more clarity. Any type of transition can be appropriately used in essay answers. Preoutlining, enumeration with key phrases, transitional words and phrases, and paragraph linking are particularly appropriate.

7. Write all that is relevant and no more. Some exam questions seem to invite long, rambling answers that contain options, personal experiences, bits of information from the course, quotations from the professor, and so on. Avoid the tendency to pad your answers, digress, or make things up, hoping that they might be right. Answers of this type waste your time in the exam and your professor's reading time. Read the question in Figure 13.1. The student could have gotten off the subject in responding to this question. Instead she marked the important words in the question, numbered its parts, and then wrote a brief outline in the margin before she began to compose her answer. In her answer she used material that she learned in the course itself, came right to the point in the first sentence, and wrote a tight, efficient, and complete answer that is supported with examples. She received full credit when the professor graded it.

After you finish writing:

1. Proofread and neatly edit your work. Don't take time to recopy. Instead, read your answer as though you were the reader

The question

phys. arous.	1. (How) do you know what you
labeling	"feel"?
ex: speech	2. (Discuss.)
date	

The answer by Sandra Sweeney

One knows what one is feeling by two methods. The first is physiological arousal. The body becomes aroused and feels different (maybe increased heart rate, sweating, respiration, stomach pain, and so on). However, since there are no really clear differences in physiological arousal between various emotions, one must also label the feeling. This is done by analyzing the situation for clues that may lead the person to identify appropriately what he or she's feeling and to recall past similar experiences for additional clues. For example, if one is about to make a speech in front of an audience, past experience labels the butterflies in the stomach as stage fright. If one experiences those same butterflies when getting ready for a date, past experience helps to label those feelings as excitement. The physiological symptoms in both situations are identical, however.

Figure 13.1 An essay question from a psychology class with a student's full-credit answer.

instead of the writer. Cross out words that don't make sense and add words when necessary. Use a $\wedge$ to show where words should be inserted. If you write only on the right-hand pages of your exam booklet, you can add afterthoughts on the left-hand pages. Use a line and a $\wedge$ to show where this material should be inserted. Make sure you have written complete sentences. Improve punctuation and spelling.

2. Recheck the question and your answer to make sure you have answered all the parts.

THE STANDARDIZED EXAM

Most of the same rules for taking other types of exams apply to taking standardized exams. The following suggestions can also help you do your best.

1. Get a good night's sleep and eat a light meal before the exam.
2. Bring what you need: the admission ticket, pencils, erasers, Kleenex, lifesavers, gum, a sweater in case the room is cold.
3. Get to the test center at least ten minutes early so that you can take a seat and settle in.
4. Listen carefully to the instructions given by the examiner and work the sample problems even if they seem easy or obvious.
5. Work fast and answer the questions you know first. Mark those you do not know so that you can find them again easily.
6. If you are answering questions on a passage, read the questions first and then look for the answers in the passage.
7. Find out if it is permissible to mark, circle, or underline as you read. Do so, if it is permitted, to help you concentrate and identify important instructions and bits of information.
8. Read all parts of every question carefully before marking the answer.
9. Keep track of time and continue to work quickly to answer as many questions as possible.
10. Guess if there is no penalty.
11. Check your work.

LEARN TO CONTROL EXAM ANXIETY

You may at times experience some exam anxiety. Research suggests that 25–50 percent of students experience sufficient anxiety to lower their test scores. If you are highly test-anxious, you are likely to be a somewhat nervous individual to begin with, and you may also be inclined to "negative self-talk," which can make you feel even worse. Examples of negative self-talk are, "I can't do this," "I didn't study enough," "There isn't enough time," "Everyone else is smarter and knows more," and so on. You can combat the tendency to indulge in such thoughts by reminding yourself that they are very difficult to prove and by replacing them with positive ones. "I've studied this material well, and it's fresh in my mind," "I can concentrate," "I don't know the answer to this question, but that happens all the time, I'll come back to it later," "I have already answered some questions successfully," and "I'm really doing well on this test."

Another characteristic of highly test-anxious students is that they usually have poor study skills. The emphasis in both this chapter and the last has been on careful and systematic preparation for exams. Such preparation is the best way to deal with exam anxiety.

Besides preparing well there are a few other ways to keep anxiety at a tolerable level while you are taking an exam. Get a good night's sleep the night before; exhaustion intensifies nervous feelings. Arrive at the exam a few minutes early. Do not talk to other class members who may be ventilating their own anxieties about the exam. Instead, find a place to work in the examination room where you feel comfortable, get out the materials you will need to take the exam, and spend the last few minutes glancing through your study sheets.

When you begin the exam, you should feel somewhat nervous if you are to do a good job. Your body is creating this energy to help you deal with your exam, to help you recall more, invent your own ideas, organize your responses more rapidly, and write faster.

During the test, use your energy to concentrate on the requirements of the exam and on what you know. Avoid looking at the other students in the room or wondering how they are doing. If you have a question about the test, ask it. Work first on the parts of the exam that you know best to build confidence. If you should become uncomfortably tense, stop for a few moments, and do some slow, deep breathing. It also helps to stretch and yawn a couple of times, and say the words "calm" and "relaxed" to yourself a few times. Then go back to the test and concentrate on reading, analyzing, underlining, and numbering the parts of each question carefully before you answer it.

If, after following these suggestions, you continue to experience much anxiety during a test, visit your Counseling Office. A number of techniques to help students with this problem have been developed, and you may be able to solve your anxiety problem by spending a few hours with a counselor.

MANAGE THE TESTING CONDITIONS

Focus on and recognize negative factors in the test environment to help minimize their negative effects on you. External distractions, for instance, can break your concentration. They include noise outside the room, people moving through the room, an uncomfortable temperature in the room, a desk that is too small, or an exam proctor who moves around excessively. Internal distractions can also interfere with concentration. They include daydreaming, worry about failure, hunger, thirst, boredom, or a blank mind. When you find yourself bothered by external or internal distractions, recognize them and then consciously refocus your attention on the test to keep them from unduly interfering with your exam performance.

A recent study has identified a number of "testing cues" that either enhance or impede students' test performance. These cues include environmental factors, the instructor's testing policy, and even the format of the test itself. Of the fifty-five cues originally identified in this research, seventeen were found to be "potent," meaning that there was 90 percent agreement among the students studied that these cues were extremely helpful or disruptive. Furthermore, it was found that the disruptive cues sent students' blood pressure up, caused their pulse rate to quicken, and kept them from working well on their tests. Here are the potent disruptive and helpful testing cues.

Disruptive Testing Cues

1. When a teacher is *not* specific about the test content.
2. When a teacher does not state in advance information about the test format.
3. When a teacher gives additional assignments before the test, such that there is no time to study.
4. When a teacher fails to give feedback on a previous test.
5. When a teacher *frequently* makes corrections during the exam concerning format or content.
6. When a teacher describes in advance the content and format of a test but you find a *surprise* during the test.
7. When there is no choice of essay questions.
8. When a desk is too small and you must continuously fold and shuffle papers.
9. When the room is too hot or cold.
10. When you have too many tests in one day.

Helpful Testing Cues

1. When a teacher allows you to drop the lowest test.
2. When a teacher provides copies of old exams.
3. When a teacher gives a list of possible questions.
4. When a teacher shows interest in students.
5. When a teacher reviews a test to show students the correct answers or allows students to keep the test when the class has a comprehensive final.
6. When the test format is multiple-choice but space is provided to work problems for partial credit.
7. When the test format is of good quality.[3]

Being aware of the items on these lists should help you minimize the negative effects of disruptive cues and use the positive cues to improve your test performance. It is usually easier to cope with negative influences when we can recognize and understand them.

LEARN FROM YOUR MISTAKES

Study all returned exams, analyze them for errors, and work to avoid making the same errors again. Professors often identify the errors students make by writing comments in the margins of the exam. Here are some of the comments that professors write most frequently on exams. They were found by reading through the margins of more than fifty exam booklets:

Who?	Too vague	Give other reactions
What?	Discuss	What about other points?
Where?	For instance?	What opportunities?
When?	What time?	Give an example
Why?	Be specific	Why this disjointed exposition?
How?	What kind?	What is the significance?
	Irrelevant	

Next time you write an exam, keep this list of comments in mind and write an answer that won't prompt such responses from your professor.

[3] See William J. Kermis, "The TCIQ: An Identification by Intensity of Potent Testing Cues in Science," *Journal of Research in Science Teaching*, Fall 1984, pp. 609–621.

Another list designed to help you avoid making errors on exams contains the common mistakes that students make. It was compiled from more than a hundred student exams. Become familiar with this list of errors as well as the cause and solution for each of them. Try to avoid making them yourself when you take exams.

THE EIGHT COMMON ERRORS STUDENTS MAKE ON EXAMS

Error 1. Answering with the wrong list or the wrong concept.

Example: Listing the steps for surveying a book when asked to list the steps for surveying a chapter.

Cause: Memorizing material as separate lists and ideas rather than getting an overall view of the material by organizing it on study sheets and learning it as an organized mass of material. Failing to think about the lists while learning them.

Avoid by making study sheets with clear titles and topic headings.

Error 2. Writing a sketchy answer.

Example: Writing only three facts about the War of 1812 in lecture notes and writing only that much information in response to an essay question on the topic.

Cause: Skimpy lecture notes and skimpy study sheets.

Avoid by taking complete lecture notes and making complete study sheets.

Error 3. Answering a question in the wrong way.

Example: There is an anecdote about a medical student who studied the stomach and got an essay exam question about the heart. He began, "The heart lies near the stomach. The stomach is composed of . . ."

Cause: Careless, hasty reading of the question and the desire to write about what you have studied, whether or not the professor asks about it.

Avoid by reading the question well, marking and numbering its parts, and referring back to it from time to time as you write. Ask the professor to clarify a difficult question, if this can be done without giving away the answer.

Error 4. Not knowing the key terms either as they appear in the question or as they are needed in the answer.

> *Example:* Not knowing the meaning of *writ of habeas corpus* in a question that asks about its purpose.

> *Cause:* Neglecting to isolate and learn key terms throughout the semester.

> *Avoid* by writing key terminology on lists or cards and learning what these terms mean before an exam.

Error 5. Not knowing how to apply the material from the course to new situations (occurs in math and science as well as in liberal arts classes).

> *Example:* Being able to list the clues to finding main ideas but not being able to find examples of these clues in a passage.

> *Cause:* Not thinking enough about the material being learned during the semester.

> *Avoid* by inventing original examples, applying what you have learned to new situations, looking for fresh relationships, and writing your insights and ideas in [square brackets] in lecture notes, textbooks, and on study sheets.

Error 6. Leaving out important material such as parts of the question, supporting details, or ramifications and implications.

> *Example:* The question asks the student to summarize the arguments in a passage, to agree or disagree with them and say why, and to anticipate other arguments that might be used. The student summarizes and agrees, but forgets to say why and forgets to anticipate other arguments. The answer, which is good as far as it goes, receives only 50% credit.

> *Cause:* Not reading the question well enough and not knowing how much information to include in the answer.

> *Avoid* by writing all you can that is relevant to the question. Use plenty of detail and examples. Reread the question when you have finished writing your answer to check whether you have answered all parts.

Error 7. Writing long, rambling answers that are inefficient, redundant, and full of irrelevant material.

Example: The student begins, "This is an important question. In answering this question, I am reminded of some of the reading assigned this semester . . ." This student has begun to write before she has begun to think.

Cause: Neglecting to plan and make brief outlines of answers before beginning to write.

Avoid by making brief outlines next to exam questions, adding to them as thoughts occur to you during the exam, and following them when you compose your answers. Also, write a first sentence that comes right to the point.

Error 8. Failing to proofread answers before turning them in.

Example: Answers are characterized by omitted words, sentence fragments, ideas that don't make sense, and simple errors like writing *to* for *too.*

Cause: Running out of time because you haven't watched it carefully enough.

Avoid by leaving enough time at end of exam to edit answers. Cross out material that does not contribute to the answer. Neatly add material that does. Make sure you have written complete sentences and that your handwriting is legible. Correct all remaining errors.

Figure 13.2 shows a student's answer to an essay question that contains at least six of the common exam errors. Take a look at it so that you can see how these errors appear in the context of an exam answer. This, in turn, should help you avoid making these errors yourself.

Whenever you do poorly on an exam, check the common errors to see how many of them contributed to your poor grade. If you are still baffled by your failure, go to your professor and ask how you can improve on your next exam. Do not go in defensively and suggest that your exam was graded unfairly. Then little can be accomplished. Rather, approach your professors with the attitude that you want to do better next time. Then they will help you.

As you study your failures in exam taking, begin to generalize from your errors. Note the mistakes that you make over and over again. Start trying to correct these errors, and improvement will come gradually. Remember that exam writing is a skill that takes time and effort to develop.

Errors:

1. Failed to mark and number parts of question. Then did not answer all parts of it (error 6).

2. Did not make a jot outline. Answer is poorly organized (error 7).

3. Did not start with a sentence that comes right to the point (error 7).

4. Confused key terminology. Wrote *summarizing* when meant *surveying* (error 4).

5. Padded the answer with irrelevant material (error 7).

6. No example included (errors 2, 5, and 6).

7. Failed to proofread and correct run-on sentence (error 8).

QUESTION

Name and describe the steps used in reading and remembering a chapter in a textbook. Give a specific example of how you have used each step in reading one of your taxtbooks.

ANSWER

Remembering what you have read is a difficult task. You can read something and in the next 24 hours completely forget it. This is why summarizing a chapter first, then reading it is quite a help. Go back within the next 24 hours and look over the chapter again, this way everything should be clear to you. Reciting and grouping will also help you to remember. Group words you don't know with familiar words of your own. Recite vocabulary words and anything that you feel you should remember. Underline important phrases and things that show the most importance in the chapter so when test time comes around you will have the main ideas of the chapter all right up in front of you. Summarize and then read the chapter or chapters before the exam. Remembering for most people is hard, that's

Figure 13.2 An essay answer that contains some of the common errors.

why if you can develop good habits for remembering what you read, you will have less trouble and a chance of knowing quite a bit if not all of what pops up on an exam. When summarizing through a chapter read all titles, headings, and subheadings, all pictures and diagrams and the summary at the end of the chapter. If you can teach yourself these things then you will have every-thing all set if you can master these things, well, you know what they say, a bird in the hand is worth two in a bush. Get good study habits and reread what you read the first time.

Figure 13.2 (cont.)   An essay answer that contains some of the common errors.

At the Very Least . . .

This chapter has presented some ideal ways of taking examinations. If you cannot follow all of these suggestions, *at the very least,* do the following:

1. Before the test
   a. Study and learn the material.
   b. Get enough sleep.
   c. Get to the exam with time to spare and with the materials you need.
2. During the test
   a. Read and analyze questions before answering them.
   b. Jot outlines for essay answers.
   c. Watch the time.
3. After the test
   a. Proofread your answers and edit them.
   b. Make certain you answered all parts of every question.

SUMMARY

Study well for all exams so that you begin each of them with a full and orderly mind. When you are handed the exam, read it through quickly to see what you will have to do. Then plan how to use your time so that you will complete the entire exam, not just part of it. Other general rules for exams are: (1) read each question carefully, mark the important parts, and answer it exactly; (2) do the easy questions first and the more difficult ones later; and (3) answer all parts of all questions as completely as possible. For essay questions write a brief outline for each question. When you answer the question, use good organization, write on the question and nothing else, make the answer tight and efficient by eliminating any padding or digression, and use as much supporting material as you can—lots of examples, diagrams, descriptions, quotations, and citations from the text and lectures. Leave time to proofread all answers on all exams before you turn them in. Work to keep your anxieties at a tolerable level during the exam and learn to ignore distractions. Finally, study all returned exams, identify your mistakes, and try to avoid making the same mistakes again.

EXERCISES

A. Monitor Your Comprehension of This Chapter.

Write quickly, in phrases rather than complete sentences, the information in this chapter that you understand and remember. Look back through your marginal notes and summaries and add what you left out. Is anything in the chapter unclear? Jot it down to ask about in class. Has reading the chapter caused you to think of new insights or examples of your own? Jot them down.

B. Class Exercises.

1. **Individuals and Whole Class.** Each student should prepare an essay question over some of the material studied so far in the course. These questions should either be read aloud in class or put on the board. The class should analyze what is required to answer each of these questions completely and well in order to receive maximum credit.

2. **Whole Class.** Read the following question that actually appeared on a history exam, and answer the questions below.

Write an essay defining and describing the changing mood, temper, and lifestyle of the lost generation of the 1920s. Your essay should cover the everyday character of this change using George Jean Nathan and H.L. Mencken as your central examples.

a. What should your answer look like when you are finished?
b. What are the question words that tell you what to do?
c. How would you outline an answer?

d. Check to see if you have omitted any parts of the question.

e. Read the lecture notes about the lost generation in Figure 5.5, pages 65–66. Do they contain sufficient information to enable you to answer this question completely?

3. *Small Groups.* Read the following essay question, mark it, and reword it, using four positive statements that describe exactly what you must do to answer it completely. Review pages 232–233 or an example.

> Choose one of the cognitive styles discussed in class and discuss its meaning, how it is measured, and at least one "real world" behavior to which it relates.

4. *Individuals.* If you completed Class Exercise B2 at the end of the last chapter, you have made study sheets on "How to Read a Textbook," "How to Take Lecture Notes," and "How to Prepare for an Exam." If you did not, make them now. You will practice writing essay answers on those three topics.

5. *Individuals.* Study your study sheet on "How to Read a Textbook" for ten minutes. Then take thirty minutes to plan and write an answer to the following question:

> Name and describe the parts of the process used to read and remember a chapter in a textbook. Give a specific example of how you have used each part in reading one of your textbooks.

Submit your study sheet with the exam answer either to another student or to the instructor for evaluation. The following Evaluation Guide can be used to score the answer.

Evaluation Guide for Reading Question

(1)
Question 1: Name and describe the parts of the process used to read, re-
(2)
member, and think about a chapter in a textbook. Give a specific example

of how you have used each part in reading one of your textbooks.

Elements in Answer	*Points*
1. Preread the chapter. Include backgrounding, the 6 steps for surveying, predicting, and asking questions	20
2. Read the chapter—mention main ideas, supporting details, and transitions	10
3. Underline, make marginal notes, and summarize	10
4. Remember the chapter and think about it. (mention at least five strategies for 5 points each, such as recite, associate, elaborate, etc.)	20

Elements in Answer   *Points*

5. Specific example of how each part of the process was
    used in own text. 5 points for each part.   20
6. Study sheets submitted   10
7. Essay form used and handwriting legible   5
8. Question marked, brief outline made before answering   5
                                                                  ———
                                                 TOTAL   100

When you receive your evaluated exam, answer the following questions to
help you with further self-evaluation.

1. Was your study sheet sufficiently complete and well-organized to help
    you answer this question?
2. Did you read and mark the question?
3. Did you write a jot outline to help you organize your answer?
4. Did you write in essay form?
5. Did you answer all parts of the questions and answer each part fully?
6. Did you organize your answer and make the organization clear with
    transitions?
7. Did you understand the terminology in the question and use it correctly
    in your answer?
8. Did you come right to the point in the first sentence?
9. Did you use examples and other details? Were they effective?
10. Did you pad your answer with irrelevant material?

6. ***Individuals.*** Study your study sheet on "How to Take Lecture Notes" for
    ten minutes. Then take thirty minutes to plan and write an answer to the
    following question:

    > Name and briefly explain five ways to improve your lecture note tak-
    > ing in class. Describe in detail what you do with your notes after you
    > have taken them. Give a specific example of how you use the left-hand
    > margin.

    Submit your study sheet with the exam answer either to another student or
    to the instructor for evaluation. The following Evaluation Guide can be
    used to score the answer.

    ———————————————————————————————————————

    ### Evaluation Guide for Lecture Note Question

    Question 2: Name and briefly explain five ways to improve your lecture note-
    taking in class. Describe in detail what you do with your notes after you have
    taken them. Give a specific example of how you use the left-hand margin.

Elements in Answer	Points
1. Name and give a brief explanation of five of the suggestions made in Chapter 4 (ignore distractions, label notes, attend class, etc.). 7 points each: 3 for name, 4 for explanation.	35
2. Read, revise, underline, make marginal notes, summarize, cover, and recite within 24 hours.	35
3. Specific example of how student has used margin (student may draw a diagram or describe).	20
4. Submitted study sheets.	5
5. Marked question, made outline.	5
TOTAL	100

When you receive your evaluated exam, answer the ten self-evaluation questions listed in Class Exercise 5.

7. *Individuals.* Study your study sheet on "How to Prepare for and Take Exams" for ten minutes. Then take thirty minutes to plan and write an answer to the following question:

> Describe in detail the procedure given in this book for studying for and taking objective, quantitative, and essay exams, beginning with the first day of class until you turn in the completed exam. Give two examples of common errors you have make in writing exams.

Submit your study sheet with the exam answer either to another student or to the instructor for evaluation. The following Evaluation Guide can be used to score the answer.

Evaluation Guide for Exam Question

Question 3: Describe in detail the procedure given in this book for studying ⁽¹⁾

for and taking objective, quantitative, and essay exams, beginning with the ⁽²⁾

first day of class until you turn in the completed exam. Give two examples ⁽³⁾

of common errors you have made in writing exams.

Elements in Answer	Points
1. Studying for: Master Study Sheet (15 points) and Study Sheets (25 points) - detailed descriptions.	40
2. Taking: reading question, using time, proofreading (15 points), plus at least two suggestions for taking each of three types of exams (25 points).	40
3. Two examples of common errors (10 points)	20
TOTAL	100

BONUS POINTS: Submitted study sheets (5); marked
question (5); outlined answer (5).   15

115 total
possible points

When you receive your evaluated exam, answer the ten self-evaluation
questions listed in Class Exercise 5.

Now look at pages 250–252 at the end of this chapter and read a student's answer to this question that received full credit. How does your
answer compare with hers?

8. *Individuals.* Write a self-analysis of the errors you made in the three
practice exams along with a description of how you will avoid making these
errors in the future.

C. Application Exercises

1. *Pairs of Students.* Bring to class an essay question and your answer from
another class. Exchange your question and answer with another student.
Discuss answers to the ten evaluation questions in Class Exercise 5.

D. Topics for Your Learning Journal

1. Give some examples of the negative self-talk that sometimes goes through
your mind when you are taking an exam. How can you turn these negative
thoughts into positive ones?

2. Look back at the list of disruptive testing cues. Which do you find particularly distracting? What can you do to minimize their negative effects?

3. Make a list of suggestions that would help you personally to lower test
anxiety.

4. List the internal and external distractions that you find most distracting
when you are taking a test. How can you minimize their negative effects?
What helps you refocus your attention on the test?

5. What suggestions from this chapter will you use this semester to help you
take exams in your other classes?

A full-credit answer to Class Exercise B7 (exam question) by student Rose Marie Bechtel.

Beginning with the first day of class, the key word is *organization.* Whatever
you decide to use to organize all your materials, make sure it will keep
everything, notes, handouts, tests, and so on, in one place so that you can
find them easily. Notebooks should be regular sized and are all right if the
class is strictly a straight lecture, no handouts. However, if you do get
handouts, a folder or binder with pocketed dividers would serve you better.

Notes for each class should be as complete as you can possibly make them. Date notes always, especially if you use loose leaf paper, and put them in a folder or notebook. Label the main sections of your notes in the margin and mark them. This means underline things that are important. Check out all the words you don't know. Ask the professor to explain anything that is really unclear to you. Leave some space at the end of each day's notes for summaries and for your own ideas or thoughts. Review your notes as soon after each class as possible.

Read your textbook thoroughly: introductions, chapters, summaries, everything. Take marginal notes and underline main ideas, important dates, people, events. Write your own summaries at the end of each chapter. This makes review easier.

If you get a large number of handouts, date them and keep them in order and in the same place with your notes. Mark these up also and review them periodically.

If you write essays or a term paper or anything of this nature, keep it. Usually the professor will have written some comments or suggestions that will be helpful, especially for essay tests.

Any old tests that are returned to you should also be kept. Try to learn from your mistakes and keep in mind any of the suggestions written on these. Also keep quizzes and review sheets for the same reason.

You should also keep notes on outside readings. These include library assignments, newspaper or magazine articles, maybe impressions of a movie or play you were required to see for class. Now, the time comes and a test is announced, but remember you are organized already.

First using either your text, lecture notes, or class syllabus as a central organizing factor, write a Master Study Sheet for the course up until the final point that the test will cover. The Master Study Sheet makes you see the course as a whole rather than as isolated pieces of information.

Next, taking each item on the Master Study Sheet, write a standard study sheet for each item. The notes on these sheets will make you remember other details, information. They will jog your memory and give you something to build on.

While you study think about how the professor thinks. Does he think in contrasts—remember and think about that while you study. Some of your study sheets should reflect the way he thinks. Study until the last possible minute.

For the objective test: Read it all. First answer all the ones you know, marking the ones you skip, so you can go back to them. If you are stuck on a multiple-choice question, try to decide ahead of time what the answer is and look for that answer. Know your terminology, and look for qualifying words such as *all, always, never, sometimes*. Go over it carefully when you're through. If you have a good reason to change an answer, change it.

For quantitative exams: Read it all, work the ones you know first. If point values are given, work the ones with the highest point values first. Show all the steps you used to arrive at your answer. You are showing the professor what you know, so be logical and clear. Check to see that you have used all the information given, and that your answer is in the form requested in the problem. Check your arithmetic.

For essay exams: Read thoroughly. If the question has more than one part, number the parts. Underline the word or words that tell you what to do. Jot down ideas as you read. Make sure you do what the question says to do, that is, discuss, explain, contrast, compare. Answer each question as clearly and completely as possible. When you finish, proofread. Check spelling, punctuation, sentence structure. Have you answered all the parts of the question? Check carefully.

Two of my main problems are reading the questions completely, and when I do, reading things into them that aren't there. This happens most frequently in objective tests.

For example, I'll start reading this question: What is the immediate treatment for a person who has swallowed a noncorrosive, fast-acting poison but has a heart condition?

I'll read to the "but" when I'm in a hurry. The answer is to induce vomiting, but the qualification (the heart condition) makes that answer wrong.

Or the following question was also on a first-aid test.

You're out with a friend in the woods. He falls and breaks his neck, and, at the same time, a sharp piece of wood pierces his chest, causing a sucking wound. Would you leave him to go get help or have him hold a dressing and go for help?

When I answered this question, I thought, what if he's unconscious, and that made me write the wrong answer. I read something into the question that was not there, and, consequently, answered the question in the wrong way.

PART FIVE

Writing Papers and Giving Reports

14 | *Writing College Papers*

When you have finished reading this chapter, you will know the following:

1. How to interpret a writing assignment.
2. How to think before you write.
3. How to write, rewrite, revise, and proofread.
4. How to prepare final copy, including notes and bibliography.

INTERPRETING THE WRITING ASSIGNMENT

Professors make writing assignments to see if you can initiate and complete independent, creative projects that involve reading, thinking, and writing about a subject. Sometimes professors describe in detail how to complete the assignment. At other times, you have to make most of the decisions about how to proceed. Papers assigned to you may range from two pages of your ideas about something discussed in class to a fifteen- or twenty-page term paper that requires considerable library research. Furthermore, you are likely to encounter paper assignments in any college class, including liberal arts, engineering, business, math, and the sciences. You will write more papers your junior and senior years than you will while you are a freshman or sophomore.

Assignments for written papers are often the most complicated assignments you will receive in college. In fact, getting the assignment straight and then completing all parts of it accurately can be half the battle in writing college papers. Be sure to listen and write down every detail of a writing assignment.

Once you have recorded the assignment in complete detail, you need to determine exactly what is required of you. Look up or ask about the meanings of unclear words, understand the details, and break a complicated assignment into manageable parts. It may be useful to restate the assignment in the form of a series of positive statements as in the example on pages 232–233. Then plan deadlines for completing each part. It is taken for granted that you will spend several hours more on a college writing assignment than you would on a comparable high school assignment.

FOLLOW A PROCESS IN WRITING PAPERS

Allow time in your plan for doing a writing assignment to follow a process in writing. A process has some built-in features that will help you write a good paper. The remainder of this chapter describes a writing process that progresses in stages: from *prewriting,* to *writing* and *rewriting,* and, finally, to *revision* and *proofreading.* At every stage you will be writing, but not all of this writing will be turned in. A good paper requires a lot of thought and decision making and these can be accomplished best by writing lists, outlines, ideas, and, finally, the paper.

Be forewarned that the writing process is a creative act that is, by its nature, often spontaneous, inspired, and difficult to see as clearly defined in stages. In actual practice the various stages of the process will at times overlap, backtrack, repeat themselves. Understanding the process will help you get started and prod you to continue until your work is finished. You should avoid trying mechanically to follow steps in a process without thinking. Creative powers interacting with the discipline and motivation that the writing process provides will help you write a paper that will ultimately satisfy both you and your instructor.

PREWRITING ACTIVITIES

1. Decide What to Write About

Paper topics are sometimes assigned by professors. More often, however, the professor expects you to select a topic that has been generated by the reading for the course, the lectures, or the discussion in the course itself, or, you might be given a completely free choice of topic. Free choice is most likely to occur in writing classes. The assignment will also usually specify what sort of purpose you are to fulfill in the paper: explaining, arguing, persuading, or describing.

When you are expected to participate in the topic selection, you should at the outset think about several things at once. You will want to write about a *subject* that is appropriate for the *audience* who will read your paper. This *audience* may be the professor and other similarly informed professionals. Or, the audience might include your classmates, particularly if you will be presenting the paper orally in class. You should also select a topic that is appropriate to the *occasion*. An informal, superficial, and trite topic is far less appropriate to the college classroom than a scholarly, formal topic that can be treated with thought and in detail. Finally, you should think about the *purpose* of the paper and select a topic that will help you meet it. Are you expected to give information only? Then select a topic that you can find enough information about. Are you expected to argue? Then you will need a topic that you can argue both for and against before you reach a conclusion. If the purpose is to be persuasive, you will need to select a topic that you believe in if you are to persuade others to accept your point of view. Or, if you are assigned to describe, you must search for a topic that lends itself to extended description and explanation.

When you are assigned to select a topic that is generated by the course itself, examine your lecture notes, reading notes, and notes on class discussions for ideas. While you were taking these notes, you may have already identified possible paper topics by writing *P*s by paper topics in the margins. List these topics along with the various issues and questions that have been raised in the course. Such questions might include, "Does collective bargaining have a future?" in a management course, "What is an effective type of consumer research?" in a marketing course, "Can the dangers of nuclear power plants be resolved?" in a physics course, or "What does the narrator reveal about his own personality?" in a literature course.

If you are in a skill-building class, such as a writing class, it won't have its own subject matter like history, sociology, or psychology. Consequently, you may be given free choice of topic. In this case, begin by making a list of your hobbies, interests, future educational or professional plans, and interesting ideas and information from your other classes. Consider what you have read lately in a magazine, newspaper, or book, or what you have heard in conversations that has caught your interest. Think about experiences you have had that might interest others.

When you look back at your lists, whether generated by the course or by free choice, select one item that is appropriate to your audience and the occasion, and that will help you fulfill the purpose of the assignment. Select, also, a topic that you can get information about. If you want to read original newspaper and magazine commentary on the building of the Panama Canal, check to see if your library can make such material available to you. If you can't find the material you need, you should modify or change your topic. You should also choose a topic that you have sufficient background to handle. If you are a freshman in biology, do not choose a difficult topic from microbiology. If you do, you may find yourself tangled in complicated terminology and difficult concepts that you have insufficient education to understand. When you have studied more, you will be able to tackle such material. For the time being stick with material you have the background and education to read and write about with ease.

2. Focus Your Topic

The topic of your paper may quickly emerge as narrow and well defined, but this is unlikely. In most cases you will need to choose one aspect of a broad subject on which to write. You cannot write a good five-page paper on "Collective Bargaining"; "Should Collective Bargaining Be Adversarial: Advantages and Disadvantages" might be a better possibility.

One way to narrow and focus your topic is to choose a broad subject that interests you, like computers or solar energy or Indians. Write it on a piece of paper. Then brainstorm this topic by making a quick list of everything you know *about* the subject that is interesting to you. For instance, suppose that you want to write a three- to five-page research paper about Indians. Figure 14.1 shows the results of some brainstorming about Indians.

Take a look at this list. Some of the items on it are still too broad or too general to be good subjects—for example, "religion" or "language." You could write chapters on each of these subjects, and you only have to write five pages. Some are more specific and would be easier to work with, such as "The Indians' Theories Concerning the Origin of Life." Broad or narrow, however, at this point you have a list of topics that interests you. Now choose the item on your list that most appeals to you as a paper topic. Let's say you decide you like "The Quality of Indian Education" best.

At this point in the paper-writing process this topic looks narrow enough to handle in the allotted space. It is something about the general subject of Indians, and your present knowledge makes you think that you could deal with it adequately in five pages. You remind yourself, however, as your work with this topic progresses, that it may need to be narrowed further. Indeed, you may find that you can handle only one aspect of it.

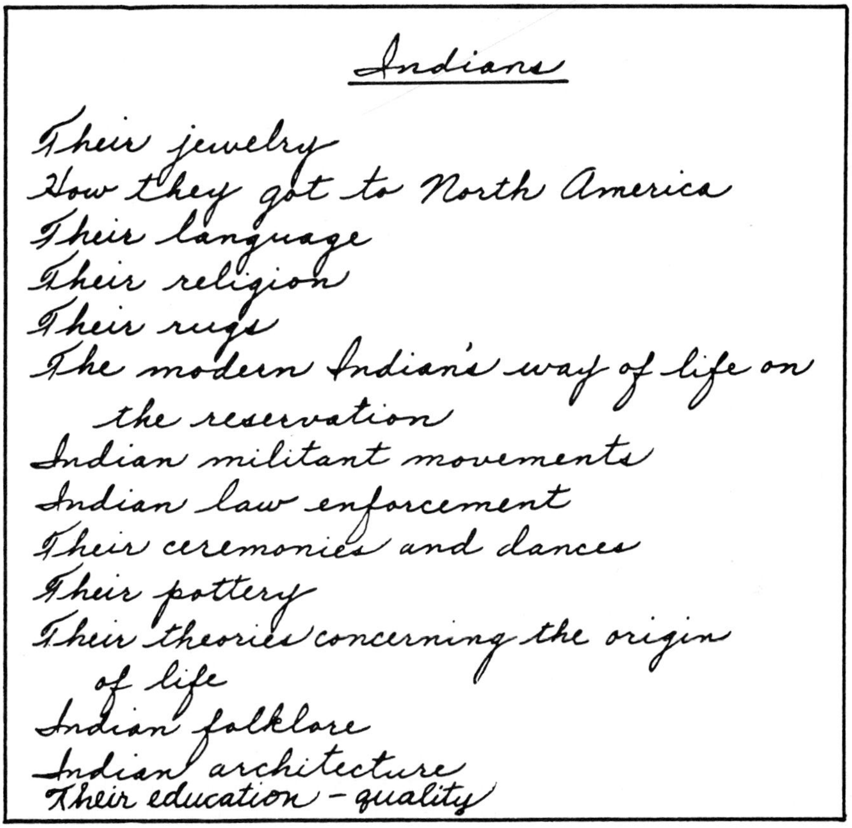

Indians

Their jewelry
How they got to North America
Their language
Their religion
Their rugs
The modern Indian's way of life on
    the reservation
Indian militant movements
Indian law enforcement
Their ceremonies and dances
Their pottery
Their theories concerning the origin
    of life
Indian folklore
Indian architecture
Their education – quality

Figure 14.1   Results of brainstorming.

3. Ask Some Questions

Determine now what you already know about your topic and what additional information you will need to know to write about it. This activity will save you hours of inefficient, misdirected research in the library and will also help to establish you as the author of your paper. By writing down ideas that will later be incorporated into your paper, you will not, as so many students do, go to the library, copy material out of books, string it all together, and turn in a dull hodgepodge of other people's accounts and opinions.

There are several specific questions you can ask to start thinking creatively and independently about your topic. As you consider these questions, actually write out answers to them.

a. *What ideas do I already have about this subject?* What opinions do I hold? What facts do I know? How do these facts and opinions relate to the subject and to each other?

b. *What sources can I consult?* Has the professor mentioned any books or articles during the semester that might get me started? Who can I ask for help in finding good sources?

c. *What must I read to get some general background information so that when I begin to do research, the subject will make sense?* Will it be adequate to consult an encyclopedia, or should I skim through a couple of background books?

d. *How will my audience influence my writing?* If I am writing for my professor, I need to consider his background and knowledge. On the other hand, if this paper will be presented to other students, I will probably need to give more background information.

e. *What examples and other forms of supporting material might I use?* Do I know of any examples from my own experience that I might include in my paper? Brainstorm for examples and other support.

4. Use Other Ways to Invent Ideas

You now know several ways to invent ideas for your paper. You know how to evaluate and draw on your past knowledge and experience, you know how to brainstorm and list ideas, and you know how to ask questions to help you generate subject matter. There are other techniques to help you develop ideas. You might use any or all of them during these early or even the later stages of the paper-writing process. They include reflecting and thinking about your topic, discussing your ideas with others, listening to a speaker on your topic, observing, or interviewing. Write down the ideas that are developed through these activities so that you will not forget them. Begin to group them under some tentative headings.

Reading is another way to generate ideas about a topic. Read the textbook or books and articles in the library that are about your topic and that will help you think about it. The next chapter explains how to do the library research required for a research paper assignment. For now, however, just read. As you read, make connections with what you already know, and think of implications, applications, examples, and ideas. Ask questions to guide further research, write everything down as fully as possible with details and explanations.

If you think you may want to quote or paraphrase any of the material you are reading, even at this early stage, xerox it and attach it to your notes. Make certain you write the author, source, publisher, date, and page numbers at the top of the xeroxed sheets.

Figure 14.2 provides an example of a paragraph and the ideas it triggered in a student's mind.

From <u>American Indian Quarterly</u>, Vol. XI, no. 4,
Fall 1987, p. 275.

JIM CROW, INDIAN STYLE

Orlan J. Svingen

IN JUNE OF 1986, Judge Edward Rafeedie ruled that "official acts of discrimination . . . have interfered with the rights of Indian citizens [of Big Horn County, Montana] to register and vote." Civil rights expert and ACLU attorney Laughlin McDonald later observed in the *San Francisco Examiner* that racism against Indian people in Montana was even worse than he had expected. "I thought I'd stepped into the last century," McDonald explained. "Whites were doing to Indians what people in the South stopped doing to blacks twenty years ago." Big Horn County Commissioner and area rancher Ed Miller "longs for the good old days" when Indians remained on the reservation. Angered by Rafeedie's ruling, Miller threatened to appeal the decision to the Supreme Court. "The Voting Rights Act is a bad thing," Miller complained. "I don't see no comparison with Negroes in the South." Before Janine Windy Boy and other plaintiffs filed suit against Big Horn County, "things were fine around here," Miller lamented. "Now they (Indians) want to vote," he exclaimed. "What next?"[1]

---

[1]Bill Shaw, "Whites vs. Indians in Montana, Where Racism Still Reigns." San Francisco Examiner, Oct. 5, 1986; New York Times, June 31, 1986.

Why are Indians the last minority to vote? Does this have to do with tribal laws and tribal voting, Indian culture, or <u>education</u>? Can all Indians <u>read the ballot</u>? Find out about the voting history of Indians and how it compares to other minorities. What is threatening about Indians voting? Does this problem exist outside of Montana?

Figure 14.2 Example of paper ideas and questions triggered by reading.

If your college has a writing center that is equipped with writing tutors, use them to help you think through your paper. They will be able to ask the kinds of questions that will help you invent ideas. Another source of information is the library. The next chapter explains how to do the library research required for a research paper assignment.

5. Learn to Listen to Your Subconscious Mind

Inventing and thinking about the ideas in a paper you are writing is partly a conscious and partly an unconscious process. When you have spent time working intensively on ideas for a paper, you should then set them aside for awhile. When you return to your ideas later, you will often discover new insights and see connections that eluded you before. Your subconscious mind has been at work while your conscious mind was busy with something else. Learn to take advantage of the work done by your subconscious mind. Your best ideas, for example, may come to you when you first wake up. Be prepared to jot them down and add them to the other ideas you have generated during prewriting stages of paper writing.

6. Shape Your Paper by Outlining

Think of an outline as a *tool* to help you organize all the material you have accumulated up to that point and as a *guide* to help you write. With an outline in front of you, you will not be puzzled about what to write next because your outline will tell you. By the time you have an outline, you will have thought through your paper from beginning to end. When your outline is done, very often the hardest part—the original thinking—of your paper is done.

Outlining can be done in several stages during prewriting, and each revised outline will be more complete than the last. Your *first outline* can be written early during prewriting activities and can be no more than a list of three or four main heads that you might use in your paper. You might also at this time write out a thesis or purpose sentence, such as the following: "The purpose of this paper is to examine the current status of the education of modern American Indians and then to evaluate it." You realize that, as your paper grows, you may want to change this sentence. It may, on the other hand, become the final thesis sentence for your paper. If you get an idea for the introduction, make a note of this also on the early outline.

At this time you can also begin to think about an organizational plan for your paper. If your material seems to fit into topics or categories, you can use a topical pattern. If it more naturally can be discussed step by step or as it occurred over a period of time, use a chronological pattern. Or, if you are writing a persuasive paper, you may prefer to use a problem-solution or cause and-effect pattern. Argumentative papers are often organized by stating the issue, giving the arguments for and against, and, finally, stating your position and supporting it.

You should not attempt library research without some sort of brief *tentative outline to guide your research.* Without such a guide, you may find yourself reading everything in the library on your topic—and wasting a lot of time. A tentative outline focuses and directs your reading so that you read to support your thesis and fill in the information gaps. Your research outline, a somewhat extended version of your first brief outline, should have a tentative thesis written at the top along with the possible main heads, some subideas and examples if you have thought of them, and a brief description of how you plan to go about your research. As you do research, continue to add to and revise this outline, including your thesis, if necessary.

When you have finished all prewriting activities, including library research, you should make a *final outline.* It can be elaborate and detailed and contain cross-references to every xeroxed article or note card you have made. Or, at the other extreme, it can be a few notes jotted on the back of an envelope. You will have to learn to make the kind of outline that works best for you.

For a research paper, one way of doing a final outline that is quick and does the job, is to write the headings and subheadings on lined notebook paper, section by section. Leave plenty of space between each section so that you can paper-clip the research cards or the xeroxed materials that you intend to use in that section to the side of that section of the outline itself.

In some classes you will be told to turn in a particular type of outline, such as a sentence outline, along with your final paper. When this is the case, follow your professor's instructions for the form of such an outline exactly.

As you go through the prewriting activities, it is essential that you *write everything down.* When you first begin to think about a subject, you are often more creative than at any other time. If you do not make a record of your initial creative thoughts, you will forget them, or, worse, as you pursue your research, other people's ideas will intrude on your own until eventually you will forget that you ever had any original ideas about your subject. With all of your notes, research materials, lists, ideas, and your outline spread out in front of you to refer to, you can now write your paper.

WRITING AND REWRITING ACTIVITIES

Your object, at this next stage, is to get a first draft of your paper. It does not have to be perfect. It only has to be good enough to work with later.

There are two ways of drafting a paper. Use the one that works best for you. The first way is to write rapidly and keep writing. You will be working to capture the flow of ideas represented by your outline. To do this you will have to get them down on paper as quickly as you can. You will be thinking fast as you move through your outline this time, and you should write fast enough to keep up with your thoughts. Do not stop to reread. Do not worry about sentence structure, word choice, punctuation, or misspellings at this point. You will take care of these things later.

If getting the first sentence on the page seems to be difficult, write a phrase. After you put down a few phrases, you will usually begin to write in sentences. If you are writing smoothly and then suddenly get blocked, unable to figure out how to express an idea, write phrases again. Leave blank spots if you cannot immediately think of the right word. Later you can complete sentences and add and change words.

A second way of composing a first draft is to do a considerable amount of rereading and rewriting as you write. Rewriting while writing is an excellent skill to learn because your paper will require less revision later. Writing and rewriting involves constantly going back to read what you have just written and making improvements at once. For instance, as soon as you write a word, you may think of a better one. Go ahead and substitute the better word. Or, you may start a sentence that becomes confused and refuses to end as you had hoped. If you can think of a better way to write it, do so immediately. At the end of each paragraph, reread the entire paragraph and make additional changes and improvements. Your draft, when you finish writing it, will look like the material in Figure 14.3.

Writing requires making one decision after another: about what to say next, what word to select, how to start a sentence, how much to write. Follow this second method of writing the first draft only if you can do so without belaboring these decisions. Your object is to get your thoughts on paper as soon as possible. If rewriting decisions are slowing your writing down so much that you lose your train of thought, then revert to the first method of writing quickly without rereading and rewriting. You can always go back and rework material when it is finally down on paper.

> can
> Outlining ~~should~~ be done in several
> stages during ~~the~~ prewriting ~~activities~~,
> and each revised outline will be more
> complete than the last., ~~until you~~
>   eventually
> ~~finally,~~ You will ^ ~~have a final outline~~
>   ~~to be used~~
> ~~that is complete~~ enough ^ ~~to guide your~~
> ~~writing.~~
> no   e
> ¶ 'Your first outlin~~ing effort~~ can be
>   written early   during
> ~~a list of done early in the~~ pre-
>   activities   no more than
> writing ~~process~~ and can be ^ a list
> of three or four main heads that you
> might use in your paper.

Figure 14.3   Example of writing and rewriting done as simultaneous activities.

USING SOURCE MATERIAL

As you write, remember that *you* are the author of this paper. Your ideas will shape and structure the paper. If you are writing a research paper, use the research materials you have taken from other sources to explain, clarify, or lend more weight to what you are saying.

You will learn how to take research notes in the next chapter. Basically, however, your notes will be of two sorts: the direct quote, which is copied word for word, and the paraphrase, which is a rephrasing in your own words of someone else's ideas. When you use either of these types of material to support your ideas and observations, you must let your reader know where they came from originally. There are two ways to give credit to the original author: by using footnotes and bibliography or by using in-text citations and a list of works cited.

1. Footnotes and bibliography You may footnote borrowed material at the bottom of the page or on a final sheet at the end of the paper where all endnotes can be listed together in consecutive order. Figure 14.4 shows the footnote method. Notice also how a direct quotation can be interwoven with one's own statements. The quoted material is acknowledged with a footnote at the bottom of the page. When you use this method of acknowledgment, attach a bibliography at the end of your paper. A bibliography lists by author and in alphabetical order the works you have quoted or paraphrased in your paper. Use the format illustrated in Figure 14.5 to prepare a bibliography.

2. In-text citations and a list of works cited A simpler way of acknowledging sources is to place notes in parentheses in the text itself and cross-reference them to an alphabetical list of works cited at the end of the paper. This method is now preferred to the older footnote and bibliography method.

All that is required is that you place in parentheses the author's last name and the page number on which the material appeared at the end of the quote or paraphrased material. Figure 14.6 illustrates

In 1972 the Indian Educational Act was passed by Congress and the next year the National Advisory Council on Indian Education was appointed by the President. The purpose of both government acts was to improve the quality of Indian education. In the Council's third annual report to Congress, there is evidence that some progress toward improvement has been made, but the Council also admits that severe problems still remain:

} you explaining factual information that is general knowledge and does not need to be quoted

"Dropout rate among Indian youth is the highest in the country. Delinquency among Indian youth is the worst among all other youth groups. Suicide rate is among the highest of any group in our society. Poverty is rampant on Indian Reservations as is alcoholism, mental illness, and a general state of hopelessness."[1]

} National Advisory Council supporting what you have said

[1]National Advisory Council on Indian Education, *The Third Annual Report to the Congress of the United States* (Washington, D.C.: U.S. Government Printing Office, March 1976), p. 23.

} footnote telling reader where you found quoted information

Figure 14.4 The footnote method of acknowledging a source.

List of Works Cited

Dippie, Brian W. The Vanishing American. Middletown:
    Wesleyan UP, 1982.
''In the Wake of the Siege at Wounded Knee.'' U.S. News and
    World Report. 21 May 1973: 112-113.
Jacoby, Alvin M., Jr. Now That the Buffalo's Gone: A Study
    of Today's American Indians. New York: Knopf, 1982.
LaFarge, Oliver. ''The Enduring Indian.'' Scientific
    American. February 1960: 37-44.
National Advisory Council on Indian Education. The Third
    Annual Report to the Congress of the United States.
    Washington, D.C.: Government Printing Office, March,
    1976.
Taylor, Theodore W. The Bureau of Indian Affairs. Boulder:
    Westview Press, 1984.

Figure 14.5   Sample list of works cited.

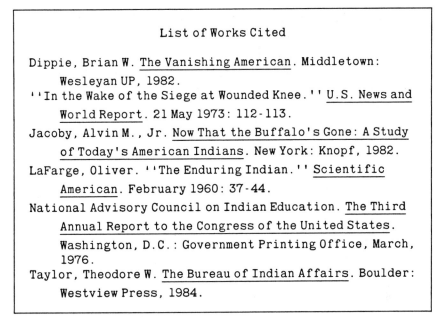

The basic purpose of education for Indians has not always been clear and consistent. For many years government-run Indian schools pressured Indians to abandon their native culture and to assimilate with the dominant American culture. John Collier, a reformer who agitated in favor of Indians and their culture from the early 1920s until his death in 1968, had a different idea. He believed that instead of effacing native culture, Indian schools should encourage and revitalize it. (Dippie 276, 325).

} *you talking*

} *paraphrased support for what you have said*

in-text citation telling reader where you learned about Collier's ideas

Figure 14.6   The in-text method of acknowledging a source.

this method of citation and also shows how paraphrased material can be interwoven into the context of one's paper. The reader who wants to know more about the source will consult the "List of Works Cited" attached to the end of the paper where the full bibliographical reference is listed. Figure 14.5 is an example of a list of works cited. It contains a full reference for the book by Dippie that is only briefly cited in the text.

To help you prepare your in-text notes and also to put together your final list of works cited, buy yourself a good handbook for doing research papers. Your bookstore will have several of them. The form used in this chapter is that provided by *The MLA Handbook for Writers of Research Papers,* 3d ed., 1988, published by the Modern Language Association. Another widely used handbook for preparing papers is the *Publication Manual of the American Psychological Association,* 3d ed., 1983. This handbook also teaches an in-text citation format that includes the author's last name and the date of publication: (Jones, 1981). The important thing is to choose one form to acknowledge your research sources and then use it consistently throughout your paper. Your instructor may insist on a specific form or style of citations.

REVISION AND PROOFREADING ACTIVITIES

As soon as you have a complete draft of your paper, put it aside for a few hours or overnight before you begin revision. The few hours delay will give you the insight necessary to create a polished final product. You rarely have such insight right after you have finished writing the first draft.

As part of the revision and final proofreading activities, be sure to include the following:

1. Check the organization.   Read through fairly rapidly to see if your ideas are presented in an order that makes sense. You may want to move an entire section or a part of a section to another place in your paper. Cut out any material that is off the subject or that does not contribute to the development of your topic.

2. Make sure that each main section of the paper contains a clear topic sentence.   This will help make your main ideas stand out. Support main ideas with subideas and/or supporting detail.

3. See if you have enough transitions.   Use transitions to make the organization of the main ideas clear to your reader. Refer back to Chapter 9 if you need to review types of transitions. Make certain, also, that your paragraphs are linked together so that your reader can follow your thought processes from one paragraph to the next. You can link paragraphs by putting in the first sentence of each paragraph words or phrases that refer back to the idea in the preceding paragraph. Then your reader can see how each paragraph relates to the one that precedes it. Paragraph linking is also illustrated in Chapter 9.

4. Read your introduction to make sure that it introduces what you have written.   When you have made sure that the organization of the body of your paper is logical and is made clear to your readers through the use of topic sentences and transitional material, go back and read your introduction to make sure that it introduces what you have written. It will help your readers to understand your paper if you provide them with an initial mental focus by writing a purpose or thesis sentence toward the end of your introduction. It does not need to be elaborate, but it should clearly state what they can expect as they read your paper. The sample first page of a paper in Figure 14.7 has a thesis sentence at the end of the first paragraph.

5. Take a look at your summary or conclusion.   If your paper is short, you will not need a detailed summary, or restatement, of your ideas, but you will want to write a concluding point that will provide a note of finality for your paper. Choose your concluding point with care.

6. Work to improve your sentences.   Make sure you have used complete sentences. If a sentence does not make sense to you, it won't to your reader either. Rewrite it to state exactly what you want to say.

Work for variety in sentence structure. If all of your sentences start with a subject, change some of them so that they begin with clauses. Vary their length. Your style will then be less monotonous. Delete sentences and words that do not contribute to what you are trying to say.

7. Locate and correct all remaining errors, including spelling, punctuation, and incorrect words.   Punctuate each sentence correctly. Look up every word that looks like it might be incorrectly spelled. Save time by using a spelling dictionary that gives no meanings but simply lists words alphabetically. If you do not like a word you have used, consult a dictionary or thesaurus and read through some synonyms to see if you can find a more appropriate word.

8. As a final check, read your paper out loud.   Pretend now that you are the reader instead of the writer. Locate and change all remaining errors. Many mistakes that your eye has missed will offend your ear.

Missy Spresser
Professor Shaw
Engl. 3101
April 15, 1990

                    The Education of the American Indian:
                          A Current Evaluation

        All Americans are at least vaguely familiar with the
plight of the American Indian. Cutbacks in federal programs for
Indians have made their problems even more severe in recent
years. Josephy reports, "By the end of 1981 it was estimated that
cutbacks in federal programs for Indians totaled about $500 mil-
lion" or more than ten times the cuts affecting their non-Indian
fellow Americans. Additional cuts seem to be threatened in the future. This reduced funding is affecting almost all aspects of
reservation life, including education (257-258). If the Indians
could solve their educational problems, solutions to many of their
other problems might not be far behind. In this paper the current
status of Indian education will be described and evaluated and
some ways of improving this education will be proposed.
        Whether to assimilate with the dominant American culture or
to preserve Indian culture has been a long-standing issue in Indian education. After the Civil War full responsibility for Indian
education was turned over by the government to churches and mis-
sionary groups. The next fifty years became a period of enforced
assimilation in all areas of Indian culture, but especially in religion and education (Jacoby 83-84).
        John Collier, a reformer who agitated in favor of Indians
and their culture from the early 1920s until his death in 1968,
had a different idea. He believed that instead of effacing native
culture, Indian schools should encourage and revitalize it (Dippie
276, 325).
        Pressure to assimilate remains a potent force today, how-
ever. More and more Indians are graduating from high school and
college and becoming eligible for jobs in the non-Indian society.
"When Indians obtain the requisite skills many of them enter the
broader American society and succeed." At present approximately 90
percent of all Indian children are educated in state public school
systems (Taylor 136, 155).
        How well these children compete with the members of the
dominant society, however, is another matter.

Figure 14.7   An example of the first page of a research paper

PREPARATION OF THE FINAL COPY

When you have completed revision and proofreading activities, you can type your paper and turn it in. Use standard 8½-by-11-inch paper. Leave one-inch margins at the top, bottom, and sides of each page. One inch from the top of the first page, by the left margin, type the following items with double spacing between each of them: your name, your instructor's name, the course number, and the date. Double-space again and center the title. Quadruple-space, indent five spaces, and begin typing your paper. There is no need to number the first page. From page 2 on, however, type page numbers in the upper right-hand corner one-half inch from the top. Type your last name before the page number on all pages. Keep a carbon or Xerox copy of the entire paper for yourself. Professors do not mean to lose papers, but they sometimes do. When they do, they expect you to be able to provide a second copy.

Figure 14.7 shows the completed first page of the paper on Indian education that has been used as an example in this chapter. All source material has been acknowledged with in-text citations. Notice that only the page numbers are required in the first citation since the author's name is included in the text.

Figure 14.5 is an example of a list of works cited that should be the last page of your paper. Included on this list are books, an unsigned article, a signed article, and a government document with a corporate author (The National Advisory Council). In-text citations for these various types of references would be as follows:

Books: author and page number (Jacoby 72).

Unsigned article: a short version of the title and page number ("In the Wake" 112).

Signed article: author and page number (LaFarge 43).

Corporate author: name and page number (National Advisory Council on Indian Education, 12).

A better way to cite this last source would be to include the name of the council in the text: "According to the National Advisory Council on Indian Education . . . (12)."

WRITING ON COMPUTERS

Many colleges now have computer labs or writing centers with computers that are available to students to help them prepare their papers. Set aside a few hours to learn to write on a computer, and you will never want to use a typewriter again. Software packages are available that help you brainstorm and generate ideas for papers at prewriting stages. Other software is available that enables you not only to type and make corrections in your paper, but also to check its spelling, grammar, proofread for certain types of errors, and even consult a thesaurus if you cannot think of the best word.

The feature most students like best in using computers is the help provided with revisions. Corrections and changes can be made in the machine. Paragraphs can be moved, words changed, sentences rewritten, passages deleted. Then fresh copy, with all corrections included, can be printed. Erasers, white-out, cutting and pasting, typing and retyping, illegible hand-written drafts all become things of the past. Most students write the first draft, print a copy of it, edit the printed copy with a pen or pencil, enter the corrections into the machine, and then print the final draft.

At the Very Least . . .

This chapter has described the ideal way of writing a paper. If you can't follow all of these suggestions, *at the very least:*

1. Write down your topic and brainstorm for ideas.
2. Make some sort of an outline that shows your ideas and the order in which you will treat them.
3. Write, revise, and proofread the paper. Make certain it is *absolutely free of errors.*

SUMMARY

You can make paper writing easier and more successful if you follow a process. Analyze the assignment first and divide your work into manageable steps. Use prewriting activities to help you select a topic, generate ideas, and organize your paper. Write your paper rapidly, capturing the flow of ideas on your outline. Do as much rewriting as you can while you write. In writing research papers, acknowledge all materials from outside sources with footnotes or, preferably, with in-text citations. List sources in a bibliography or in a list of works cited at the end of your paper. Revise and proofread your paper, type it, and turn it in. Learn to use a computer to help you write your papers if one is available.

EXERCISES

A. Monitor Your Comprehension of This Chapter.

Write quickly, in phrases rather than complete sentences, the information in this chapter that you understand and remember. Look back through your marginal notes and summaries and add what you left out. Is anything in the chapter unclear? Jot it down to ask about in class. Has reading the chapter caused you to think of new insights or examples of your own? Jot them down.

B. Class Exercises.

1. *Small groups.* Select a topic from the list in class exercise 2 below. Brainstorm the topic for 10 minutes. All members of the group should participate, and one member should record the ideas. Follow the rules for brainstorming:
   a. Do not question, disagree, or otherwise evaluate any contribution.
   b. Write everything down without comment.
   c. Go for quantity rather than quality; in other words, make a long list.
   d. Expand and elaborate on each other's ideas.
   e. Get it all down even if you write only a word or phrase to record each idea.
   f. Stop when you reach the time limit.

2. *Individuals.* Gain insight into the paper writing process by practicing each part of it. Use a computer to write your paper if one is available.
   a. Select a topic from the following list and brainstorm by quickly listing ideas and examples that you could include in a two-page paper.

      1. How to organize study materials.
      2. How to survey a textbook.
      3. How to survey a chapter.
      4. How to take notes on a college textbook.
      5. How to take lecture notes.
      6. How to study lecture notes.
      7. How to discover the student's responsibilities in a college class.
      8. How to remember more.
      9. How to concentrate when you don't want to study.
      10. Some places to study.
      11. How to solve your time problems.
      12. How to study for an exam.
      13. How to analyze your personal learning style.
      14. How to analyze a professor's teaching style.
      15. Support services at your university.

16. How to choose a topic for a paper or oral report.
17. How to keep track of assignments.
18. Why and how to acknowledge material in a paper.
19. How to outline a paper or oral report.
20. How to "map" a section of material.
21. How to use the dictionary.
22. How to improve your vocabulary.
23. How to revise a paper.
24. How to read and take notes on a math text.
25. How to take lecture notes in math.
26. How to take part in class discussion.
27. Why it is important to read the introduction or preface to a book.
28. How to find the main idea in a section of material.
29. How to brainstorm a topic.
30. How to improve the quantity and quality of your own creative thinking.
31. How to take essay exams.
32. How to take objective exams.
33. How to take quantitative exams.
34. Common exam errors and how to avoid them.
35. How to proofread and correct an exam or paper.

b. Briefly outline the paper and write a rough draft.
c. Do as much rewriting as you can and still keep your train of thought.
d. Revise, proofread, type your paper, and make three copies of it to bring to class.

3. *Small groups.*
Work as an editing group. Proceed as follows. Authors distribute copies of their papers to the other members of the group and read their papers aloud. As they listen, group members write suggestions for revisions on their copies of the paper, discuss these changes with the author, and, finally, return all copies to the author for final rewriting.

4. *Individuals and Evaluation Partners.*
Do a final rewriting of your paper and submit to another student for evaluation. Use the following Evaluation Guide to assign a score.

Evaluation Guide for a Paper

Instructions: Find the description in each area that best describes the paper you are evaluating. Give 1, 2, or 3 points in each area. Twenty-one points indicates an excellent paper. Fourteen to twenty indicate some revision is needed. Thirteen or less points indicates a need for significant revision.

Points

_____ *Assignment*

3- You followed the assignment perfectly, completing all parts, leaving nothing undone.

2- You left out two or three details in completing the assignment.

1- You have not fulfilled the requirements of the assignment.

_____ *Topic and Focus*

3- You selected a good topic and focused it by making a clear statement about it early in the paper. You focused the topic with a good title.

2- The focus is not entirely clear. Either the title does not describe what the paper is about, or there is no sentence used to focus the topic.

1- This paper does not have a clear topic and focus.

_____ *Organization*

3- The organization of this paper is clear and logical. Transitions are used to emphasize ideas and to help the reader move smoothly from one idea to another.

2- This paper may be organized, but the organization is not clear because of insufficient transitional material.

1- The organization in this paper is not apparent. Rather, this is a disorganized collection of ideas about the subject.

_____ *Development*

3- The ideas in this paper are well developed with explanations, examples, and other supporting details.

2- This paper has some details, but it tends to remain at the general level and to be somewhat unclear.

1- There are virtually no details in this paper. Rather, this is a collection of general statements about a subject.

_____ *Beginning and End*

3- The paper has a title, an introduction, and either a summary or a concluding point at the end.

2- The paper is lacking either a title, an introduction, or an appropriate ending.

1- The paper has no clear beginning or end.

_____ *Sentences*

3- All of the sentences are complete, and there is sufficient variety in sentence structure.

2- There are one or two incomplete or run-on, unpunctuated sentences. There is not much sentence variety.

Points

1- There are many incomplete sentences, and there is virtually no sentence variety.

_____ *Errors*

3- There are no spelling, punctuation, or other errors in this paper.

2- There are a few errors.

1- This paper is full of errors, and it is, consequently, very difficult to read.

Total points _____

Comments:

5. *Individuals, Editing Groups, and Evaluation Partners*

Write a paper that includes all parts of the writing and final evaluation process as described in Class Exercises 2, 3, and 4, with the following changes.

a. Select a topic of your own instead of using one on the list.

b. Do some library research. Chapter 15 will help you learn how. Quote or paraphrase material in your paper from at least one book and one article. Document your sources and include a List of Works Cited as demonstrated in this chapter.

c. Add the following component to the *Evaluation Guide for a Paper:*

_____ *Research and Source Material*

3- Source material from both a book and an article is smoothly incorporated into the text and is documented according to an accepted format (MLA or APA).

2- Source material is not clearly related to the rest of the text and there are errors in documentation.

1- Source material is unrelated to the text and documentation is inaccurate.

A perfect score for a research paper is 24 points. Sixteen to twenty-three points or less indicates a need for revision.

C. Application Exercises.

1. Follow all of the suggestions for prewriting to help you get started on a paper for another class.

2. Write, rewrite, revise, and proofread the paper using suggestions from this chapter.

D. *Topics for Your Learning Journal*

1. Write topics, issues, or major questions that have been dealt with in each of the classes you are taking this semester. Put stars by the ones that would make good paper topics.

2. Write and rewrite a paragraph on the following topic: "Writing a paper is (fun, easy, difficult, terrifying, impossible) for me." Supply your own adjective. Reread and improve each sentence as you write it. Then reread and rewrite the entire paragraph until you are satisfied with it.

3. The writing process is not always described in exactly the same way by everyone, nor does everyone practice it in exactly the same way. Write a description of your version of the writing process. Include everything you do, beginning with the early stages of thinking about the topic until you turn in the final copy.

15 | Doing Library Research

When you have finished reading this chapter, you will know how to:

1. Get organized for research.
2. Build a bibliography.
3. Find research materials in a university library.
4. Take research notes.

GET ORGANIZED FOR RESEARCH

Begin library research by getting organized to do research. You will collect materials in the library either by xeroxing them on the copy machine and filing them in folders labeled according to the main topic units in your paper or by hand copying or paraphrasing material on index cards. If you select the xerox method, buy file folders or a letter-size expanding file and some small self-adhesive tags for the pages of books and articles that you want to xerox. Bring along some pens or pencils. Finally, take plenty of change to feed the library xerox machine or pay the copy center. You will also need some 4×6 cards for your bibliography. If you select the card method for research notes, buy a package of 4×6 cards, take all of your notes on them, get together three or four pens or pencils, and buy an appropriate file to use to organize your note cards. Cardboard expanding files used for canceled checks will work. Expanding files are good for keeping both note cards and xeroxed materials organized because you can label the tabs on the pockets with your main heads, as shown in Figure 15.1. Then it is easy to file your materials where they belong as you acquire them. Buy a roll of self-adhesive labels, which you can peel off and use if you want to change the headings on these tabs. Whatever filing system you use, make sure that it is easy to

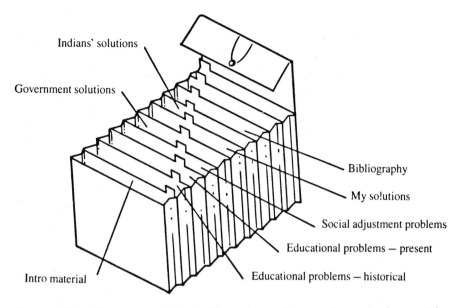

Indians' solutions

Government solutions

Bibliography

My solutions

Social adjustment problems

Educational problems — present

Intro material

Educational problems — historical

Figure 15.1 How a canceled check file can be used to organize research materials.

carry around and that it is big enough to hold all of your xeroxed materials or note cards. Before you file your materials, make certain that you have included complete source information on each piece so that you won't have to go back and look it up again. This means writing the author's name, the title, and the place and date of publication on each individual source.

START WITH THE BIBLIOGRAPHY

Your first job when you go to the library to begin research is to accumulate a list of sources, or bibliography. If you remember that *biblio* means "book" in Greek, it will be easier to remember that a bibliography is a group of books and articles about your subject. Use the ideas you jotted down while prewriting to help you start locating materials. Consult the card catalog and various indexes in the library to help you find material. (There is information later in this chapter on how to use these devices.) As you locate books and articles on your topic, consult them to see if they contain bibliographies themselves that will lead you to additional sources.

Make a record of bibliographical items before you locate the items themselves in the library or start taking any notes on their contents. For the paper on Indian education, for example, you would need a record of all the books and parts of books on this subject that are available in the library. You would also need a record of magazine and journal articles written on your subject. You might also see if some newspaper articles are available. Finally, you might get the names of some government publications that would describe official government action concerning Indian problems. Do not worry if your bibliography seems long. When you actually look for these materials in the library, you will not find all of them. Some will be checked out; others will not be in your library's holdings.

As you accumulate sources, keep your "tentative outline to guide research" handy, and find materials that are relevant to that outline. Do not record books and articles that are not about some part of your subject. Library research takes a lot of time. Every source you record should be one you might use.

Write each bibliographical item on a separate card. A bibliography card for a book should include author, title, place of publication, publisher, date of publication, and call number so that you can later locate it in the library. Figure 15.2 provides an example. A bibliography card for an article should include author (if one is listed), title of article, name of publication, volume (unless it is a weekly publication, in which case the date of publication is sufficient), page numbers, and location in library. Figure 15.3 provides an example. Here are two additional examples of how to write

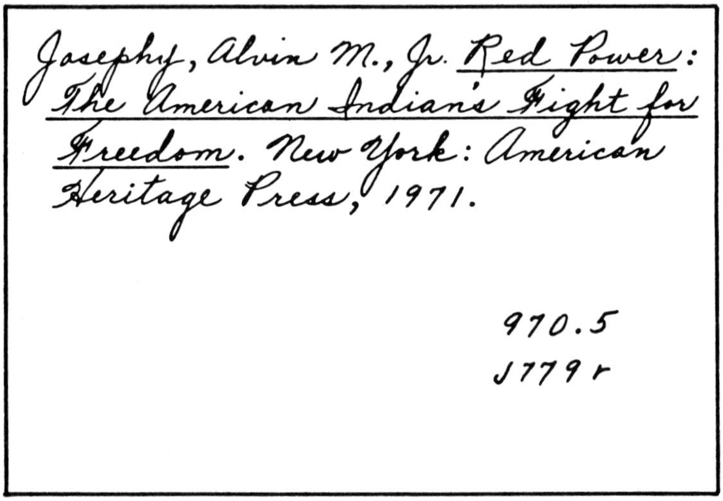

Josephy, Alvin M., Jr. *Red Power: The American Indian's Fight for Freedom.* New York: American Heritage Press, 1971.

970.5
J779 r   Call number for location

Figure 15.2 A bibliography card for a book.

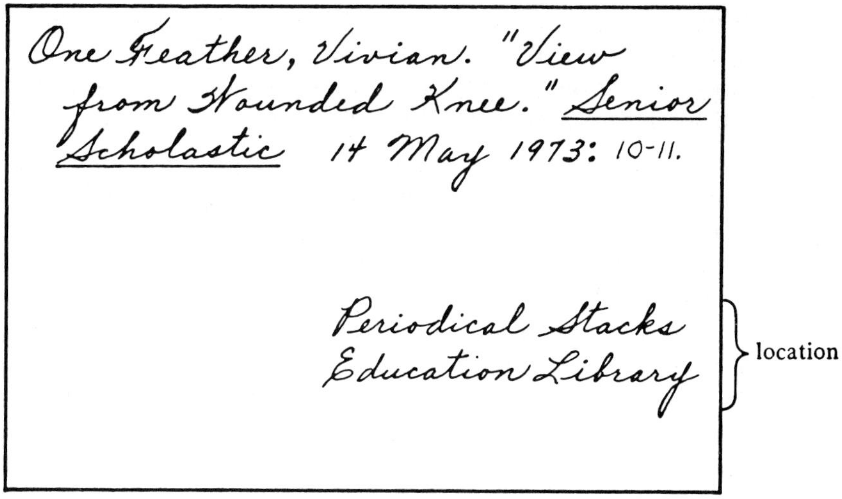

One Feather, Vivian. "View from Wounded Knee." *Senior Scholastic* 14 May 1973: 10-11.

Periodical Stacks Education Library } location

Figure 15.3   A bibliography card for an article.

complete bibliographical information for an article in a magazine or journal in which you would include the volume number:

> Gosling, J. T., and A. J. Hundhausen. "Waves in the Solar Wind." *Scientific American* 236 (1977): 36–43.

and, for an article in a newspaper in which the date of publication is sufficient:

> Cowen, Edward. "World Oil Shortage Is Called Inevitable." *New York Times* 17 May 1977: 1.

These examples follow the Modern Language Association (MLA) style. If your professor asks you to use another style, such as that recommended by the American Psychological Association (APA), you should get a copy of that style book and follow the slightly different form as you write your bibliography.

You make bibliography cards as suggested above for several reasons. They serve as a guide to the next step in your research process, which is to find the sources listed on your cards and then to read and xerox these sources or to take notes on them. Whenever you take notes on a source, you will *not* need to write out more than a short title on the xeroxed page or on your note card to identify the source, since the complete information will be on your bibliography card. As an alternative to short titles, some people number their bibliography cards and write the corresponding number on their xeroxed pages or note cards to identify the source of the note. Later, you will use the information on your bibliography cards when you write your in-text citations or footnotes. Finally, with all your sources on cards, it is easy to alphabetize them and type a list of works cited or bibliographical listing to append to your paper. Until you are ready to write acknowledgments and to assemble and type the list of works cited, however, keep all these cards in the back bibliography section of your expanding file, where you can easily find them during the research process. Or, put a rubber band around them and keep them in some other safe place.

In order to accumulate a complete bibliography, you will need to use various parts of the library. Take fifteen minutes in a new library to find out how it is laid out. Begin by locating an information desk, a reader's advisor, or someone at the circulation desk who can answer questions. Tell this person that you are new to the library and ask if a map or directory is available. If you get one, use it, look around, and ask questions of your resource person. Make certain you can answer all of the questions in Class Exercise B1 at the end of this chapter.

Now you are ready to get to work on your bibliography and research. A good place to start is to locate some books on your topics.

HOW TO FIND BOOKS

To find books, you go first to the card catalog. Nearly all libraries have card catalogs. A few have book catalogs, and even more are acquiring computer indexes. If your library's holdings are on the computer, it is still useful to know how to use the card catalog as a back-up system when the computer is down. The card catalog contains drawers of three-by-five cards, arranged alphabetically, which give you information about the books in the library and tell you where to find them. Most books are represented in the card catalog by at least three cards. One card lists the book under the last name of the author, one under the title of the book, and one, or sometimes several, under various broad subjects. Books of fiction often do not have subject cards. Figure 15.4 shows examples of the author, title, and subject cards for one book.

Learn to read and understand the cards in the card catalog. Notice how the author is written on one line and the title below, with only the first word in capitals. The call number enables you to locate the book in the library. When you find one book on your topic, look at the bottom of the catalog card for other subject headings under which your book is listed. Then look under those headings to find other books that might be related to your subject.

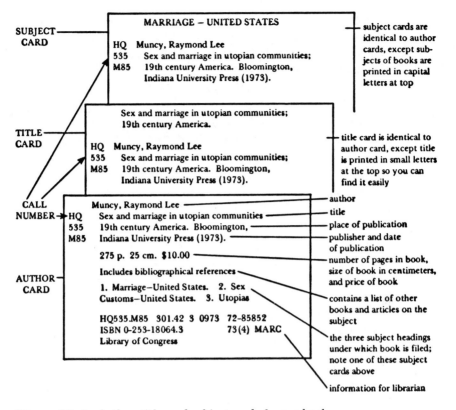

Figure 15.4   Author, title, and subject cards for one book.

The computer index has all the information you would find in the card catalog stored in the computer. You read the information about your book on the screen of a computer terminal rather than on a card. Terminals may be located throughout the library. Computer indexes are "user friendly" and tell you, usually on the screen itself, exactly what you must do to use them. Special advantages of computer indexes are: (1) their terminals may be placed throughout the campus as well as in the library; (2) they not only give the usual information about a book but also its current status, such as whether it is checked out, on reserve, or on order; and (3) they enable you to search by author, title, subject, or by combinations of these. Usually you will need to copy the information about your book off the screen. Some libraries, however, are able to provide a printed copy of all the books they own on a particular subject. You have to ask for this service, and there will usually be a fee to pay.

If you have trouble figuring out broad subject headings related to your topic, go to the reference room and ask for the Library of

Congress *List of Subject Headings* (it may also be available near the public catalog). This is the list librarians use to catalog books by subject. Write down those subject headings that might lead you to books on your topic.

For those books that look useful, write out bibliography cards as described above. When you write down the call number, write down all of it, to the last decimal point, or you will have trouble locating your book. When you have made your bibliography cards, the next step is to discover how to get the books. A directory is usually in plain sight in the lobby. It tells you on what floor and in what general area on that floor you will find a book with a specific call number. On each floor of the library you will find other directories to help you locate material there.

If you cannot find a book on the shelves, there are a number of things you can do. First, look around a bit on the shelves—above, below, and from side to side—to see if someone put it back in the wrong spot. If you still cannot find it, look at the other books in the area. They will be on or near your topic also, and one or more might serve as well as the one you were trying to find. You can also go to the circulation desk and ask if your book has been checked out, placed on reserve, or lost. If it's on reserve, you can read it in the *reserve section.* If it is lost, the library can trace it and try to find it for you. If it is checked out, you can find out when it is to be returned and then ask that it be held for you. The library will notify you when it comes in, and you can pick it up at the circulation desk.

HOW TO FIND ARTICLES

In order to find articles in the library you need to consult the various *indexes to periodical literature.* They tell you in which magazines and journals articles on your subject can be located. There are a number of indexes to periodical literature. Here is a list with descriptions of the ones you will be most likely to use.

1. The *Readers' Guide to Periodical Literature* lists by author, title, and subject all the articles printed in nearly 160 magazines of interest to the general public. The *Readers' Guide* was preceded by *Poole's Index to Periodical Literature,* which is the *Readers' Guide* of the nineteenth century. It indexes articles in magazines that go back to 1815. Many of these articles may be available in your library on microfilm.

2. You will usually find the *International Index,* the *Social Sciences and Humanities Index,* and the new separate *Social Sciences Index* and *Humanities Index* shelved together. You will not get confused if you remember that they are all the same index—only the names have been changed. These indexes lead you to scholarly articles and book reviews in the social sciences—anthropology, economics, environmental science, geography, law and criminology, medical sciences, political science, psychology, public administration, and sociology—and in the humanities—archaeology, classical studies, folklore, history, language, literature, political criticism, performing arts, philosophy, and religion and theology.

3. The *Education Index* will lead you to articles about education in more than two hundred different periodicals.

4. The *Engineering Index, Art Index, Applied Science and Technology Index,* and *Industrial Arts Index* are other specialized indexes that lead you to magazine and journal articles in the fields indicated by their titles.

5. *Abstracts,* like periodical indexes, list articles on particular subjects. They also list the books on these subjects. They give short summaries of both books and articles. Abstract periodicals are available in psychology, biology, philosophy, folklore, geography, history, anthropology, sociology, and other subjects.

6. The *Biological and Agricultural Index* is useful to biology and agriculture students.

The first time you look into a periodical index you will probably need some help in reading it. But once you learn to read one index, you can read the others, since most of them are similar in format. Here is an entry from the *Readers' Guide to Periodical Literature.* Under the general heading "Women" and the specific subheading "History" the following article is listed:

> What ought to be and what was: women's sexuality in the nineteenth century. C. N. Degler, bibli f Am Hist R 79:1467-90 D'74.

The title of the article and its author are listed first. "Bibli f" means that there are bibliographical footnotes in this article that will lead you to other sources of material on this subject. The article appears in the magazine abbreviated as "Am Hist R." You will have to consult the Abbreviations of Periodicals Indexed at the front of the book to find out that this abbreviation stands for the *American Historical Review.* You will need the full name of the magazine before you attempt to find it in the periodical stacks. After the name of the magazine, some numbers are listed. The first number, 79, is the volume number. All issues of the *American Historical Review* published in the year this article was printed were bound together at the end of that year as volume 79. After the volume number is a colon, followed by the page numbers 1467–1490. Finally, the date is listed. Only one month begins with D, and the year is 1974.

Here are three other bits of advice to help you use periodical indexes efficiently. First, take five minutes to read the title page and preface to find out how the index is arranged, how often it comes out, what sort of material is indexed, whether or not it includes summaries of each item indexed, what abbreviations are used, and if there are any other pointers to help you use it. Second, remember that all periodical indexes come out periodically themselves, like the magazines and journals they index. In choosing the particular volume of an index to use, look in indexes printed at the time that the subject was of the greatest current interest. Finally, consider the point of view of the index you are consulting. If your subject is air pollution and you want popular articles of general interest, look in the *Readers' Guide*. If you want an engineering or scientific point of view, look in the *Engineering Index* or the *Applied Science and Technology Index*.

When you have completed your bibliography cards for the articles you wish to consult, you then need to find where the journals themselves are located. Some libraries catalog their periodicals and shelve them with the book collection. Others place them in periodical stacks, which may be "open," so that you can walk through and search for your own periodicals, or "closed," so that you will have to send a library employee for what you want. Before you enter these stacks, find the directory to them. It may be a Linedex, which is a revolving, upright card file, or a Serial Holdings List, which is a list of all periodicals, as well as their locations, owned by the library. Look up the stack number of the periodical you want, find the magazine, then the volume, then the month, and finally the pages where the article appears, in that order.

HOW TO FIND MATERIAL IN MICROFORM

You now know how to find books and articles when they are in volume form. More and more materials, including rare or old books, magazines (*Time* and *Newsweek,* for example), journals, and newspapers are now being put in microform because they take up less space than they did in their original form. You will know that *books* are in microform when the card catalog call number includes one of the microform abbreviations: *mic, mf, mc,* or *mfc.* Similarly, if you see one of these abbreviations next to the name of a *periodical* in the Linedex, the Holding List, or the card catalog, you will need to look for the periodical in microform.

You read microform material on machines that enlarge the tiny photographed images of pages so that you can see them easily. The first time you use one of these machines you will have to ask the microform librarian for help. But after the first time, you will probably be able to manage the machine yourself. If you find a page you need to copy, copy machines for microforms are available in most libraries.

With the aid of the card catalog and Linedex, you will have no trouble finding out about and reading *books* and *magazines* on microfilm. The Linedex and card catalog will not help you, however, in locating material in *newspapers.* There are special indexes to help you find material in microformed newspapers. Here are the most important and most useful of them:

1. *Newsbank* will lead you to newspaper materials published after 1970 on almost any contemporary subject you can think of (drug abuse, student protests, abortion, birth control, air and water pollution, and so on). *Newsbank* articles are drawn from 150 newspapers representing 103 major cities in the United States. To locate several newspaper articles on your subject, consult the *Newsbank* index first. It will lead you to a microfiche card that may contain fifteen to twenty different articles on your subject.

2. *The New York Times Index* differs from *Newsbank* in that it goes back further in time (to 1851), it indexes only one newspaper, and that entire newspaper is microfilmed each day. For each year there is a separate volume. To use *The New York Times Index,* look up your topic at the time it was in the news. Articles are arranged under the topic in chronological order.

The New York Times Index not only lists the titles of the articles, it also gives summaries or abstracts of them. Thus, from the *Index* itself you can get a capsule of a story or series of stories. If you want more detail, the *Index* tells you which issue of the *Times* you need to find on microfilm in order to read the entire story.

3. Indexes for the *Wall Street Journal* and for the *Christian Science Monitor* are also available. Usually you can find your local newspapers on microfilm in the library too. These will go way back if you live in an old town or city. Ask your librarian what sort of index is available to help you locate stories in these newspapers.

4. For a different point of view you can look up your topic in the *Index to the Times (London).* From 1962 on this index is available in

bound volumes. Prior to 1962, and going back to 1790, the index is on microfilm. The newspaper itself, also on microfilm, goes back to 1785.

HOW TO USE OTHER SOURCES OF INFORMATION IN THE LIBRARY

In doing research you will not always limit yourself to information from books, magazines, journals, and newspapers. You may also want to find out *biographical information* about someone, locate information in *governmental publications,* get help with your own *bibliography* building, find an *essay, play, short story,* or a *poem,* or even check on the *history of a word.* There are volumes to help you do all these things, and they are usually located in the reference room.

1. *Biographical information* can be obtained from a variety of volumes, including the *Biography Index,* the *Dictionary of American Biography,* the *Dictionary of National Biography, Current Biography,* and the various *Who's Whos* (in America, the South and the Southwest, International, and so on).

2. If you are interested in locating information in *government publications,* there are two main indexes you can consult—the *Public Affairs Information Service Bulletin* and the *Monthly Catalog.* The relatively new *Index to U.S. Government Periodicals* is also a useful guide. See if your library also owns the periodicals it indexes, called *U.S. Government Periodicals,* which are on microfiche and are arranged by subject like *Newsbank.*

3. If you have been through the card catalog and some of the indexes to periodicals and still want to expand your bibliography, use the *Bibliographic Index.* It will tell you where to find bibliographies on your topic that have been published either as parts of books, pamphlets, in periodicals, or as separate books.

4. Sometimes you want to locate an *essay, short story, play,* or *poem* that you know is published in some anthology, but you do not know which one. To find an essay, look in the *Essay and General Literature Index;* to find a play, look in the *Play Index;* to find a short story, use the *Short Story Index;* and to find a poem, look under the author, title, or first line in *Granger's Index to Poetry.* If you want the original source of a familiar saying or quotation, look it up in *Bartlett's Familiar Quotations.* These are only examples; other sources for such materials are also available.

5. Finally, you should know about the biggest and most complete *dictionary* of them all, the *Oxford English Dictionary.* You would use the *O.E.D.* if you wanted to study the history of a word: to learn

its origin and see how it has changed in spelling and meaning over the years.

There are many other sources of specialized information in the reference room. Your best guide is the reference librarian, who can usually tell you where to look to find literally any type of information about anything.

HOW TO DO A COMPUTER SEARCH

Most libraries now offer a computer search service that permits you to search the world's literature, in addition to that possessed by your library, for information on your topic. In doing computer searches, your library works through a vendor, such as Dialogue, or Bibliographic Retrieval Service (BRS), to access large data bases that can provide you with lists of sources on your topic within seconds. To use them effectively, you will need to make a tentative outline with a research question or tentative thesis and a list of main ideas. Use this to come up with some key words that describe the information you are seeking. There are some special advantages of computer searches: (1) the information is the most current available; (2) the search can be done much faster than by hand and more thoroughly since combinations of subjects and/or authors can be used at once; (3) you can specify that the search be done in scholarly or popular literature, that it cover a particular time period, and even that it be confined to a particular language; (4) you will end up with a printed bibliography. In fact, when the data base includes abstracts, you will be provided with an annotated bibliography. Expect to help the library to pay for your search since computer time is expensive. Since you are searching the world's literature, you cannot expect your library to have all of the sources on the computer list. Use the interlibrary loan service to order missing material from another library. Expect such an order to take two to three weeks' time.

WHENEVER IN DOUBT IN A LIBRARY, ASK QUESTIONS

Librarians do not mind being asked questions. Here are some examples of the types of questions you might ask the readers' adviser or the reference librarian while you are doing research, and some examples of the answers you might receive. As you read the questions, cover up the answers, which are in the right-hand column, and see how well you can provide answers of your own. There are often several places to search for information. See if, on the basis of this chapter, you can anticipate some of the answers provided or even add additional sources of your own. Note also that some additional indexes and other sources are mentioned beyond those discussed thus far in this chapter.

Questions	Answers
I am interested in divorce laws in various states. Where could I find a sampling of current legislation?	In *Newsbank*. Look under the broad category of "Social Relations," and the subcategory "Divorce and Divorce Laws." You will find articles from newspapers from various states which you can then read on microfiche.
I am doing a paper on the "open classroom." Where can I find information on it?	Look up "open classroom" in the *Education Index*. It will lead you to articles on the subject. The ERIC (Educational Resources Information Center) microfiche collection would also have information on the subject.
I want to know the latest scientific research about DNA. Where do I find it?	Look up DNA in the subject index in the back of the most recent volume of *Biological Abstracts*. There will be list of articles with the abstract number beside them. Look up the abstracts by their numbers in the volume and read the summary of the research. Also take a look at *Microbiology Abstracts*.
How can I find out the current birth and death statistics?	Look in the *Public Affairs Information Service Bulletin* for census statistics put out by the government. *The American Statistics Index, The Statistical Abstracts of the United States*, and the *World Almanac* are useful sources for locating statistical information also.
I am interested in memory, and I want to find the latest articles about it.	If you want scholarly articles, consult the *Social Sciences Index* or *Psychological Abstracts*. If you

Questions	Answers
	want popular articles, consult the *Readers' Guide to Periodical Literature.*
Where can I find the latest information on the world food crisis?	The *Public Affairs Information Service Bulletin* will lead you to government and other publications not always listed in the *Reader's Guide.* The *Readers' Guide* is another good source. For more scholarly information consult the *Social Sciences Index.*
I want to do a paper on Hemingway. Where do I look for critical articles and books about his work?	Look in the *Humanities Index* and the *Social Sciences and Humanities Index.* Look also in the card or computerized catalog. Books *by him* will be cataloged *first.* The books *about him and his work,* which are what you are looking for, will be cataloged *second.* In the computer you can also ask for books *by him* and *about him.*
I am doing a paper on Wordsworth for my English class. I do not want to read a whole book about his life. Where can I get some quick biographical information?	Look in the *Dictionary of National Biography.* It will not only give you the pertinent facts of his life, but it will also provide you with a bibliography to help you get started on your research. Any general encyclopedia will also provide information about Wordsworth.
How can I find out how people felt about the Panama Canal when it was first being built.	Look in *Poole's Index to Periodical Literature* for the years during which and just after it was built.

EVALUATE THE RESEARCH MATERIAL YOU HAVE SELECTED

One of your concerns in doing research is to select the books and articles that will give you the most informed, detailed, up-to-date, reliable, and intelligent information available. Here are some suggestions to help you pick the best sources. When you first pick up a book or article, check introductory material and/or headnotes to get some idea of its quality and the author's general competency. Notice also *when* the material was published. Sometimes you will need the most recent material available, or you may want material published at the time your topic was of greatest concern to the most people.

You can find out still more about a book and its author by reading some book reviews in the *Book Review Index,* the *Book Review Digest,* or the *Technical Book Review Index* in the library. Reviews will give you some idea about how the book was originally received by experts in the field. You might also consult a biographical dictionary to get additional information about the author.

Your professors can also tell you about the reputation, quality, and general worth of books and articles written in their own fields. In fact, asking your professors for the titles of some of the best books and articles on their subjects is often one of the best ways to start research.

Finally, you can compare passages on the same subject in several different books to judge which seem better than the others. If one or two of the books seem to be more accurate and to contain fuller explanations and more documentation than the others, you would probably be safe in choosing those books as the best of the several available.

HOW TO TAKE RESEARCH NOTES

When you have gathered together a variety of the best research sources your library has to offer on your subject, you are then ready to begin reading and taking notes. Keep your tentative outline handy so that you will not read off your subject. Furthermore, as you read, make any necessary changes in your tentative outline. You may find that one item on the outline interests you more than the others. Early in your research, then, recast your paper. Revise your outline, relabel some of the tabs in your file, and then read for material to fill in the new, revised outline.

Don't try to read each book and article you have selected all the way through. You will find the material you need more rapidly and accurately if you survey all books and articles you use before you take any notes from them and then consult the index. Use the methods for surveying described in Chapter 8. Look especially for the chapter or chapters that are relevant to your research. During this process you may also spot one or two chapters that set forth the author's major theories in the book. By reading or surveying these chapters, you can often gain almost as much information as you would by reading the entire book.

As you read and take notes, think about the final outline for your paper and solve as many organizational problems as possible as you go along. One student made a fifteen-page final outline for a paper intended to advocate certain legislation *before* he began his research. When he began to read, he found the legislation had already been passed. His fifteen-page outline was useless. He had to shift his focus to ways in which the new legislation could be made generally known to the public, and redid his outline. His mistake was making an elaborate outline before he began to read. A brief, tentative outline would have saved him time. You cannot know how your subject may shift and change until you get into your reading. Then you need to be alert enough to shift and change with it.

Every once in a while you should take the cards or xeroxed material from behind a heading, read through them, and put them in a sequence that seems logical to you. Move some of them to other sections if it seems appropriate to do so, or create new sections. As you move your research materials into sequential order, you are continuing to shape your paper while you do research. You will not make the mistake, so commonly made by students, of accumulating a pile of dozens of articles or note cards, all loosely related to your subject, with no idea of how to use them in your paper.

In addition to jotting the subject at the top of each article or card, it is also important to indicate briefly, below the subject, the source of that information. The author's last name is usually enough; if you have two or more sources by the same author, write the title of the source in brief form. You may have numbered your bibliography cards. Then all you need write on the note card is the corresponding number. You can be brief because the complete information about the source is on the bibliography card.

The material you xerox or write on note cards will be of three types. First, there is material that you want to quote exactly as the author wrote it. Draw a box around material you want to quote from xeroxed material or copy it on your card exactly as it appears in your source. Put quotation marks around copied material so that you can later incorporate this material in your paper as a direct quote. It's a good idea to double-check for accuracy all direct quotes you record. Figure 15.5 shows a card that contains a direct quote from a book. Notice that the numbers of the pages on which the material originally appeared are written at the end of the quote. Make certain that the page numbers are on xeroxed material. Note, also, that only one side of a card is used. Never take notes on both sides of a note card. You need to be able to lay cards out on your desk to see patterns of ideas. If a quote is too long to fit on one card, use two. Write a brief title with the abbreviation *cont.* on the second card, and number the cards.

You will not always want to quote directly for the sources you are researching. You should quote exactly when the material is particularly well expressed or when the author is well known and you prefer to use his or her exact words. More often, however, you will paraphrase, or put into your own words, what the author has said. The paraphrased note is the second type of research note you will take. Figure 15.6 provides an example from a magazine article. In paraphrasing it is important to read and rephrase the material carefully so that you will not change the author's meaning and thus misrepresent the material. Indicate paraphrasing on your note card by omitting the quotation marks and by writing *paraphrase* on the card. You must clearly state on the card the source and page number of the paraphrased material. Even though you have changed the wording, you must let your reader know its origin. If you

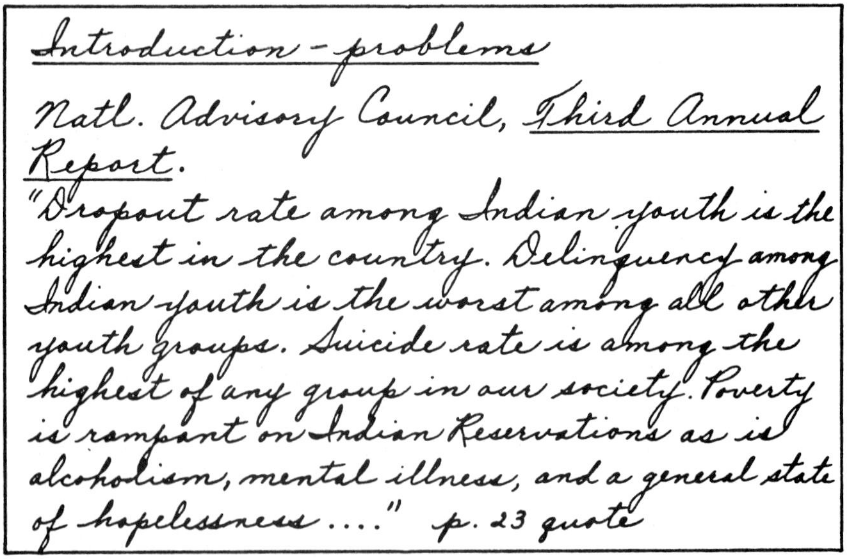

Introduction – problems

Natl. Advisory Council, Third Annual Report.
"Dropout rate among Indian youth is the highest in the country. Delinquency among Indian youth is the worst among all other youth groups. Suicide rate is among the highest of any group in our society. Poverty is rampant on Indian Reservations as is alcoholism, mental illness, and a general state of hopelessness ...." p. 23 quote

Figure 15.5   First type of note card: Direct quote from a book.

> *Introduction - statistics*
>
> *U. S. News - Wounded Knee Siege*
> *1970 U. S. Census statistics for Indian*
> *families on reservations:*
> *Ave. family income: $1500 (less than half*
> *present poverty level)*
> *Unemployment: 40 - 80 %*
> *Life Expectancy: 44 years (compare 64 for*
> *other Americans)*
> *Infant mortality 3 times greater than*
> *for other Americans*
> *p. 113 paraphrase*

Figure 15.6   Second type of note card: Paraphrased note from an article.

are working with xeroxed material instead of cards, you may be able to paraphrase material into the body of your paper as you are writing it.

A third type of note you will make as you do your research will have *mine* or *me* written at the top. On these cards or sheets of paper record ideas that occur to you as you read and work with your subject. Usually the more of these you have, the better. For some papers it is essential that you have ideas of your own. For others that are more purely research papers, the notes on sources will be more important. Figure 15.7 provides an example of this third type of note card.

Continue to read or skim through the material in your bibliography, continue to xerox or take notes, to label and file them, and your paper will take shape. Check occasionally to see if one area of your paper is sketchy and another too detailed. At any one point during your research you may decide to delete a meager section and divide a large section into subsections. Or you may decide to do more research on the meager section.

When you have finished your research, read through all your research materials. Make sure they are all labeled. Put them in the sequence that you will follow in writing your paper. After you have finished your paper, reorder the bibliography cards alphabetically and use them to compile the final bibliography or list of works cited.

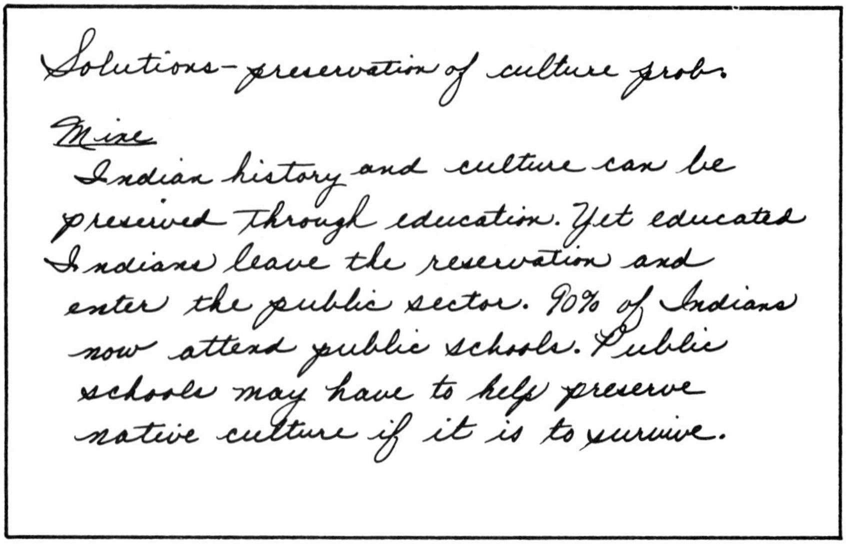

Solutions—preservation of culture prob.

Mine

Indian history and culture can be preserved through education. Yet educated Indians leave the reservation and enter the public sector. 90% of Indians now attend public schools. Public schools may have to help preserve native culture if it is to survive.

Figure 15.7 Third type of note card: Your original idea.

At the Very Least . . .

This chapter has described some complete and thorough ways of doing library research. If you do not use all of these ways, *at the very least* do the following:

1. **Learn to use the computer index or the card catalogue and find a book.**
2. **Learn to use periodical indexes and find an article. Start with the *Reader's Guide.***
3. **Learn to read material on the microform reader. Start with *Time* and *Newsweek.***
4. **Xerox research materials or take notes on cards, writing one idea or piece of information per card. Write the source, page numbers and titles on all research materials.**

SUMMARY

Use your tentative outline to guide your research. Look for bibliographical items relevant to headings on this outline. Each source in your bibliography should be recorded on a separate card. A complete bibliography usually includes the names of books, magazine and journal articles, and materials from other sources, some of which might be in microform. Once you have found that your library owns the sources in your bibliography, you then need

to find them, evaluate their relative worth, and either xerox parts of them or take research notes on them. If notes are taken on cards, then each card should contain only one item of information. Research materials are of three types—direct quotes, paraphrases, or your own ideas. As you accumulate research materials, label and organize them as you go along. Then it will be relatively easy to make your final outline and write your paper.

EXERCISES

A. Monitor Your Comprehension of this Chapter.

Write quickly, in phrases rather than complete sentences, the information in this chapter that you understand and remember. Look back through your marginal notes and summaries and add what you left out. Is anything in the chapter unclear? Jot it down to ask about in class. Has reading the chapter caused you to think of new insights or examples of your own? Jot them down.

B. Class Exercises.

1. Individuals or Small Groups. Become acquainted with the library at your institution by visiting it and answering the following questions.

1. Where is/are the library/libraries at your institution located?
2. Is the Main Card Catalog in your library a card catalog or is it computerized? If it is computerized, where are the terminals? If it is a card catalog, where is it located? Describe the organization of the catalog and how to use it.
3. Where are the books themselves?
4. Where are the indexes to periodicals? Where is the Reader's Guide to Periodical Literature?
5. Are there any computerized indexes to periodical literature? Which ones are they? Where are they? What types of material do they index? How and for what purposes might you use them?
6. Where is the Serials Holdings List of the periodicals your library owns and their call numbers?
7. Where are the periodicals (magazines and journals) themselves?
8. Are the periodical and book stacks "open" so that you can go into them, or are they "closed" so that you will have to send a library employee for the material you need?
9. Where are the microforms? How do you check them out? Where are the microform readers?
10. What do the abbreviations *mic, mf, cc, mfc* in the Serial Holdings List or the card catalog stand for?
11. Locate and name one newspaper index in the microform section.

12. Where is the reference room? Give three examples of material you can find there.

13. Where is the reserve section? What is its purpose?

14. Where are the government documents? Give three examples of materials you can find there.

15. Where is the circulation desk where you check out a book? What do you have to do to check out a book, and how long can you keep it out?

16. Give three examples of library materials which may *not* be check out.

17. Where is the copy center or the xerox machines?

2. *Individuals or pairs. Finding books.* Select a topic that interests you or that you have to research anyway. Go to the card or computerized catalog and find the names of three books on the topic. Make a bibliography card (Figure 15.2) for each of these books. Check the directory to find where these books are located. Then go to that area and find *one* of them. Survey the book as you were taught to do in Chapter 8. Then locate a chapter that has a useful treatment of your topic. Survey it as you were taught to do in Chapter 8. Make two note cards. One of these note cards should contain a direct quote (Figure 15.5). The other should contain a paraphrase (Figure 15.6).

3. *Individuals or pairs. Finding articles.* Use the periodical indexes to look up three articles about your topic. Make a bibliography card (Figure 15.3) for each article. Use the Serial Holdings List, or whatever other system your library uses, to help you locate the periodicals in which these articles appear. Find *one* of the articles, survey it for five minutes, and write two note cards, one a quote and one a paraphrase. You should now have an idea of your own about your topic. Record this idea on a third note card (see Figure 15.7).

4. *Individuals or pairs. Using microforms.* Look up your topic in one of the newspaper indexes. Find three newspaper articles about your topic and write a bibliography card for each of them (Figure 15.3). Find a copy of *one* paper in which one of these articles appears and read it on the microform reader. Write *one* note card, either a quote or a paraphrase. Write another note card that contains an observation or idea of your own.

5. *Individuals.* Organize the cards that you prepared for exercises 2, 3, and 4, secure them with a rubber band, and turn them in. The sequence should be as follows:

   a. 1 cover card. Write your name and your topic on it
   b. 3 bibliography cards for books
   c. 2 notecards for books—a direct quote and a paraphrase
   d. 3 bibliography cards for articles
   e. 3 notecards for articles—a direct quote, a paraphrase, an idea of your own
   f. 3 bibliography cards for newspaper articles in microform
   g. 2 notecards for microforms—one quote *or* paraphrase and one observation or idea of your own

Total: 17 cards.

C. Application of Skills

1. Go to the reference section of the library, select any reference book, and write a short essay about it. Include the book's title and information about its purpose, organization, and how it might be useful to you. Add one interesting bit of information from the book.

2. Look up *The New York Times* on the microform reader for the day you were born. Write a paragraph about what else was going on in the world that day.

3. Browse through any section of the library and write the authors and titles of five books that look like they might be interesting to read. Describe why you think they might be interesting to read.

D. Topics for Your Learning Journal

1. What is the most pleasurable experience you have had while doing library assignments? Describe and say why.

2. What was the most frustrating experience? Describe and say why. Can you make it less frustrating next time?

3. Describe how you may be able to use the library in each of the other classes you are taking this semester.

16 | Giving Oral Reports

When you have finished reading this chapter, you will know the following:

1. How an oral report is different from a written report.
2. How to give an interesting oral report.
3. How to adapt a paper for oral presentation.

THE DIFFERENCE BETWEEN ORAL AND WRITTEN REPORTS

To make an oral presentation clear and interesting to the class, you will need to know the main differences between oral and written style. Here they are.

1. Oral reports have fewer main ideas than written reports.   Listeners, unlike readers who can go back and reread, have only one chance to get the main ideas. If too many of them are presented in a short time, the listener tunes out and misses most of them. It is better for your audience to understand a few ideas well than not to understand anything you say.

2. Oral reports contain more supporting material than do written reports.   The reason, again, is that the listener has only one chance at the ideas being presented. If these ideas are accompanied by multiple examples and perhaps a diagram on the blackboard or some other type of illustration, the listener will be more likely to understand and remember the main ideas.

3. Oral reports have more transitional material than written reports.   Transitions, you will remember (and if you don't, review Chapter 9), are used to show when a speaker or writer is leaving one idea and introducing the next. Furthermore, transitions emphasize ideas and sometimes state how one idea relates to another. One uses more of them in oral reports than in papers because they make the main points more obvious for the listener. A preoutline in the introduction will help your listeners identify your main ideas. Enumeration plus the use of a key phrase is one of the bluntest and most obvious ways to make your main ideas stand out. It is particularly effective for the listeners who, remember, get the main ideas when they hear them the first time or miss them altogether. You can also include internal summaries in your report. Ideas stand out when you stop occasionally to restate what you have said so far, and then introduce your next topic. Finally, although your written paper may have ended with a conclusion, your oral report will be more effective if you end with a summary, or a repetition of your main ideas.

The transitions described here might seem rather blunt and obvious if they were used in quantity on the printed page. Listeners will not find them so. Instead, with the added transitional material, they will be much more likely to grasp the main ideas of your report. And when listeners are getting the ideas, they are almost always attentive and interested.

4. Oral reports are more repetitious than written reports. Speakers not only repeat ideas in preoutlines, internal summaries, and final summaries, they also repeat key phrases ("these differences," "these changes and adaptations"), whenever necessary, so that the listeners will know at all times exactly what is being talked about. It is not uncommon for speakers to repeat a complicated main idea right after they have said it the first time, in slightly different language, so that the audience will get two chances at it.

5. Oral reports contain more personal pronouns (I, you, us, we) than do written reports. The speaker directly addresses the listening audience because it is there, immediately present. The speaker may even refer to audience members by name. Write a few personal pronouns into your report to establish a less formal, more personal rapport with your audience.

6. Oral reports contain more direct questions to the audience than do written reports. The purpose of such questioning is to create greater audience involvement. Questions invite the members of your audience to think through their own experience and to begin to anticipate what you might say. They become more involved and interested.

7. Oral reports sometimes have less perfect sentence structure than do written reports.   You can use your voice, rather than syntax or punctuation, to emphasize an important idea. A dangling participle, for instance, may dangle to the eye but not to the ear. "Having wasted time all day, there was no time left for either study or play," looks bad on the printed page. It makes sense, however, when said aloud, and would not stand out in an oral report as a particularly gross error. In speech you can also get away with a whole string of short sentences that would make a written report appear choppy and abrupt.

8. Finally, oral reports are much less formal and are more conversational than written papers.   The reason for this difference is, again, that the audience is present. Consequently, in an oral report, it is better to say, "Let's not forget" rather than "It should be noted that," and "I think" rather than "According to this writer." In fact, your report will go better if you look away from your speaking notes as frequently as possible to speak to your audience as though you were in a conversation with them.

HOW TO PREPARE AN ORAL PRESENTATION

1. Begin by thinking about your audience.   Your oral report will need to fulfill the requirements of the assignment. But you should also consider the interests of the audience and how much they already know about the topic. Select a topic that will be interesting to them and provide background information if you need to so that they can understand you.

2. Make a Speech Outline.   You will deliver your speech from a speech outline. It will help you see your main points easily, and it will help you achieve fluent delivery.

A speech outline is somewhat different from other outlines in the following ways:

a. Write the introduction in complete sentences exactly as you intend to give it. Include a purpose sentence to give focus to your report, and underline it on your outline so that you won't forget to emphasize it in delivery.

b. Write out all the main headings that introduce main ideas and the major transitions in complete sentences. These are important parts of the report, and you don't want to muff them in delivery.

c. Write out the summary and/or the conclusion in complete sentences just as you intend to say it. It is another important part of your report.

d. List all subideas and supporting details as phrases on the outline.

Figure 16.1 is an example of a speech outline for a five-minute speech. Study it and use it as a model. It also gives a review of some of the ideas in this chapter.

Introduction written out. Engages audience by appealing to interests and experience.

How to Prepare a Speech Outline

How many times have you listened to a speech without clearly understanding what the speaker was talking about? How many times have you been unable to follow the line of thought? I had an experience like this in a recent communications class. The students were assigned to give five-minute oral reports on articles they had read. Even though they were supposedly learning to communicate better, they actually did not communicate at all. They read their papers, they never looked up, and some of them spoke so softly we could not hear them. I could not tell you now the topic of a single one of those speeches. These speakers could have made interesting and memorable presentations if they had spoken from speech outlines. I want to describe how to make a speech outline to help you prepare your next oral report.

Purpose sentence underlined for emphasis

A good outline plus a little practice can help you give a report that your audience will find interesting and that they will also remember. There are four areas of concern in making speech outlines.

Transition written as sentence.

First main head written as sentence.

I. Speakers first need to concern themselves with the main heads that state the main ideas on the outline. They need to decide how many main ideas they can have and what these ideas should be.

Figure 16.1 An example of a speech outline for a five-minute speech.

Subideas and supporting details written as phrases.

A. How many.
  1. 2–4 for a 5-minute speech
  2. 5–7 for a 20-minute speech
  3. Audience forgets more
  4. Can't go back

B. What should they be
  1. Jot down ideas first
  2. Write in complete sentences on outline
     a: For example, write: "The American Revolution had a global impact, but scholars disagree on what that impact was."

Transition and main head.

II. Second, speakers need to concern themselves with the subheads and supporting material on the speech outline.

A. Both—phrases

Subideas and details

  1. For example, write: "European view, then and now" and list details in phrases.

B. Examples and details create interest—use lots of them

Transition and main head

III. Third, speakers need to concern themselves with transitions as they prepare the speech outline.

A. Purposes of transitions
  1. emphasize ideas
  2. move from one idea to another

Subideas and details

B. Need lots of clear, obvious transitions. Write in sentences.
  1. For example, write: "We have looked at the way Europeans viewed the American Revolution. Now let's look at the way Americans themselves viewed it. And let's divide these views into two parts: the views expressed at the time of the revolution and modern views. First, then . . ."
  2. Listeners can anticipate what's coming

C. Use transitions at beginning, middle, end.

Transition and main head

IV.   Finally, and this is the fourth area, speakers need to concern themselves with the summary or conclusion of the speech.

Figure 16.1 (cont.)   An example of a speech outline for a five-minute speech.

Subideas
and details

A. Final summary helps audience remember
  1. For example, write: "We have examined two views of the American Revolution, the European and the American. The Europeans regarded it as less revolutionary than the French revolution. Americans have traditionally regarded it as the force that gave birth to the country."
B. Concluding point.
  1. Emphatic
  2. What want audience to remember.
    a. For example, write: "There may have been no America as we know it without the revolution."

Summary.
Write in
complete
sentences.

I have described four important areas of concern for speakers to pay attention to when they create speech outlines: the main heads, the subheads and supporting details, the transitions, and the end of the speech. Write an effective speech outline on a topic that interests your audience, practice it a few times, and your oral report will be a memorable success.

Figure 16.1 (cont.)   An example of a speech outline for a five-minute speech.

3. Talk through your report.   Use the outline to guide you. When you come to the heads and subheads that are listed as phrases only, explain them as complete thoughts. If anything on the outline is unclear or makes your report sound choppy or awkward, revise the outline.

4. Plan a visual aid or a handout.   Any oral presentation will be more interesting and memorable if you use some visual aids. Blackboards and actual specimen examples are good, as are prepared charts, diagrams, graphs, or a list of main points on poster board. Opaque or overhead projectors, videotapes, films, and cassette tapes can also enliven an oral presentation. In order to use visual aids successfully, there are three important rules to remember:

a. Make them BIG enough so that everyone in the room can see them easily.

b. Pull them out only when you are actually going to refer to them. If they are out during your entire speech, they will distract your audience.

c. Keep them simple. Audiences cannot study complicated visual aids and listen to you at the same time. Visual aids should highlight and emphasize your remarks. Some of the same rules apply for hand-outs. Keep them clear and simple and do not give them your audience until you want them to look at them. Make certain that you bring enough so that each member of the audience receives one.

5. Practice.   When you have finished planning and writing the outline for your oral report, *practice* the report silently to yourself at least two times and out loud to the wall at least once. Now underline your main heads, and look away and say them to yourself until you learn them. Then practice your speech a few more times until you can give it without looking at your outline. Glancing at your outline a few times as a reminder is permissible. But do not read it.

Practice will ensure fluent delivery, which is important if you are to keep your audience's attention. It will also keep you from getting excessively nervous while you are giving your report. Time your report so that you will not go overtime. Speak loudly so that your audience can hear you, and look them in the eye. Put some energy into your delivery and work to develop a genuine sense of communication with your audience.

HOW TO ADAPT A WRITTEN PAPER FOR ORAL PRESENTATION

At times you will be asked to present a written paper orally in a class. Do not *read* the paper unless the professor specifically tells you to do so. It is extremely difficult and usually very boring to listen to someone read a paper. Instead, make a copy of your written manuscript and adapt it for oral presentation by marking up the manuscript itself. Use the following suggestions.

1. Go through the paper and underline and number the most important ideas. Cross out the less important ones. Consider how many you can explain well in the time you have.

2. Think of additional examples, informal comments to audience members, and other details and jot them in the margin. Remember, you will need more examples and detail, probably, than you have in your written paper.

3. Write in some obvious transitions so that your main ideas won't be lost on your listeners. Write in the margins or between the lines if there is space.

4. Write a summary at the end. You will probably need one.

5. If the manuscript gets too messy to use, write a speech outline.

Practice as you would for any oral report. You may glance at the manuscript a few times when you give the report, but *do not* read from it. A hand-out or a visual aid will make your report more interesting to your audience.

At the Very Least . . .

This chapter has presented some ideal ways of doing an oral report. If you cannot follow all of the suggestions, *at the very least* do the following:

1. Plan and make a brief outline of your report.
2. Rehearse it until you can give it fluently.
3. Don't go overtime.
4. Use eye contact and work to communicate with your audience.

SUMMARY

Since listeners cannot go back and reread, they must get the ideas in an oral report when they hear them the first time. Make it easier for your listeners to understand your points by limiting the number of main ideas in your oral reports, by adding supporting material and transitions, by repeating important phrases and ideas, and by summarizing main points. Make your oral reports more interesting by using personal pronouns, by asking questions of your audience, by speaking as though you were conversing with them, and by using visual aids. Adapt a written report for oral presentation by writing the changes to oral style in the margins or by rewriting the entire report in speech outline form. Finally, practice oral reports so that you will be fluent and not excessively nervous when you give them. Do not read to the audience. Look at them instead and develop a genuine sense of communication.

EXERCISES

A. Monitor Your Comprehension of This Chapter.

Write quickly, in phrases rather than complete sentences, all of the information in this chapter that you understand and remember. Look back and add what you left out. Is anything unclear? Jot it down to ask about in class. Has reading the chapter caused you to think of new insights or examples of your own? Jot them down.

B. Class Exercise

1. *Individuals.* Look back at pages 273–274 and choose a topic from the list in Class Exercise B1. Write a speech outline for a five-minute oral report. Use the outline in Figure 16.1 as an example. Practice and deliver the report to your class. Use a visual aid during the report.

2. *Individual Evaluations.* Class members should be assigned to evaluate each other's reports. The following Evaluation Guide may be used.

Evaluation Guide for Oral Reports

Instructions: Record the numbers of the items that give the best descriptions. Underline the sentences that describe the report best. The perfect score is 9.

Points

_____ *The Speech Outline*

3. The topic on the outline is clear and well focused in the introduction. The introduction gives background information and engages the audience. The main points are clear, in a good sequence, and there are not too many of them. There are sufficient transitions, examples and other details, and a good summary and concluding statement.

2. The topic is fairly clear but it is not explained well enough in the introduction. There are too many main points, or too few, or those that are there are not easy to find. There are not enough transitions or examples. There is no summary or no clear concluding point.

1. It is difficult to figure out what this report is about. The ideas do not stand out. There are no transitions or examples.

_____ *The Oral Report*

3. The report was clear, fluent, and interesting. The speaker had practiced and did not read the outline. Eye contact was good. The speaker was energetic and communicated the main points so that the audience could recognize and remember them.

2. The speaker did not know the report very well and looked at the outline too much. Eye contact was poor. We could not hear very well. The main points did not stand out well because they were not well enough emphasized.

1. The report was too short, it was difficult to figure out what it was about, and it was clear that the speaker had not spent enough time preparing it.

Points

_____The Visual Aid

   3. The visual aid (or handout) was not too complicated, it was introduced when it was used in the speech, and it was easy to read.

   2. The visual aid (or handout) was hard to read, complicated, and did not help clarify the main points in the speech. Furthermore, it was displayed throughout the report rather than when it was needed.

   1. The visual aid (or handout) was of poor quality and it did not help clarify any of the speaker's main points.

C. Application of Skills

1. Listen to a live speech or listen to one on television. Write a critique of the speech. Say what was good about it and what could have been improved. Get ideas for critiquing the speech from the Evaluation Guide in the last exercise. Also use your own judgment.

D. Topics for Your Learning Journal

1. Either by yourself or as a class project, describe the qualities that you admire in an excellent speaker. Describe the qualities that irritate and distract you in a poor speaker. Which excellent qualities could you incorporate into your own speaking style?

2. Write your reaction to the statement, "Stage fright is really just excess energy that you can learn to channel to make a more forceful speech." Write a positive plan for dealing with this excess energy so that it helps rather than hinders you.

PART SIX

Summary

17 | Evaluating Your Skills and Setting More Goals

When you have finished reading this chapter, you will know the following:

1. The reading and study skills that are working well for you now.
2. The reading and study skills that you still want to improve.
3. A plan for continuing to develop your reading and study skills.

As you have read the chapters and worked the exercises in this book, you have been in the process of changing some of the basic ways in which you read and learn. This is usually a slow and complicated process for most students. To begin with, you cannot make many changes all at once. You proceed gradually to try out and add new methods to add to your usual ways of doing things. Some of the new methods that you have learned while reading this book have made immediate sense to you, you have accepted them, and you now practice them regularly. Others you may have tried a few times, but perhaps not enough times to remember them or make them habits. Still others may have seemed odd, difficult, or not useful to you at this time.

This chapter provides you with the opportunity to review all of the methods, the skills, and strategies taught in this book and to reconsider all of them in respect to their present or potential use to you. As you read through the following list, evaluate the status of your present use of each item on the list. Do this on your own. Then participate in the class exercises at the end of the chapter to compare your accomplishments and goals with those of your classmates.

Instructions:

1. Read the list, consider each item, and make a judgment about what you do now. Check one of the columns:

    (1) *I have accepted and use this item regularly;*

    (2) *I have tried this item a few times, it works for me, but I need to use it more to make it a habit;*

    (3) *This item has promise, but I haven't really tried it. I want to work with it more.*

2. When you have evaluated the present status of each item, write an explanation in the space provided of how you do or do nor use it.

3. As you go through the list, *circle the numbers of the top priority items* for continued use and improvement and *make a check by the items you are unlikely to use* at least at present. Say why. **Notice that the chapter numbers are in parentheses after each item to help you with review.**

Example: Here is an example of what a section might look like when you finish with it.

Item	Use Regularly	Need to Practice	Need to Try	Explanation
ADAPTING TO CLASSES				
1. Analyze the organization of each class (4)	✓			I analyze the syllabus and follow it. I organize my notes.
2. Analyze your responsibilities in each class (4)	✓			I know what the tests will cover and what to do and by when. I write it down.
③ Take advantage of outside help (4)			✓	I need to use the math and writing lab.
✓4. Analyze the professor's teaching style (4)				Only have two - they are similar in style
5. Adapt your style of learning to particular classes (4)		✓		Need to take more notes in history class.

Item	Use Regularly	Need to Practice	Need to Try	Explanation
ADAPTING TO CLASSES				
1. Analyze the organization of each class (4)				
2. Analyze your responsibilities in each class (4)				
3. Take advantage of outside help (4)				
4. Analyze the professor's teaching style (4)				
5. Adapt your style of learning to particular classes (4)				
ASSIGNMENTS				
1. Understand and record assignments accurately on assignment sheets (3)				
2. Write due date for each assignment (3)				
3. Divide long assignments into short steps (3)				
4. Do assignments regularly and on time (3)				
CONCENTRATION				
1. Have a regular place to study (3)				
2. Recite and write while studying (2, 11, 12)				
3. Reward yourself for starting and finishing an assignment (2)				
4. Solve problems instead of worrying about them (2)				
5. Set priorities for assignments (3)				
6. Work to finish assignments rather than to put in time (3)				
7. Avoid distractions while taking notes or studying (2)				

Item	Use Regularly	Need to Practice	Need to Try	Explanation
8. Read summary of previous class just before next class (5)				
9. Label lecture notes in left-hand margin to force concentration (5)				
10. Take marginal notes while reading (10)				
DISCUSSION IN CLASS 1. Prepare for discussion (7)				
2. Take some notes on discussion (7)				
3. Listen well, and when you contribute, keep on the subject (7)				
EXAMS, PREPARING FOR AND TAKING 1. Allow yourself plenty of time to prepare for an exam (12)				
2. Make Master Study Sheets to organize your exam studying (12)				
3. Make study sheets by topic when studying for exams (12)				
4. Study in groups (12)				
5. Write questions and answer them (12)				
6. Create a reference book from your textbook for open book exams (12)				
7. Recite (12)				
8. Prepare for a standardized test when you must take one (12)				
9. Read all exam questions thoroughly, noting important words (13)				

Item	Use Regularly	Need to Practice	Need to Try	Explanation
10. Answer the questions you know first (13)				
11. Proofread exams carefully (13)				
12. Show all your work on quantitative exams (13)				
13. Use what you have learned from the test itself to help answer difficult questions (13)				
14. Write brief outlines for essay questions (13)				
15. Manage your time during an exam (13)				
16. Come right to the point in essay answers; don't pad or digress, but do support your answer (13)				
17. Work to ignore distractions (13) 18. Work to control exam anxiety (13)				
19. Learn from your errors on exams (13)				
GOAL PLANNING 1. Set long-term goals that are specific, measurable, realistic, and challenging (1)				
2. Set short-term goals to help you meet your long-term goals (1)				
3. Have some alternate goals in mind (1)				
4. Declare a major and generate a degree plan (1)				
GROUP WORK 1. Prepare for group work (7)				
2. Adhere to instructions and time limits (7)				

Item	Use Regularly	Need to Practice	Need to Try	Explanation
3. Assume leadership if necessary (7)				
4. Include all group members in the discussion (1)				
LEARNING STYLES				
1. Analyze your learning style (4)				
2. Vary your study method to correspond to your learning style (3, 4, 5, 10, 12)				
3. Create a work environment that suits your work style (3)				
LECTURE NOTE TAKING				
1. Make notes into chapters with title at top (5)				
2. Outline lecture notes as much as possible (5)				
3. Be an active, aggressive note taker (5)				
4. Always attend lectures (5)				
5. Take complete lecture notes (5)				
6. Develop abbreviations and symbols for note taking (5)				
7. Put your own ideas into your lecture notes (5)				
8. Write in ink and on one side of paper (5)				
9. Make your handwriting more legible (5)				
10. Revise notes within 24 hours (5)				
11. Label notes in margin, cover notes, then learn, using labels as cues (5)				
12. Write brief summaries of your notes (5)				

Item	Use Regularly	Need to Practice	Need to Try	Explanation
13. Dictate summaries of your notes into a tape recorder (5)				
14. Map your notes (5)				
15. Recite your notes with another student (5)				
LIBRARY RESEARCH				
1. Know how to find books, articles, and other materials in the library (5)				
2. Ask questions whenever you get confused or can't find something in the library (15)				
3. Survey a book or article before taking research materials from it (15)				
4. Evaluate how competently written your research sources are (15)				
MATH AND PROBLEM-SOLVING COURSES				
1. Write in lecture notes both problems on blackboard and verbal explanations given by professor (5)				
2. Make math strategy cards (14)				
3. Make math fact cards (10)				
4. Write definitions of math symbols and specialized vocabulary on definition sheets (10)				
MEMORY				
1. Look for a logical pattern of ideas in material you wish to remember (11)				
2. Associate the unfamiliar with the familiar (11)				

Item	Use Regularly	Need to Practice	Need to Try	Explanation
3. Reduce and simplify difficult material (11)				
4. Make lists, diagrams, or "maps" of materials to be learned (10, 11)				
5. Write and recite when you study more than you read and listen (2, 11)				
6. Visualize and draw diagrams and pictures (11)				
7. Think up your own examples (11)				
8. Memorize facts for some classes (11)				
9. Make up sentences, rhymes, or words to help you remember (11)				
10. Memorize just before you go to sleep (11)				
11. Review every week or two (11)				
MONITORING READING COMPREHENSION AND LEARNING				
1. Monitor your reading comprehension and seek clarification for difficult passages				
2. Monitor your learning until you are confident you have learned what is required				
MOTIVATION				
1. Have a reason for going to college (2)				
2. Rely on both internal and external motivation (2)				
3. Use positive self-talk when doing difficult tasks (2)				
4. Find something interesting in boring classes (2)				

Item	Use Regularly	Need to Practice	Need to Try	Explanation
5. Work yourself out of dead ends (2)				
ORAL REPORTS 1. Give all oral reports in oral style (16)				
2. Speak from a speech outline when giving an oral report (16)				
3. Rehearse all oral presentations and observe time limits (16)				
4. Enliven oral reports with visual aids (16)				
ORGANIZING IDEAS 1. Recognize the organization of a course (4)				
2. Recognize the organization of a lecture (5)				
3. Recognize the organization of a book (8)				
4. Recognize the organization of a chapter (8)				
5. Organize your own ideas in writing a paper (14)				
6. Organize your own ideas in doing a speech or oral report (16)				
7. Organize materials by topics on study sheets for exam preparation (12)				
8. Organize essay exam answers before you begin to write (13)				
ORGANIZING STUDY MATERIALS 1. Organize lecture notes, class materials, and reading materials so you can find them (3)				

Item	Use Regularly	Need to Practice	Need to Try	Explanation
READING				
1. Draw on background knowledge (8)				
2. Make predictions (8)				
3. Ask questions (8)				
4. Survey a book before you read it (8)				
5. Survey a chapter before you read it (8)				
6. Identify the main idea in paragraph or section of material and note how it is developed (9)				
7. Jot down main ideas in margin (2, 10)				
8. Analyze how ideas in a chapter are organized (9)				
9. Write summaries at end of sections or chapters of textbook material (10)				
10. Map the main ideas (10)				
11. Recite main points in a chapter as soon as you've read it (11)				
12. Isolate and define unfamiliar concepts in your textbooks (6, 10)				
13. Take summary notes on library reading (10, 15)				
THINKING ABOUT NEW MATERIAL				
1. Ask questions to stimulate critical thinking (11)				
2. Elaborate on new ideas (11)				
3. Read to generate your own ideas (11)				
4. Write ideas in detail to help you think about them (11)				

Item	Use Regularly	Need to Practice	Need to Try	Explanation
5. Talk to others to clarify ideas (11)				
6. Discover and use the time that is most productive for creative thinking (3)				
7. Take positions but keep an open mind (11)				
8. Put own ideas in [square brackets] in lecture notes (5)				
9. Write own ideas in margins and on flyleaves of text-books (11)				
10. Write own ideas before doing research for a paper (14)				
11. Write own ideas on study sheets (12)				
12. Present original material in exam answers (13)				
13. Think about what you are learning both inside and outside of class (3, 5, 11)				
TIME MANAGEMENT 1. Make a Time Analysis Worksheet (3)				
2. Make Time Management Worksheets (3)				
3. Learn during class time (3)				
4. Study when you're most alert and get off to a fast start (3)				
5. Use small amounts of time such as hours between classes (3)				
6. Find enough time to put in one, two, or three hours outside of class for every hour in class (3)				

Item	Use Regularly	Need to Practice	Need to Try	Explanation
VOCABULARY				
1. Learn concepts as well as words (6)				
2. Use context clues to understand unfamiliar words and concepts (6)				
3. Analyze Greek and Latin word parts as clues to a word's meaning (6)				
4. Isolate, write on vocabulary sheets, and learn the specialized and general vocabulary for each course (6)				
5. Know and use vocabulary terms when taking exams (6)				
6. Use a dictionary or glossary regularly (6)				
7. Consult a thesaurus for synonyms (6)				
WRITING PAPERS				
1. Select, narrow down to manageable size, and focus a subject for the paper (14)				
2. Invent ideas for your paper with prewriting activities (14)				
3. Make a tentative outline to guide research (14)				
4. Take research notes on cards or xerox them (15)				
5. Collect research that includes direct quotes, paraphrases, and your own ideas (15)				
6. Make an outline to guide your writing (14)				

Item	Use Regularly	Need to Practice	Need to Try	Explanation
7. Compose rapidly when writing a paper; do some rewriting as you write (14)				
8. Revise for organization, sentence structure, words, and punctuation (14)				
9. Read paper aloud when revising (14)				
10. Eliminate all writing errors before submitting paper (14)				
11. Write and revise your paper on a computer (14)				

EXERCISES

A. Class Exercises

1. *Individual.* Review the items. Select five areas in which you have improved the most and list them. Then select the five top priority items that you have circled for improvement and write a plan for improving each of them.

2. *Small groups.* Individual group members should compare their lists of the 5 items most improved and the 5 areas for improvement. The recorder should combine the lists, make a tally of duplicate items, and report to the class on the evaluation and goal plans of the group.

3. *Whole class.* Make some generalizations about how the entire class has improved and how it would like to continue to improve.

B. Topic for Your Learning Journal

1. For your final journal entry, evaluate your present strengths and weaknesses as a student and set some goals for your own future improvement. Make certain they are realistic and that you want to do them.

Appendix

The three reading selections that follow provide you with the opportunity to practice the reading process as it has been described in this book. The instructions that accompany each passage invite you to employ the process as you preread, read and take notes, make maps and summaries, and think about what you have read.

All three passages are drawn from current college textbooks, and they represent the subject areas of psychology, chemistry, and history. All passages, furthermore, are longer than the short practice exercises in the text. To read them, you will need to integrate the skills and strategies that you have learned. Completing these longer exercises should help you transfer the reading instruction provided in this book to the real reading that you must do for your other college courses.

Instructions for Reading Selection One from Psychology

Prereading Activities

1. Background the title, "Long Term Memory and Forgetting," by making a list of what you already know about the subject.
2. Survey the chapter by reading the first and last paragraphs, reading the headings, and circling the important words that appear in boldface type.
3. Predict what you think the chapter will be about.
4. Ask one question that you would like to answer as you read.

Reading Activities

1. Look for main ideas as you read. Underline selectively and jot the important ideas in the margin.
2. Write a very brief summary at the end of each section of material that identifies the main point only of that section.
3. Underline the context clues in the passage that define the words you circled while you were surveying. Write a V in the margin to identify each of these words and their meanings.

Post-Reading Activities

1. Write a one-page summary, in phrases only, of the entire selection. (refer back to page 174 for an example).
2. Make a map of the selection. Which do you prefer, summaries or maps?
3. Ask questions to stimulate critical thinking:
   a. How does this relate to what you already know?
   b. How is the information in this passage useful and valuable to you?

Long-Term Memory and Forgetting[1]

Think of your **long-term memory** as a vast storehouse of information containing names, dates, places, what Johnny did to you in second grade, and what Susan said about you when you were 12. Psychologists are not certain how much of what you experience and think about becomes stored in long-term memory.

How Much of What We Experience or Think Is Stored in Long-Term Memory?   Some psychologists argue that every perception and idea is stored permanently. The only question is whether we shall receive appropriate stimulation to help us retrieve this information. These psychologists often point to the work of neurosurgeon

[1] Excerpts from *Essentials of Psychology*, Second Edition by Spencer A. Rathus, copyright © 1989 by Holt, Rinehart and Winston, Inc., reprinted by permission of the publisher.

Wilder Penfield. By electrically stimulating parts of the brain, some of his patients reported fairly vivid remembrance of things past.

Other psychologists such as Elizabeth Loftus note that the memories "released" by Penfield's probes were not perfectly detailed. Patients also seemed to recall more specifics of events that were important to them. We may be more likely to store permanently those perceptions and thoughts that are important or meaningful to us. We recall material better when we pay more attention to it and encode it in a meaningful, rehearsable form.

How Accurate Are Long-Term Memories?   Memory is not like the scanning of an old photograph. Instead, memory tends to be **reconstructive** and less than fully accurate. Even the words we use in encoding our memories make a difference. In another study Loftus and Palmer showed subjects a film of a car crash and then asked them to fill out questionnaires that included a question about how fast the cars were going at the time. But the language of the question varied, so that some subjects estimated how fast the cars were going when they "hit" one another, and others estimated their speed when they "smashed" into one another. Subjects reconstructing the scene on the basis of the cue "hit" estimated a speed of 34 mph. Subjects who watched the same film but reconstructed the scene on the basis of the cue "smashed" estimated a speed of 41 mph!

Subjects in the same study were questioned again a week later: "Did you see any broken glass?" Since there was no broken glass shown in the film, yes answers were errors. Of subjects who had earlier been encouraged to encode the accident as one in which cars "hit" one another, 14 percent incorrectly answered yes. But 32 percent of the subjects who had encoded the cars as "smashing" into one another reported, incorrectly, that they had seen broken glass.

How Much Information Can Be Stored in Long-Term Memory? There is no evidence for any limit to the amount of information that can be stored in long-term memory. New information may replace older information in the short-term memory, but there is no evidence that memories in long-term memory are lost by displacement. Long-term memories may last days, years, or for all practical purposes, a lifetime. From time to time it may seem that we have forgotten, or "lost," a memory in long-term memory, such as the names of elementary or high school classmates. But it is more likely that we simply cannot find the proper cues to help us retrieve the information. If it is lost, it usually becomes lost only in the same way as when we misplace an object but know that it is still somewhere in tho house or apartment. We cannot retrieve it, but it is not eradicated or destroyed.

Transferring Information from Short-Term to Long-Term Memory How is information transferred from short-term to long-term memory? By and large, the more often chunks of information are rehearsed, the more likely they are to be transferred to long-term memory. But pure rehearsal, with no attempt to make information meaningful by linking it to past learning, is no guarantee of permanent storage.

A more effective method is purposefully to relate new material to information that has already been solidly acquired. Relating new material to well-known material is known as **elaborative rehearsal**.

You may recall that English teachers encouraged you to use new vocabulary words in sentences to help you remember them. Each new usage is an instance of elaborative rehearsal. You are building extended semantic codes that will help you retrieve their meanings in the future. When I was in high school, foreign-language teachers told us that learning classical languages "exercises the mind," so that we would understand English better. Not exactly. The mind is not analogous to a muscle that responds to exercise. But the meanings of many English words are based on foreign tongues. A person who recognizes that *retrieve* stems from roots meaning "again" (*re-*) and "find" (*trouver* in French) is less likely to forget that *retrieval* means "finding again" or "bringing back."

Before proceeding to the next section, let me ask you to cover the preceding paragraph. Now, which of the following words is correctly spelled: *retrieval* or *retreival?* The spellings sound alike, so an acoustic code for reconstructing the correct spelling would fail. But a semantic code, such as the spelling rule "*i* before *e* except after *c,*" would allow you to reconstruct the correct spelling: retrieval.

Organization in Long-Term Memory The storehouse of long-term memory is usually well organized. Items are not just piled on the floor or thrown into closets. We tend to gather information about rats and cats into a certain section of the warehouse, perhaps the animal or mammal section. We gather oaks, maples, and eucalyptus into the tree section.

As we develop, we tend to organize information according to a *hierarchical structure.* A **hierarchy** is an arrangement of items (or chunks of information) into groups or classes according to common or distinct features. As we work our way up the hierarchy, we find more encompassing, or **superordinate**, classes to which the items below belong. For example, all mammals are animals, but there are many types of animals other than mammals.*

When items are correctly organized in long-term memory, you are more likely to recall accurate information about them. For instance, do you remember whether whales breathe underwater? If you did not know that whales are mammals or knew nothing about mammals, a correct answer might depend on some remote instance of rote learning. You might recall some details from a documentary on whales, for example. But if you *did* know that whales are mammals, you would be able to "remember" that whales do not breathe underwater by reconstructing information you know about mammals, the group to which whales are subordinate. Similarly, you might "remember" that whales, because they are mammals, are warm-blooded, nurse their young, and are a good deal more intelligent than, say, tunas and sticklebacks, which are fish.

Had you incorrectly classified whales as fish, you might have searched your memory and constructed the incorrect answer that they do breathe underwater.

FORGETTING

What do DAR, RIK, BOF, and ZEX have in common? They are all **nonsense syllables.** Nonsense syllables are meaningless syllables three letters in length. Their usage was originated by German psychologist Hermann Ebbinghaus (1850–1909), and they have been used by many psychologists to study memory and forgetting.

Since they are intended to be meaningless, remembering nonsense syllables should depend on simple acoustic coding and rehearsal, rather than on elaborative rehearsal, semantic coding, or other ways of making learning meaningful. Nonsense syllables provide a means of measuring simple memorization ability in studies of the three basic memory tasks of *recognition, recall,* and *relearning.* Studying these memory tasks has led to several conclusions about the nature of forgetting.

Recognition   There are many ways of measuring **recognition**. In one study of high school graduates, Harry Bahrick and his colleagues interspersed photos of classmates with four times as many photos of strangers. Recent graduates correctly recognized persons who were former schoolmates 90 percent of the time, whereas subjects who had been out of school for 40 years recognized former classmates 75 percent of the time. But a chance level of recognition would have been only 20 percent (one photo in five was of an actual classmate), so that even older subjects showed rather solid long-term recognition ability.

In many studies of recognition, psychologists ask subjects to read a list of nonsense syllables. Then the subjects read a second list of nonsense syllables and indicate whether they recognize any of the syllables as having appeared on the first list. Forgetting is defined as failure to recognize a nonsense syllable that has been read before.

Recognition is the easiest type of memory task. This is why multiple-choice tests are easier than fill-in-the-blank or essay tests. We can recognize or identify photos of former classmates more easily than we can recall their names.

Recall Psychologists often use lists of pairs of nonsense syllables, called **paired associates**, to measure **recall**, a second memory task. Subjects read through the lists, pair by pair. Later they are shown the first member of each pair and asked to recall the second. Recall is more difficult than recognition. In a recognition task, one simply indicates whether an item has been seen before or which of a number of items is paired with a stimulus (as in a multiple-choice test). But in a recall task, the person must retrieve a syllable, with another syllable serving as a cue.

Retrieval is made easier if the two syllables can be meaningfully linked, even if the "meaning" is stretched a bit. The image of a WOMan smoking a CEG-arette may make CEG easier to retrieve when the person is presented with the cue, WOM.

It is easier to recall vocabulary words from foreign languages if you can construct a meaningful link between the foreign and English words. The *peso*, pronounced *pay-so*, is a unit of Mexican money. A link can be formed by finding a part of the foreign word, such as the *pe-* (pronounced *pay*) in *peso*, and construct a phrase such as "You pay with money." When you read or hear the word *peso* in the future, you recognize the *pe-* and retrieve the link or phrase. From the phrase, you then reconstruct the translation, "a unit of money."

A similar method for prompting recall involves the use of acronyms. As noted in our discussion of THUNSTOFAM,* acronyms are words that are constructed from the first letter or letters of the chunks of material to be retrieved. In Chapter 2 we saw that the acronym SAME can help us recall that sensory neurons are also called *a*fferent neurons, and *m*otor neurons are also termed *e*fferent. In

---

* An acronym for THe UNited STates OF AMerica.

Chapter 3 we saw that the acronym ROY G. BIV can help us recall the colors of the visible spectrum.

Relearning: Is Learning Easier the Second Time Around?
Relearning is a third method of measuring retention. Do you remember having to learn all the state capitals in grade school? What were the capitals of Wyoming and Delaware? Even when we cannot recall or recognize material that had once been learned, we can relearn it more rapidly the second time, such as Cheyenne for Wyoming and Dover for Delaware. Similarly, as we go through our 30s and 40s we may forget a good deal of our high school French or geometry. But we could learn what took months or years much more rapidly the second time around.

Since time is saved when we relearn things we had once known, this method of measuring retention is also known as measuring **savings**. Quickly, now: What are the capitals of Wyoming and Delaware?

The Tip-of-the-Tongue Phenomenon: An Example of Cue-Dependent Forgetting   Have you ever been so close to recalling something that you felt it was "on the tip of your tongue"? But you still could not quite put your finger on it? This is a frustrating experience, such as reeling in a fish but having it drop off the line just before it breaks the surface of the water. Psychologists term this experience the **tip-of-the-tongue (TOT) phenomenon**. The TOT phenomenon appears to be an example of **cue-dependent forgetting**. That is, the information seems to be there, but the cue that could retrieve it is missing. As a result, the memory is inaccessible.

In one TOT experiment, Brown and McNeill defined some rather unusual words for students, such as *sampan,* which is a small riverboat used in China and Japan. Students were then asked to recall the words they had learned. Since the terms remained somewhat exotic and unelaborated,* students did not have well-developed cues for retrieving them. Students often had the right word "on the tips of their tongues," but many reported words similar in meaning, such as *junk, barge,* or *houseboat.* Other students reported words that sound similar, such as *Saipan, Siam, sarong,* and *sanching.*

Brown and McNeill concluded that our storage systems are indexed according to cues that include both the sounds and the meanings of words, according to both acoustic and semantic codes. By scanning words that are similar in sound and meaning to the word

---

* Students, that is, had not had the opportunity to engage in elaborative rehearsal of the words—to use them in various contexts.

that is on the tip of the tongue, we often eventually find the right cue and retrieve the word for which we are searching.

State-Dependent Memory   Sometimes the cue for retrieving a memory is physiological or emotional rather than cognitive. Drugs, for example, alter our physiological response patterns. They can influence the production and uptake of neurotransmitters involved in learning and memory and can modify the general state of alertness of the body. It also happens that material that is learned "under the influence" of a drug may be most readily retrieved when the person is again under the influence of that drug.

Our moods may also serve as cues that aid the retrieval of memories. Feeling the rush of love may trigger images of other times when we had fallen in love. The grip of anger may prompt memories of frustration and rage. Gordon Bower ran experiments in which happy or sad moods were induced in people by hypnotic suggestion and the subjects then learned lists of words. People who learned a list while in a happy mood showed better recall when a happy state was induced again. But people who had learned the list when a sad mood had been induced, showed superior recall when they were saddened again. Bower suggests that in day to day life, a happy mood influences us to focus on positive events. As a result we shall have better recall of these happy events in the future. A sad mood, unfortunately, leads us to focus on and recall the negative. Happiness may feed on happiness, but sadness under extreme circumstances can develop into a vicious cycle.

WHY PEOPLE FORGET

When we do not attend to, encode, and rehearse sensory input, we may forget it through decay of the trace of the image. Material in short-term memory can be lost through displacement, as may happen when we try to remember several new names at a party.

According to **interference theory**, we also forget material in short-term and long-term memory because newly learned material interferes with it. The two basic types of interference are *retroactive interference* (also called *retroactive inhibition*) and *proactive interference* (also called *proactive inhibition*).

Retroactive Interference   In **retroactive interference** new learning interferes with the retrieval of old learning. A medical student may memorize the bones in the leg through rote repetition. Later he or she may find that learning the names of the bones in the arm makes it more difficult to retrieve the names of the leg bones, especially if the names are similar in sound or in relative location on each limb.

Proactive Interference   In **proactive interference** older learning interferes with the capacity to retrieve more recently learned material. High school Spanish may "pop in" when you are trying to retrieve college French or Italian words. All three are Romance languages, with similar roots and spellings. Old German vocabulary words would probably not interfere with your ability to retrieve more recently learned French or Italian because many German roots and sounds differ markedly from those of the Romance languages.

In terms of motor skills, you may learn how to drive a standard shift on a car with three forward speeds and a clutch that must be let up slowly after shifting. Later you learn to drive a car with five forward speeds and a clutch that must be released rapidly. For a while you make a number of errors on the five-speed car because of proactive interference. (Old learning interferes with new learning.) If you return to the three-speed car after driving the five-speed car has become "natural," you may stall it a few times. This is because of retroactive interference (new learning interfering with the old).

Repression   According to Sigmund Freud, we are motivated to forget painful memories and unacceptable ideas because they produce anxiety, guilt, and shame. (In terms of operant conditioning, anxiety, guilt, and shame serve as negative reinforcers. We learn to do that which is followed by their removal—in this case, not to think about certain events and ideas.) In Chapter 9 we shall see that psychoanalysts believe that repression is at the heart of disorders such as **psychogenic amnesia.**

Childhood Amnesia   In his clinical investigations of patients' early experiences, Freud discovered that patients could not recall events that happened prior to the age of 3 and that recall was very cloudy through the age of 5. Freud labeled this phenomenon **childhood amnesia.** Many of us have the impression that we have vivid recollections of events during the first two or three years after birth, but studies in which attempts are made to verify these memories by interviewing independent older witnesses show that they are inaccurate.

Childhood amnesia has nothing to do with the fact that the events are of the distant past. Those of us who are in our 30s, 40s, and older have many vivid memories of childhood events that occurred between the ages of 6 and 10, although they are many decades old. But 18-year-olds show steep declines in memory once they attempt to recall events earlier than the age of 6, even though these events are fewer than 18 years away.

Freud attributed childhood amnesia to the repression of the aggressive and sexual impulses that he believed young children had toward their parents. However, the events lost to childhood amnesia are not weighted in the direction of such "primitive" impulses; they include the most pedestrian, emotionally bland incidents. The effects of childhood amnesia are too broad, too nonselective, for Freud's hypothesis to hold water.

Childhood amnesia probably reflects the interaction of physiological and cognitive factors instead of psychoanalytic factors. For example, a structure of the limbic system (the hippocampus) that is involved in the storage of memories does not become mature until we are about 2 years old. Too, myelination of brain pathways is still occurring for the first several years after birth, contributing to the efficiency of memory functioning for the general processing of information. From a cognitive perspective, children usually cannot use language until about the age of 2. Since they are lacking language, they cannot label objects and events.

Those early childhood memories we are so certain we can "see today" are probably reconstructed and mostly inaccurate. Or else they may stem from a time when we were much older than we thought we were.

Retrograde and Anterograde Amnesia   In **retrograde amnesia**, a source of trauma, such as a head injury or an electric shock, prevents people from remembering events that took place before the accident. In **anterograde amnesia**, there are memory lapses for the period following the traumatic event. In some cases it seems that the trauma interferes with all the processes of memory. Paying attention, the encoding of sensory input, and rehearsal are all impaired. A number of investigators have linked certain kinds of brain damage— as of the hippocampus—to certain kinds of amnesia, but their views remain somewhat speculative.

Some perceptions and ideas must apparently be allowed to **consolidate** or rest undisturbed for a while if they are to be remembered. A football player who is knocked unconscious or a victim of an auto accident may be unable to recall events for several minutes prior to the trauma. The football player may not recall taking to the field. The accident victim may not recall entering the car.

Now that we have looked at how and why we forget, let us consider ways of improving our ability to remember.

SOME METHODS FOR IMPROVING MEMORY

Who among us has not wished for a better memory from time to time? If we could remember more, we might earn higher grades, charm people with our stock of jokes, or even pay our bills on time. It was once believed that one's memory was fixed, that one had a good or poor memory and was stuck with it. But today psychologists have found that there are a number of ways in which we can all improve our memories, such as the following.

The Method of Loci   You might be better able to remember your shopping list if you imagine meat loaf in your navel or a strip of bacon draped over your nose. This is a meaty example of the **method of loci**. With this method you select a series of related images, such as the parts of your body or the furniture in your home. Then you imagine an item from your shopping list, or another list you want to remember, attached to each image.

By placing meat loaf or a favorite complete dinner in your navel, rather than a single item such as chopped beef, you can combine several items into one chunk of information. At the supermarket you recall the (familiar) ingredients for meat loaf and simply recognize whether or not you need each one.

Mediation   In the method of **mediation**, you link two items with a third that ties them together. What if you are having difficulty remembering that John's wife's name is Tillie? Laird Cermak suggests that you can mediate between John and Tillie as follows. Reflect that the *john* is a slang term for bathroom. Bathrooms often have ceramic *tiles. Tiles,* of course, sounds like *Tillie.* So it goes: John-bathroom-tiles-Tillie.

Mnemonics   In a third method of improving memory, **mnemonics,** chunks of information are combined into a format, such as an acronym, jingle, or phrase. Recalling the phrase "Every Good Boy Does Fine" has helped many people remember the musical keys E, G, B, D, F.

How can you remember how to spell *mnemonics*? Simple—just be willing to grant "aMNesty" to those who cannot.

The Future of Learning and Memory   Research into the biology of memory is in its infancy, but what an exciting area of research it is. What would it mean to you if you could read for a half-hour to an hour, pop a pill, and cause your new learning to become consolidated in long-term memory? You would never have to reread the material; It would be at your fingertips for a lifetime. It would save a bit of study time, would it not?

Instructions for Reading Selection Two from Chemistry

Prereading Activities

1. Background the title, "Where Are Science & Technology Taking Us?" by making a list of what you already know about the subject.
2. Survey the chapter by reading the first and last paragraphs, reading the headings, and circling the important words that appear in boldface type.
3. Predict what you think the chapter will be about.
4. Ask one question that you would like to answer as you read.

Reading Activities

1. Unless you have taken chemistry, parts of this passage may seem difficult to you. Follow some of the instructions for reading difficult material on page 147. When you have finished prereading, read the entire passage through to the end, and as you read, place a vertical line in the margin next to the passages you do not understand very well.
2. Go back and reread the entire selection. This time look for main ideas, underline them, and jot them in the margin. Pay particular attention to the details—there are many of them. What significant ideas do they support? How do the visuals function to clarify ideas? Identify technical vocabulary and define as much of it as you can by examining context. What is the function of the marginal comments?
3. Are there still passages that you cannot understand? Analyze why. What can you do to understand them better?

Post-reading activities

1. What is the main idea of the entire selection? Place it in the central position on a map. Attach the other ideas and some of the details.

2. From memory, summarize as much as you can remember about this selection. Go back and read your marginal comments and add additional ideas and details to your summary.
3. Ask questions to stimulate critical thinking:
   a. What are the problems?
   b. How can they be solved?
   c. What are the implications of these solutions?
   d. How can some of the ideas in this passage be applied to other situations?
   e. What are some of the potential effects of scientific advancement?

Where are Science and Technology Taking Us?[2]

Two major technological revolutions currently under way are the microelectronic revolution and the biotechnology revolution.

The Microelectronic Revolution

The chip, nickname for the integrated circuit, is a small slice of silicon that contains an intricate pattern of electronic switches (transistors) joined by "wires" etched from thin films of metal. Some are information storers called memory chips. Others combine memory with logic function to produce computer or microprocessor chips. These two applications would appear to make the chip, like the mind, capable of essentially infinite application. A microprocessor chip, for example, can provide a machine with decision-making ability, memory for instructions, and self-adjusting controls.

In everyday life we see many examples of the influence of the chip: digital watches; microwave oven controls; new cars with carefully metered fuel-air mixtures; hand calculators; cash registers that total bills, post sales, and update inventories; computers in a variety of sizes and capacity—all these make use of the chip. A typical microprocessor chip holds 30,000 transistors but is small enough to be carried by a large ant.

[2] Excerpts from *Chemistry, Impact on Society* by Melvin D. Joesten, David O. Johnston, John T. Netterville, James L. Wood, copyright © 1988 by Saunders College Publishing, a division of Holt, Rinehart and Winston, Inc., reprinted by permission of the publisher.

The story of the chip starts with the invention of the transistor in 1947. The transistor is a semiconductor device that acts either as an amplifier or as a current switch. Although transistorized circuits were a tremendous improvement over vacuum tubes, large computer circuits using 50,000 or more transistors and similar numbers of diodes, capacitors, and resistors were difficult to build; computers had to be wired together in a continuous loop, and a circuit with 100,000 components could easily require 1 million soldered connections. The cost of labor for soldering and the chance for defects were both high. In the late 1950s, the Navy's newest destroyers required 350,000 electronic components and millions of hand-soldered connections. It was clear that the limit to the use of transistors in super-circuits was the number of individual connections that could be linked and maintained at one time.

In 1958 Jack Kilby at Texas Instruments and Robert Noyce at Fairchild Semiconductor, working independently, came up with the solution: make a semiconductor (silicon or germanium) in the transistor serve as its own circuit board. If all the transistors, capacitors, and resistors could be integrated on a single slice of silicon, connections could be made internally within the semiconductor and no wiring or soldering would be necessary.

The Biotechnology Revolution—Designer Genes

The biotechnology revolution began after the first successful gene splicing and gene cloning experiments produced recombinant DNA in the early 1970s. In Chapter 11 we shall discuss the biochemistry of DNA and the genetic code. The present discussion focuses on the potential of recombinant DNA technology to solve three of the world's greatest problems: hunger, sickness, and energy shortages.

The process for forming and cloning recombinant DNA molecules is as follows. The basic idea is to use the rapidly dividing property of common bacteria, such as *E. coli*, as a microbe factory for producing recombinant DNA molecules that contain the genetic information for the desired product. Rings of DNA called plasmids are isolated from the *E. coli* cell. The ring is cut open with a cutting enzyme, which also cuts the appropriate gene segment from the desired human, animal, or viral DNA. The new gene segment is spliced into the cut ring by a splicing enzyme. The altered DNA ring (recombinant DNA) is then reinserted into the host *E. coli* cell. Each plasmid is copied many times in a cell. When the *E. coli* cells divide, they pass on to their offspring the same genetic information contained in the parent cell.

The commercial potential of recombinant DNA technology was recognized very early, and several biotechnology companies were started by the scientists who had done key experiments in gene splicing and gene cloning. There are more than 200 biotechnology companies, but most of them are still doing development work and have no products to sell. The risk is high, but the payoff of successful ventures will also be high.

An early benefit of recombinant DNA was the biosynthesis of human insulin in 1978. Millions of diabetics depend on the availability of insulin, but many are allergic to animal insulin, which used to be the only source of commercial insulin. Biosynthesized human insulin is now being marketed by a firm called Genentech. Biotechnology firms are also producing human growth hormone, which is used in treating youth dwarfism, and interferon, which is a potential anticancer agent.

Genetic engineers are trying to modify crops so they will make more nutritious protein, resist disease and herbicides, and even provide their own fertilizers. Researchers are also trying to use recombinant DNA techniques to produce vaccines against diseases that attack livestock.

Strains of bacteria are being developed that will convert garbage, plant waste material such as cornstalks, and industrial wastes into useful chemicals and fuels. This not only helps solve the energy shortage but also provides a way to recycle wastes and lower the accumulation of solid wastes.

A decade ago, at the beginning of the recombinant DNA era, many people, including scientists working in the area, saw danger in biotechnology. Since *E. coli* is an intestinal bacterium, what if some of the genetically engineered *E. coli* escaped and found their way into people's intestines? These fears led to an 18-month moratorium on recombinant DNA research. Although the evidence to date shows that the *E. coli* used in recombinant DNA technology is too delicate to survive outside its environment, strict regulations are still being followed in experiments with genetically engineered bacteria.

There is also a deeper ethical concern. At present no genetic engineering of human genes is being done, but the capability is there. Should we raise a child's IQ from 80 to 100? If we do this, should we raise IQs from 120 to 160? Should we alter human genes to improve health, longevity, strength, and so forth? By altering life forms, whether plant, animal, or human, are we playing God? Debates on these questions have been going on since the beginning of biotechnology and will continue. The mechanism for resolving such important questions offers a new challenge to a free society.

RISKS OF TECHNOLOGY

We have described some of the benefits of technology, but we also need to examine related risks. *Bhopal, Challenger,* and *Chernobyl* are names associated with three catastrophic accidents that remind us of technological risks.

December 3, 1984: The worst chemical plant accident in history occurred in the early morning hours at a Union Carbide insecticide plant in Bhopal, India. Over 2,000 people were killed, and tens of thousands were injured when methyl isocyanate, a deadly gas used in the preparation of pesticides, escaped from a storage tank. Several violations of recommended safety procedures contributed to the disastrous leak, including an inoperative refrigeration system to keep the methyl isocyanate cool, an inoperative scrubbing tank to neutralize any escaping gas, and an inoperative flare tower designed to burn any gas that escaped from the storage tank.

January 28, 1986: The space shuttle *Challenger* exploded 74 seconds after liftoff, killing the shuttle's seven crew members. Officials at both the National Aeronautics and Space Administration and Morton Thiokol, the rocket manufacturer, recommended launch in spite of clear and repeated warnings from Thiokol engineers about problems with the plastic O-rings used to seal joints between casing sections in the booster rocket.

April 26, 1986: An explosion at the Chernobyl nuclear plant near Kiev in the Soviet Union released large amounts of radioactive material into the atmosphere. About 25,000 persons were evacuated on April 27, and within a week a total of 135,000 had been evacuated from an 18-mile zone around the power plant. Two persons were killed in the explosion, and 29 died from radiation sickness during the next three months.

Andronik M. Petrosyants, chairman of the Soviet Committee for the Peaceful Uses of Atomic Energy, said, "The accident took place as a result of a whole series of gross violations of operating regulations by the workers." Ironically, the accident occurred in the course of a safety test. Workers had shut down automatic safety systems in order to test how long the reactor's turbine generators would continue to operate in the event of an unforeseen reactor shutdown. The six fatal errors, according to a Soviet report, were (1) shutting of the emergency cooling system, (2) lowering the reactor's power to a point at which the reactor was difficult to control, (3) exceeding flow rates by having all water circulation pumps on, (4) shutting off the automatic signal that shuts down the reactor when the turbines stop, (5) pulling out almost all the control rods from the core, and (6) shutting off safety devices that shut down the reactor if steam pressure or water levels become abnormal. When workers began the test by stopping power to the turbine, the reactor began immediately to overheat. Within seconds two explosions—one from steam pressure and one from the ignition of hydrogen gas produced from the reaction of steam with graphite, uranium fuel, and the zirconium alloy that encased the fuel—blew the roof off the reactor building and ignited more than 30 fires around the plant. The damaged reactor core and the graphite surrounding it began to burn at temperatures as high as 2500°C. The fire released into the atmosphere large amounts of radioactive material, which was borne by prevailing winds over the Ukraine and much of Europe. Other countries were not informed of the accident; the first indication that something was wrong was detected on April 28, when monitoring stations in Sweden recorded a sudden jump in levels of radioactive isotopes of krypton, xenon, iodine, cesium, and barium—the mixture that would be expected if a nuclear accident had occurred.

The long-term effects of the Chernobyl accident are difficult to predict. Estimates of an increase in cancer rates in the western Soviet Union are in the thousands. People evacuated from the Chernobyl area are subject to periodic examinations for signs of cancer and other illnesses caused by radiation. In addition, anyone who travels within 100 miles of the reactor site is tested for radioactivity. The full extent of contamination of food and water supplies is not known, but Swedish officials estimate that their country has so far lost at least $144 million in ruined food. Milk, vegetables, and water supplies will continue to be monitored for radioactive contamination.

All three of these accidents involved human error and lack of enforcement of recommended safety procedures. Years of excellent safety records in the chemical industry and the nuclear power industry do not eliminate the risks of chemical and nuclear technology. However, the risks can be reduced by the constant application of recommended safety procedures and by full utilization of technological developments.

Hazardous Wastes

Careless disposal of hazardous wastes has been the cause of many human health problems. Love Canal in Niagara Falls, Times Beach in Missouri, and Minamata Bay and Jinzu River in Japan are just a few locations where serious health problems have resulted from the improper disposal of hazardous wastes.

Love Canal, the neighborhood that in 1977 discovered it was built on a toxic chemical dump, was the first publicized example of the problems of chemical waste dumps. In the mid-1970s heavy rains and snows seeped into the dump and pushed an oily black liquid to the surface. The liquid contained at least 82 chemicals, 12 of which were suspected carcinogens.

Times Beach, Missouri, was bought by the U. S. Environmental Protection Agency (EPA) in 1983, and its 2200 residents were relocated because dioxins, a group of toxic chemicals produced in small amounts during the synthesis of a herbicide, were found in the soil at concentrations as high as 1100 times the acceptable level.

In the 1950s tons of waste mercury were dumped into the bay at Minamata, Japan. In the next few years thousands of persons in the Minamata area suffered paralysis and mental disorders, and over 200 people died. Several years passed before it was determined that these people suffered from poisoning by methyl mercury compounds. Anaerobic bacteria in the sea bottom converted mercury to methyl mercury compounds, which were eaten by plankton. The methyl mercury compounds were carried up the food chain and eventually accumulated in the fatty tissue of fish, which are a major part of the Japanese diet. Intake of methyl mercury compounds reached levels that caused the sickness now known as Minamata disease.

Itai-Itai disease, which makes bones brittle and easily broken, is caused by cadmium poisoning and was also first observed on a major scale in Japan. *Itai* means "it hurts" in Japanese and graphically illustrates the pain associated with this disease. Many cases were observed downstream from a zinc-refining plant on the Jinzu River in Japan. Cadmium is a byproduct of the zinc-refining industry and is used in various alloys and in nickel-cadmium rechargeable batteries.

What Is an Acceptable Risk?

Risk assessment for individuals involves a consideration of the likelihood or probability of harm and the severity of the hazard. Assessment of societal risks combines probability and severity with the number of persons affected. The science of risk assessment is still evolving, but it is clear that the importance of public perception of risks needs to be recognized before risk assessment can be quantified. Often there is little correlation between the actual statistics of risk and the perception of risk by the public or by individuals. For example, we are all aware that the risk of injury or death is much lower from traveling in a commercial airplane than from traveling in an automobile, yet all of us know persons who avoid airplane flights because of their fear of a crash.

What factors influence public perception of risk? Catastrophic accidents such as Bhopal and Chernobyl obviously affect public perception of risk. In addition, people tend to judge involuntary exposure to activities or technologies (such as living near a hazardous dump site) as riskier than voluntary exposure (such as smoking). In other words, persons rate risks they can control lower than those they cannot control.

No absolute answer can be provided to the question "how safe is safe enough?" Determining acceptable levels of risk requires value judgments that are difficult and complex, involving the consideration of scientific, social, and political factors. Over the years a number of laws designed to protect human health and the environment have been enacted to provide a basic framework for making decisions. The fact that three types of laws exist in this area adds to public confusion about risk assessment and its meaning.

Risk-based laws are zero-risk laws that allow no balancing of health risks against possible benefits. The Delaney Clause of the Federal Food, Drug, and Cosmetic Act is a risk-based law. It specifically bans the use of any intentional food additive that is shown to be a carcinogen in humans or animals, regardless of any potential benefits. The rationale for this law is the nonthreshold theory of carcinogenesis, which assumes that there is no safe level of exposure to a carcinogen.

The Safe Drinking Water Act, the Toxic Substances Control Act, and the Clean Air Act are **balancing laws;** they balance risks against benefits. The Environmental Protection Agency is required to balance regulatory costs and benefits in its decision-making activities. Risk assessments are used here. Chemicals are regulated or banned when they pose "unreasonable risks" to or have "adverse effects" on human health or the environment.

Technology-based laws impose technological controls to set standards. For example, parts of the Clean Air Act and the Clean Water Act impose pollution controls based on the best economically available technology or the best practical technology. Such laws assume that complete elimination of the discharge of human and industrial wastes into water or air is not feasible. Controls are imposed to reduce exposure, but true balancing is not attempted; the goal is to provide an "ample margin of safety" to protect public health and safety.

Risk Management

Those in responsible positions in business and government now have a greater awareness than they used to of the need to solve environmental problems associated with technological production and to assess the risks of technology. Most of our present environmental problems stem from decades of neglect. The Industrial Revolution brought prosperity, and little thought was given to the possible harmful effects of the technology that was providing so many visible benefits.

The chemical industry should take the lead in demonstrating its willingness to help solve the problems caused by its predecessors' lack of foresight. This should be done through cooperation, not confrontation. We need a science policy that is based on input from responsive leaders, both in industry and in government, who provide a forum from which to examine the facts and reach responsible decisions that lead to prompt action.

Is this possible? You may doubt it, but you have a responsibility to future generations to do your part in seeing that responsible action is taken. We cannot and should not "turn off" science and technology. Those who long for the "good old days" should remember what that means—diseases such as malaria, smallpox, and polio, which took many lives; no antibiotics for infections; and none of the modern fertilizers to increase crop yields needed to feed the world's population. You could add to this list many things that are of a humanitarian nature before you even start listing the technical advances that have raised the comfort level in our lives.

Risk management requires value judgments that integrate social, economic, and political issues with the scientific assessment of the risk. Determination of the acceptability of risk is a societal issue, not a scientific one. It is up to all of us to weigh the benefits against the risks in an intelligent and competent manner. The assumption of this text is that the wit to deal with environmental problems caused by uncontrolled technology is to be found in the educated public at large, not in the select group that stands to make a short-term financial or political profit. Always keep in mind that, except in the case of some radioactive wastes, the knowledge is available to "clean up" after any industrial operation; it is just a matter of cost, energy, and values.

It is apparent that we need citizens to take responsibility for being informed about the technological issues that affect society.

Albert Gore, Jr., U. S. senator from Tennessee, said in support of better science education,

> Science and technology are integral parts of today's world. Technology, which grows out of scientific discovery, has changed and will continue to change our society. Utilization of science in the solution of practice problems has resulted in complex social issues that must be intelligently addressed by all citizens. Students must be prepared to understand technological innovation, the productivity of technology, the impact of the products of technology on the quality of life, and the need for critical evaluation of societal matters involving the consequences of technology.

WHAT IS YOUR ATTITUDE TOWARD CHEMISTRY?

Before beginning the study of chemistry and its relationship to our culture, each of us needs to examine our prejudices (if any) and attitudes about chemistry, science, and technology. Many nonscientists regard science and its various branches as a mystery and feel that they cannot possibly comprehend the basic concepts and consequent societal issues. Many also have a fear of unleashed chemicals **(chemophobia)** and a feeling of hopelessness about the environment. Many of these attitudes are a result of reading about harmful effects of technology, which are indeed tragic. However, what is needed is a full realization of both the benefits of and the risks from science and technology. In the analysis of the pluses and minuses, we need to determine why harmful effects occur and whether risks can be reduced for future generations as we seek advantages offered by the human understanding of nature. This book will give you the basics in chemistry, which we hope will give you a more satisfying life through understanding and a richer, healthier life through the ability to make wise decisions about personal problems and problems that concern our world.

SUMMARY

How can we summarize this chapter as it concerns you, the student?

1. We need an informed citizenry to use and to evaluate scientific and technological advances.
2. To be informed about chemical problems requires a basic knowledge of what matter is really like and what matter does.
3. More sophisticated chemical problems require a deeper understanding of the workings (facts and theories) of chemistry.

4. You should be involved. As an educated person, you have a responsibility and a privilege.

Instructions for Reading Selection Three from History

Prereading Activities

1. The first two reading selections come from college textbooks. This third selection is an article, and consequently, it has no boldface headings. You will need to modify your prereading activities to work with this article. Do so as follows:
   a. Background the title
   b. Read the author information and the first paragraph to get an idea of what it is about.
   c. Read the last paragraph to see how the author concludes.
   d. Read the first sentence of all of the other paragraphs. Divide the essay into chunks by drawing a pencil line across the page at those points where you think the author stops talking about one idea and starts talking about another.
   e. Write a list of predictions to forecast what you think this essay will be about.
   f. Circle words and allusions to people or events that you do not understand.

Reading activities

1. Read the entire essay. See if you can recognize the organizational pattern. It will help you identify the main ideas. If you have divided this essay into chunks by drawing lines at the wrong places, erase your lines and redraw them.
2. Underline selectively, jot main ideas in the margin, and write summaries of each major chunk of material.
3. Mark passages that you cannot understand with a straight line in the margin. Analyze them to see why you do not understand them. If you trace your comprehension problem to specific words, either determine their meaning from context or look them up.

Postreading Activities

1. Make either a map or an outline of the major ideas.

2. Write a sentence that states the major idea of this essay. Then summarize, in one page, the main ideas and details used to develop this idea.

3. Use this essay to generate ideas of your own on a related subject. Can you think of other examples, either historical or contemporary, that may be different from people's usual view of them? What ideas and details would you use to develop your topic if you were to write about it?

The Revolution and the Unfree: Blacks, Women, Indentured Servants, Minors, and the Unpropertied[3]

LINDA GRANT DEPAUW (b. 1940), who teaches at George Washington University, has written extensively about women's history and the colonial era. She argued in her article that historians writing about the Revolutionary era, paradoxically enough, had focused their attention only upon a small minority of America's population in 1776. No more than 15 percent of the Revolutionary generation were free to enjoy life, liberty, and the pursuit of happiness as promised in the Declaration of Independence. Pre-Revolutionary America was a "land of the unfree," according to her, because the greatest proportion of the population lived under legal limitations that restricted their liberties. What does her interpretation do to the picture of the movement as a "Revolution by the people"?[4]

The fortune that Thomas Jefferson pledged with his life and sacred honor in support of the declaration that all men are created equal

---

[3] Linda Grant DePauw, "Land of the Unfree: Legal Limitaions on Liberty in Pre-Revolutionary America," *Maryland Historical Magazine* 68 (1973), pp. 355–368. Reprinted courtesy of the Maryland Historical Society. Footnotes omitted.

[4] Excerpts from *The American Revolution*, Fourth Edition by George Athan Billias, copyright © by Holt, Rinehart and Winston, Inc., reprinted by permission of the publisher.

and endowed with inalienable rights to life, liberty, and the pursuit of happiness, included, in the summer of 1776, almost two hundred slaves. The incongruity of a slave-owning people basing their Revolution on such exalted doctrines did not escape remark by contemporaries any more than it has escaped notice by historians. "How is it" sneered Samuel Johnson, "that we hear the loudest *yelps* for liberty among the drivers of negroes?" The Loyalist Thomas Hutchinson dryly observed that there seemed to be some discrepancy between the declaration that all men were equal and a practice that deprived "more than a hundred thousand Africans of their rights to liberty."

Even those Englishmen who sympathized with the American cause were repelled by the paradox. "If there be an object truly ridiculous in nature," Thomas Day commented, "it is an American patriot signing resolutions of independence with the one hand, and with the other brandishing a whip over his affrighted slaves." And the patriots themselves were not insensitive to it. "I have sometimes been ready to think," Abigail Adams wrote to her husband, "that the passion for liberty cannot be equally strong in the breasts of those who have been accustomed to deprive their fellow creatures of theirs." Patrick Henry confessed amazement that men as sincerely "fond of liberty" and genuinely religious as himself tolerated slavery. "Would anyone believe," he asked, "I am the master of slaves of my own purchase!"

Historians writing about the age of the American Revolution have tended to ignore the paradox more frequently than they have attempted to resolve it, but in recent years serious attention has been given to the enslaved blacks, and such New Left historians as Jesse Lemisch and Staughton Lynd have pointed out the limitations on the rights of such groups as merchant seamen and urban workers. Yet the full magnitude of the paradox is still unmeasured, for it appears that the contradiction between Lockean ideals and social practice in the year 1776 was not only more pronounced than contemporaries and traditional historians described but even exceeds the dimensions suggested by recent historians of the New Left. Had Lockean dicta been applied to all the human beings in British North America on the eve of the Revolution, and had all been permitted to enjoy the natural and legal rights of freemen, it would have been necessary to alter the status of more than 85 per cent of the population. In law and in fact no more than 15 per cent of the Revolutionary generation was free to enjoy life, liberty, and the pursuit of happiness unhampered by any restraints except those to which they had given their consent.

The unfree of Revolutionary America may be conveniently considered in five categories: Negroes, white servants, women, minors, and propertyless adult white males. These categories overlap and the proportion of the total population falling into each of the categories differed from one part of the country to another. Thus there were proportionately more women in New England than in backcountry North Carolina, many more blacks, proportionally, in Virginia than in New Jersey, and a larger proportion of disfranchised adult white males in South Carolina than in Massachusetts.

It is also true that legal limitations on liberty do not necessarily coincide either with a psychological sense of freedom or with social practices. The unfree were rarely, in fact, exploited to the full limit allowed by law. Nor has there been any attempt in this brief essay to present a precise description of legal status based on the myriad of local traditions, statutes, and common law interpretation. The following summaries claim to be correct in outline, not to have exhausted the complexities of the subject which are vast and largely unstudied. It is clear, however, that for each of the unfree groups the law placed definite theoretical limits on the rights Locke viewed as inalienable.

The black slaves, the most visible of the colonial unfree, comprised approximately 20 per cent of the colonial population, a proportion twice as great as that formed by the black population of the United States today. These slaves were legally chattel property. The law saw no self-evident right to liberty attached to the person of the dark-skinned laborer from Africa, and, indeed, the law had little concern for his right to life. The deliberate murder of a slave was not necessarily a felony in Virginia before the Revolution, for the law assumed that no one would intentionally destroy his own estate. Slaves had no right to hold property of their own and enjoyed the use of no more than the master allowed. As for the third right in Jefferson's trinity, pursuing happiness, if that took the form of taking time off from the master's work, it was a punishable offense.

There were a small number of free blacks in Revolutionary America, most of them in the North. Their status was superior to that of the slave, but they were still limited politically, socially, and economically in all of the colonies. For most legal purposes there was no distinction made between free and enslaved Negroes. They might have some time they could call their own for pursuing happiness, but they were forbidden to pursue it in a tavern. In Rhode Island a free black man could not even purchase a quart of cider.

White servants in colonial America comprised a class perhaps half as large as the slave force but unbalanced in age and sex distribution in favor of young adult males. Their status was superior to that of Negroes but still substantially below that of freemen. In many ways the servant was merely a slave with prospects of eventual freedom and whose entry into his lowly station had been more or less voluntary. When, in November 1775, Lord Dunmore attempted to lure blacks into the British army by offering them freedom as a bounty, the same offer was extended to white servants.

The servant's labor belonged to his master twenty-four hours a day, seven days a week. Like the black slave, he was a chattel. He had no property himself but what his master allowed. He could not marry without his master's permission and, like a black man, he could not drink liquor in a tavern. Running away and disobedience were severely punished, and stories of inhuman cruelty to white servants are common. Like a slave, a white servent could be sold against his will away from his wife and family or seized to satisfy his master's debts. There seems little to recommend the legislation governing servants over that governing blacks—with one exception. White servants, unlike slaves, had personal rights to life and contract rights to a minimum standard of living. They could bring suit to enforce these rights and the courts would enforce them even to the extent of freeing the servant outright.

The legal status of colonial women was determined by the tradition of the British common law with certain modifications forced by pioneer American conditions, most of which were made before the end of the seventeenth century. Blackstone's *Commentaries,* which began to circulate as an admired authority among colonial lawyers in the decade before the Revolution, described a theoretical position for English females that varied substantially from that held by free English men. Under common law, Blackstone taught, a woman ceased to exist if she married, for she and her spouse became one flesh and the flesh was his. She was no longer responsible for her debts or even for all of her personal actions. She had no legal control over any property either inherited or earned. And if her husband judged her disobedient or saucy he could chastise her as he did his children and servants. This was considered proper as he might be held responsible for her misbehavior in cases short of murder and high treason. Although divorce laws were relatively liberal for a time in the seventeenth century, a reaction in the Revolutionary era made divorce, regardless of cause, practically impossible for a woman to obtain.

The status of unmarried women, both widows and spinsters, was considerably better. By a law of 1419 known as "couverte de Baron" an unattached woman, the "Feme Sole," was entitled to engage in business enterprises on her own account. A widow was entitled to one-third of the family estate and might be willed even more. So long as she did not remarry she could invest or dispose of this property as she wished. There was, however, great social pressure on women to marry. Although women made up almost half of the total population when all age groups are included, the sex ratio of men to women in the marriageable age group (i.e., between sixteen and sixty) was extremely high—160.8 men to every 100 women. Consequently spinsters were few and they were generally propertyless dependents in the home of a male relative. Widows commonly remarried before their husbands had been buried a year—unless they were remarkably unattractive, elderly, or poor. Those in the last category, who could not support themselves on one-third of their deceased husband's estate, would be subject to the poor laws unless a male relative could be found to take them in. The poor law prescribed compulsory labor for the poor so that impoverished widows might be bound out to serve as domestics. In Wareham, Massachusetts (admittedly an exceptional case) there was an annual auction of indigent widows.

Americans under the age of twenty-one, a clear majority of the population in 1776, were legal infants, and the right to liberty of such persons was far from self-evident to the founding fathers, although they were aware that it seemed to follow, at least for older children, from the Lockean premises. It would be a mistake to confuse the class of legal minors in Revolutionary America with modern adolescents. Blackstone declared a boy of twelve fit to take an oath of allegiance and a girl of seven ready to be given in marriage. The age of discretion for most purposes fell between seven and fourteen and all children above this age group were subject to capital punishment for felonies and bore most of the responsibilities if not the privileges of adults. Children entered the labor force well before they entered their teens, and they developed a degree of maturity and experience in the world that would be considered unhealthily precocious today. The large number of men in their early twenties who served competently as field officers in the Revolutionary armies and sat in the Continental Congresses could only have appeared in a society that considered teenage boys adults even though it deprived them of full legal rights. Male children of the age of sixteen were taxable and liable for militia duty. And since the population of colonial America was generally young, sixteen being the median age, unfree males between sixteen and twenty-one comprised one quarter of the total taxable male population. In an age when the mortality rates among infants and children were high and when a youth of sixteen had less than an even chance of surviving to the age of thirty, the loss of even a few years of liberty was a significant grievance.

Furthermore, theories of child nurture in colonial days were distinctly grim, based on the still formidable patriarchical traditions that had prescribed death for a "rebellious and incorrigible son."

Obedience to parents was a duty imposed by divine as well as human law to be enforced by corporal punishment if necessary. Minors were expected to work for their parents as soon as they could walk, but they had no personal property rights before they came of legal age. Authority over children above ten or fourteen was frequently transferred from the natural parents to a master. The institution of apprenticeship was still viable at the time of the Revolution and was the usual path for a young man who did not intend to become a farmer but wished to learn a trade. Girls might also become apprenticed. Apprenticeship articles were drawn to standards set by colonial legislatures and generally required the consent of the child as well as of his parents. But children of poor or otherwise incompetent parents might be sold against their will to masters who promised, sometimes deceitfully, to provide for them adequately and teach them a trade before they came of age.

Once apprenticed, a child's labor belonged to the master as fully as did that of any servant. Even visits to his own parents could be forbidden and the free-time conduct of apprentices was subject to the same sort of restrictions that applied to adult servants or slaves. Disobedience to a master as to a father could be punished with the whip. If a child came to detest the trade his father apprenticed him to, or if the master failed to make him proficient in the craft, his entire future would be warped, for once of age and free it would be too late to begin again to acquire the skills needed to make a living.

These four groups—Negroes, servants, women, and minors—together comprised approximately 80 per cent of the two and a half million Americans in the year 1776. The legal doctrine applied to these classes excluded them from the category of persons who should enjoy the "inalienable rights" of which the Declaration speaks. But perhaps the most significant mark of their unfreedom was their usual lack of a right to vote, for the privilege of consenting to the laws was the essential right of a free man in Lockean theory. Indeed, the very word "enfranchise" was defined in the eighteenth century as the equivalent of the word "emancipate;" it meant "to make free."

Interestingly enough, the prohibition on the suffrage does not appear to have been absolute either in law or in fact for any of the unfree groups. Colonial suffrage legislation tended to be vague. Only Virginia, South Carolina, and Georgia specifically confined the franchise to white voters and there are recorded cases of Negroes, mulattoes, and Indians actually casting ballots. When in 1778 a provision excluding blacks from the suffrage was inserted in the proposed Massachusetts constitution, a citizen observed in the *Independent Chronicle* that "A black, tawny or reddish skin is not so unfavorable in hue to the genuine son of liberty, as a tory complection." Rare instances of bond servants casting votes are known and enough servants presumed to exercise the franchise in Albany, New York to necessitate their specific exclusion from participation in city elections in 1773.

Only Pennsylvania, Delaware, South Carolina, and Georgia specifically disfranchised females who otherwise qualified as property holders. When Hannah Lee Corbin protested to her brother Richard Henry Lee in 1778 that Virginia women ought not to be taxed if they had not the right to vote, he replied that "women were already possessed of that right," and, apparently, some women did vote for a time in Virginia as well as in New England and the middle colonies. But these cases were rare and it is significant that Mrs. Corbin did not know she had the franchise until her brother so informed her.

Only six states explicitly stated that voters must be twenty-one years of age (Pennsylvania, South Carolina, Virginia, Connecticut, New York, and North Carolina), and there are recorded cases of young men under legal age occasionally registering their votes.

In all likelihood, the liberality of colonial suffrage legislation was due to careless draftsmanship rather than to any desire to permit members of the unfree classes to vote. The intention was to limit the franchise to free, adult, white males and others who voted slipped through by accident as a result of laxity among election inspectors. Indeed, we know of such cases chiefly because they served as grounds for complaint in disputed elections.

A fifth group of colonial Americans, adult white males with little or no property, was deprived of the vote in colonial elections and so fell short of full liberty in the Lockean sense. But they were privileged above the other unfree groups since they were legally entitled to acquire property and were protected from physical abuse except such as was administered by public authority after trial as punishment for offenses against the state. Some of these disfranchised males were idiots, invalids, or residents of workhouses. Others were simply too poor to qualify under the arbitrary property requirements of the various electoral laws. Statistically they are the least significant of the unfree, although they have had more than their share of attention from critics of consensus history. They made up between 5 and 10 per cent of the total population. If they are added to the 80 per cent of the population in the other unfree categories, which were limited not merely in their political rights but in their rights to personal liberty and property as well, then only 10 to 15 per cent of the American population remain to qualify as "freemen" in the fullest sense.

It is curious that this startling statistic has somehow escaped comment by historians. While the enslavement of Negroes and disfranchisement of some adult white males may be noted in passing as undemocratic elements in pre-Revolutionary America, the disfranchisement and worse of the other unfree classes is accepted without remark even in our enlightened age. Thus, Elisha P. Douglass defined democracy in his *Rebels and Democrats* as "a political system in which all adult males enjoyed equal political rights." Robert Brown writes in *Middle-Class Democracy and the Revolution in Massachusetts*, "The only valid approach . . . is to find out how many adult men could vote out of the total adult male population," and he concludes that "If anything with the appearance of a man could vote there was little problem of a restricted electorate." And finally, the author of his paper casually observed in *The Eleventh Pillar*, "The important ratio is that of qualified voters to adult white males."

Today almost 65 per cent of the total population is enfranchised and in law, at least, virtually all of the people are secured in property rights and protected from physical abuse by private parties. Yet even our age finds it self-evident that women and young people should have been excluded from colonial political life. Since this is the case, we should not find it difficult to understand how the men of two centuries ago could accept the contradiction between their Lockean principles and their discriminatory practice without too much discomfort.

It would be both uncharitable and simplistic to dismiss the founding fathers as hypocrites because they tolerated this inconsistency. Some conflict between ideal principles and social practice is inevitable if the ideals are at all noble and the society composed of human beings rather than angels. Nor is such contradiction undesirable. Quite the opposite, since it induces men, who will always fall short of perfection in their day to day experience, to consider the possibility of alternative social arrangements superior to their own. Thus John Adams was vastly amused when his Abigail presumed to apply the Revolutionary slogans to the condition of married ladies. But after puzzling over her remarks for a month he realized that, indeed, he could discover no moral foundation for government that would justify the exclusion of any class of people from full participation. Of course it was "impossible", he wrote to James Sullivan, that the principle of consent should ever be carried so far. But the logic was undeniable and if it were followed to its conclusion "women will demand a vote; lads from twelve to twenty-one will think their rights not enough attended to; and every man who has not a farthing, will demand an equal voice with any other, in all acts of state." Adams seems to have predicted the long range impact of the Revolutionary doctrine accurately enough.

Again, Patrick Henry, facing up to the contrast between his words and his practice of keeping slaves, wrote, "I will not, I cannot justify it. However culpable my conduct, I will so far pay my devoir to virtue, as to own the excellence and rectitude of her precepts, and lament my want of conformity to them."

In the final analysis, however, the contradiction was tolerable to Americans because they compared the extent of liberty in their society not with the Lockean ideal but with the extent of liberty in other contemporary or historically known societies. From this perspective there was no doubt that the Americans of 1776 were remarkably free. Even the slaves, servants, women, and children of American enjoyed positions superior to those held by similar classes in other lands and other times. And surely a land in which more than 10 per cent of the population owned property and had a voice in the government was a wonder in an age when the civilized world was ruled by hereditary monarchs and property ownership was a prerogative of aristocrats. Even in England, where the political liberty of the early eighteenth century had made her people the envy of Europe, no more than 25 per cent of "the active male population" had voted in even the freest parts of the kingdom—and after the first third of the century even this electorate had dwindled. Yet, to quote J. H. Plumb, "this was England's vast singularity, a unique situation amongst the major powers of the world."

Surely the gap that separated American society from the Lockean ideal was no more impressive than that which separated colonial American society from the societies of Europe. If freedom had a home anywhere in the world in the year 1776 it was in the new United States of America. But if "democracy" implies government by consent of the governed or at least by consent of a majority of those governed and not merely of an adult white male elite, then those historians from Bancroft to Brown who have described American society of the mid-eighteenth century as "democratic" are simply wrong. The opinion of Carl Becker and many others that colonial governments "did in a rough and ready way, conform to the kind of government for which Locke furnished a reasoned foundation" is vastly overstated. And the attempts of the New Left history to view the American Revolution "from the bottom up" will be superficial so long as "the bottom" is conceived in a way that still excludes the majority of the population.

Index